Inside and Outside the Law

Law is a discourse of absolutes, and yet it is beset by ambiguities. Legality is inevitably identified with morality, and yet there is in all legal systems a zone where the legal and the non-legal become hard to distinguish, and where it is debatable how far the moral and social standing of particular groups or individuals can be equated with their legal status. Anthropology is typically concerned with the frontiers of legality, and with groups defined by the law as marginal. *Inside and Outside the Law* reflects on the ambiguities of law's authority, drawing on comparative case-studies of ethnic groups within different modern states, of groups defined as marginal through their sexual behaviour, and on analyses of the ambiguities at the heart of state authority itself.

Inside and Outside the Law will be of interest to political scientists and legal theorists, as well as anthropologists and sociologists concerned with popular conceptions of the state and its laws.

Olivia Harris is Reader in Anthropology at Goldsmiths College, University of London.

D1446830

European Association of Social Anthropologists

The European Association of Social Anthropologists (EASA) was inaugurated in January 1989, in response to a widely felt need for a professional association which would represent social anthropologists in Europe and foster co-operation and interchange in teaching and research. As Europe transforms itself in the nineties, the EASA is dedicated to the renewal of the distinctive European tradition in social anthropology.

Other titles in the series:

Inside and Outside the Law

Anthropological studies of authority and ambiguity

Edited by Olivia Harris

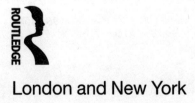

London and New York

First published 1996
by Routledge
11 New Fetter Lane, London EC4P 4EE

Simultaneously published in the USA and Canada
by Routledge
29 West 35th Street, New York, NY 10001

Typeset in Times by Routledge
Printed and bound in Great Britain by Clays Ltd, St Ives PLC

British Library Cataloguing in Publication Data
A catalogue record for this book is available from the British Library

Library of Congress Cataloguing in Publication Data
Inside and outside the law: anthropological studies of authority and
ambiguity/edited by Olivia Harris.
"Anthropological Studies of Authority and Ambiguity."
Includes bibliographical references and index.
1. Law and anthropology. 2. Culture and law. I. Harris, Olivia
K487.A57I57   1997
340′. 115–dc20   96–21564
                                                                        CIP

ISBN 0–415–12928–1 (hbk)
ISBN 0–415–12929–X (pbk)

Contents

Contributors

Ray Abrahams, University Lecturer in Anthropology and Fellow of Churchill College, University of Cambridge, is especially interested in rural society in its relation to the state. He has done fieldwork in Tanzania and Uganda, Estonia and Finland. Among his publications are *Nyamwezi Today* (1981) and *A Place of their Own* (1991) and, as editor, *Barons and Farmers in Estonia* (1994) and *Witchcraft in Contemporary Tanzania* (1994).

Thérèse Bouysse-Cassagne is the author of *La Indentidad aymara* (1987) and of other studies on Aymara and Pukina ethnohistory, as well as on Andean religions. She is Director of Research at the Centre National de la Recherche Scientifique, Paris, and at the Institut des Hautes Etudes de L'Amérique Latine.

Sophie Day, who is a Lecturer in Anthropology at Goldsmiths College, University of London, has done fieldwork in Ladakh and London and has a special interest in medical anthropology.

Marie-Bénédicte Dembour, is a Lecturer in Law at the University of Sussex. She also holds a doctorate in Social Anthropology and has done fieldwork in Belgium. She has particular interests in law, human rights, identity, colonialism and memory.

Sue Fleming, of the Department of Social Anthropology, University of Manchester, has done fieldwork in the Solomon Islands, Tonga and Mozambique. Central to her interests are problems of Third World development.

Ørnulf Gulbrandsen is Professor of Anthropology at the University of Bergen. To his earlier work in industrial anthropology, he has added an interest in cultural ecology, kinship and politics. His fieldwork among the Tswana of South Africa has yielded a number of publications, including *Poverty in the Midst of Plenty: Socio-Economic Marginalization, Ecological Deterioration and Political Stability in a Tswana Society* (1994).

Olivia Harris has researched and published widely on the Andean region. She is Reader in Anthropology at Goldsmiths College, University of London, and Visiting Professor in the Department of Social Anthropology, University of Oslo.

Stephan Palmié teaches at the Amerika-Institut of the University of Munich. He has carried out research in the USA, Cuba and Jamaica, and has taught in the Carter G. Woodson Institute of the University of Virginia.

Manuchehr Sanadjian is an Iranian anthropologist living in the UK.

Acknowledgements

I am grateful to Signe Howell for inviting me to convene a session on law for the 3rd EASA Conference in Oslo, and thus encouraging me to pursue a new line of thought, and to all those who participated in the session, in particular those who presented papers. My thanks also to the British Academy for a travel grant that enabled me to attend the conference.

At the time I started work on editing the papers for publication I little thought that the editorial process would be delayed by my own encounters with the law. In the event, the Introduction had to be written in La Paz (Bolivia), without access to bibliographic resources, in the midst of unplanned 'fieldwork'. My inadvertent participant observation of legal processes, in which I found myself on the one hand ambiguously 'inside and outside the law', and on the other working with lawyers to reformulate a particular statute which has effectively excluded many ethnic groups in Bolivia from acquiring legal status, have provided many insights. For these I thank my daughter Marina, and colleagues in the National Secretariats of Ethnic Affairs and Popular Participation, Bolivia.

In these unpropitious circumstances Heather Gibson at Routledge, and Roger Goodman of EASA, have acted with exemplary patience and understanding. Harry Lubasz made a major contribution in revising the translation of Chapter 6 and Vanessa Fleming formatted most of the chapters. My warmest thanks to all of them.

Chapter 1

Introduction
Inside and outside the law[1]

Olivia Harris

The theme of this book derives from a course I taught on 'The Politics of Tradition', which looked at the concept of custom: the ongoing tension between a concept of society grounded in rules, and one that focuses rather on social action, strategy and improvisation. 'Tradition', as a form of legitimisation deriving from the posited continuity between past and present, appears to be unchanging, and yet as anthropologists and historians have increasingly pointed out, paradoxically traditions are constantly being invented and reinvented in the name of continuity with the past and fixed rules.

On the other hand, in modern nation-states certain aspects of cultural process become fixed with a symbolic task of representing particular social identities. Minority groups are more or less obliged to reify particular practices in order to define and bound themselves as different, and thereby create a basis for making demands and claiming rights from the wider society. Both the reifications and the demands which accompany them are products of legal systems. James Clifford's study of *Identity in Mashpee* is a good illustration: the rights of the Mashpee to their land in the prime tourist area of Cape Cod (Massachusetts) depended on proving their continuous identity as Native Americans according to apparently arbitrary legal criteria (1987). It seemed to me that the relationship between Anthropology and Law was potentially more far-reaching and complex than what I had understood of the debates within the sub-field of 'the Anthropology of Law'.[2]

The theme chosen for the 3rd EASA Conference – Moralities – more or less demanded a session on law, given the importance of debates concerning the relationship between moral norms and a corpus of laws. This concern has been central to the philosophy of law, and to European philosophy more generally, illustrated by the power of Sophocles' portrayal of Antigone, or Plato's of Socrates, caught between the contradictory claims of morality and the state. Current anthropological debates around the issues of fixity and fluidity, and the invention of traditions, led me to formulate the Durkheimian theme of the relation of law and moralities in terms of its negative attributes. Laws themselves often put social actors in difficult moral predicaments by the fact that they forbid, or even criminalize, actions which for the people concerned are acceptable or desirable within their own moral code. Moreover, where particular groups or activities are defined as outside the law, or ambiguously legitimate, what are the consequences for their moral standing?

The issue of moral standing and moral action is intimately linked with concepts of the person, as the EASA conference made clear. It was striking how many of the plenary speakers invoked legal or legal-religious definitions of personhood as a way of identifying rules of social agency. A fruitful area of research at the interface of Anthropology and Law is the way that legal systems enshrine and codify particular concepts of person and agent. These concepts differ significantly between legal systems, and in turn obviously shape the practices of those who are subject to them.

It has often been argued that Western legal subjects are founded in an abstract, neutral, gender-blind individual developed from Enlightenment thought (Unger 1977; Smart 1989). Certain categories of people by such criteria are almost *ipso facto* outside the law, and to a certain extent therefore deprived of the status of legal subject: women, homosexuals, the poorly educated. The degree to which Human Rights discourse replicates this abstract individualism and avoids issues of interpersonal relationships is admirably analysed by Dembour (Chapter 2).

ANTHROPOLOGY AT THE FRONTIERS OF LEGALITY

The early history of anthropology as part of the field of comparative law is well known (Kuper 1988), and the growth and development of legal systems was a fundamental aspect of evolutionary theory. The legalist influence was retained in the enduring anthropological concern with the problem of order and the resolution of conflict in the absence of specialized institutions, derived in part from Durkheimian sociology, but with far wider ramifications. Notoriously, Radcliffe-Brown's emphasis on custom, and on society as a normative system, was strongly influenced by legal ideas.

British social anthropology to some extent polarized between a Radcliffe-Brown-inspired emphasis on rules, and a Malinowskian emphasis on social action, where social actors are individuals who continually strategize and break or bend the rules.[3] In recent years this enduring concern has been reactivated in the critique made by Pierre Bourdieu of anthropology's emphasis on structures, on norms and on codifications, thus obscuring the real texture of everyday social life (1977, 1990a). For Bourdieu, anthropologists are typically inclined twoards the 'legalist illusion' (1990b), and there is too great a respect for the written text, with all the corresponding reifications. According to this perspective, the legalist emphasis of anthropologists led them to reify custom into customary law in the same way that colonial administrations were doing (Chanock 1985; Fitzpatrick 1992). As Merry phrases it, customary law was transformed through the colonial impact from 'a subtle, adaptable, and situational code to a system of fixed and formal rules', from 'the embodied, spoken and interpreted text into a fixed, abstracted and disembodied one that was written' (1992: 365). It is clear that the twentieth century has seen the globalization of the political form of the nation-state, and a corresponding revolution in the relation of colonized peoples to law.[4]

However, the chapters of this book indicate clearly that law and formal bodies of rules regulate people's behaviour only in a rather approximate way, but the ambiguity derives from there being laws or rules which help to constitute persons/groups. Changes in rules or laws do materially affect the moral standing and capacity for action of individuals and groups. This is illustrated dramatically by Geoffrey Scarre's (1987) analysis of the outbreak of witchcraft accusations in early modern Europe. The introduction of inquisitorial procedures into municipal proceedings in the late fourteenth century, including the withholding of the identity of witnesses from the accused, and the admission of evidence from those not normally thought fit to testify made possible a dramatic increase in accusations, and threfore in the category of 'witches'. Before this, accusers who failed to substantiate their charges faced judicial penalties.

Anthropology as a discipline characteristically chooses as its field of study those who are at the frontiers of legality, and anthropologists seem to have a constitutional affinity for those whose relationship with the law is at best ambivalent. This is obvious in the early history of the discipline, which took as its object those primitive or non-European others who were by many criteria 'outside the law' as defined by their European or Euro-American rulers – their customs, their religious practices, their freedom, their lack of writing, their promiscuity and so forth. There has been an implicit anarchism running through the development of anthropological theory – for example in the influential ideas of Mauss or Evans-Pritchard on how societies can operate without the state. But it is equally true today. At a time of immense expansion of anthropological research, and the opening up of new fields and topics, I suggest that it is still true that the epicentre of the discipline remains with social groups who are defined as marginal by the mainstream society – peasants, squatters, nomads, mafia, the informal sector, migrants. The hallmark and the inspiration of our discipline is that we search for the exceptions, the anomalies, to inform our vision of the social universe. How indeed is marginality to be defined if not in relation to the law? In addition in much current anthropological debate there is a notable hostility to any form of authority, especially in the USA. The different chapters of this volume attest to marginality as a continued source of inspiration for anthropological research.

Having said this, I must also add that the characteristic movement of anthropological analysis is not so much to celebrate the marginal status of such groups, as to demonstrate that, contrary to appearances, or to the prejudices of dominant society, their lives are as much ruled by principles of order and value as are those of the mainstream. A classic example would be the functionalist approach to the study of witchcraft – a category which is par excellence 'outside the law' – and which anthropologists characteristically argued was actually part of the normal functioning of society. The early development of the 'anthropology of law' surely also reflects a similar movement: the desire to demonstrate in detail that societies which according to Western criteria have no specialized legal systems almost certainly have institutions for fulfilling legal functions, such as settlement of disputes and the sanctioning of disorder, and in some cases, moreover, have sophisticated traditions of jurisprudence.

AUTHORITY AND AMBIGUITY

Much of the work both of the anthropology of law and of critical legal theory has been concerned to demystify law: to show how rules are not, and cannot always be, obeyed, how laws are self-contradictory, how the practice of law differs from the ideal. The anthropological concern with 'law as process' aimed to get away from a stultifying concern with rules as such in order to focus on how those rules were implemented or not, how real-life situations escaped the apparent clarity of rules. Anthropologists also relied heavily on a dichotomy between local custom and national law to express the frequent clash of values and practices they observed in their research. The real-life diversity of legal systems and practices at local, national and transnational levels is recognized in legal theory under the general heading of legal pluralism, and is seen as characteristic of all contemporary societies (Fitzpatrick 1983; Griffiths 1986).

Modern law is a continuous attempt at fixity and closure which is undermined by the impossibility of its own project. As a system of codification, whether based on legislation or on case law, it is an abstraction, and in consequence actual life-situations fit into it only imperfectly. This creates a zone of moral or at least pragmatic ambiguity and of room for manoeuvre, where some form of courts are necessary to settle ambiguous disputes, where lawyers flourish, where corruption enters in, and where decisions can be made on strictly legal grounds which appear to fly in the face of common sense or everyday morality.

At the same time, a major thread in legal philosophy – that of legal positivism – emphasizes the socially contingent nature of particular laws, their historical grounding, and derives their authority not from their intrinsic link to moral rules, but to their enactment by socially recognized authorities (Raz 1979).

This work of demystifying the law, and relativizing it in terms of its ambiguities, its evident failures to match moral judgements, its contingent origins, is obviously important, and what is more, corresponds to real life experiences, as Day especially explores (Chapter 5). There cannot be many people whose respect for law is entirely untarnished by scepticism. However, the process of demys-tification runs the risk of diluting the central issue, which is that in spite of the way that particular laws can be criticized or transgressed, for example because they reflect political or sectional interests, or fail in their duty to protect their citizens, or clash with or undermine local values, in spite of the ways that laws can be manipulated or misinterpreted, there remains a sense of the transcendental value of law which it could be argued is a general human faculty. A good example of this paradox is the discourse of Human Rights analysed by Dembour (Chapter 2). The *idea* of Human Rights has a universal remit and a transcendent value which makes it a viable basis for political claims, and for criticizing particular states; at the same time we have to recognize as anthropologists that identifying universal human rights is fraught with difficulties, and that particular claims (Dembour cites the examples of rights to credit, and rights to annual holidays) are highly specific to cultural and economic circumstances.

Within legal and political theory, the concept of natural law has expressed this sense that law has an absolute status, a transcendent value. Whether based in religion and derived from God, or from a theory of instincts, or from reason, natural law sees itself as logically prior to and morally superior to the state or particular legislators, and theories of natural law were immensely influential in the 1776 USA Declaration of Independence, the 1789 Declaration of the Rights of Man in France, and as a model for the Napoleonic and Prussian legal codes.[5]

Semantically, concepts of law are closely related to those of justice, order and balance in the Indo-European tradition (Benveniste 1969). Theories of natural law offer one kind of founding myth from which the absolute status of law can be derived, and natural law assumes a direct identification between law and morality (Raz 1979: 157). However, they have an *a priori* status which accords ill with the ambiguous status of law in everyday experience. On the other hand, legal positivism offers an account of law which is too contingent to account for the apparently binding quality of law. To this end recent theories have turned to anthropology to explain the axiomatic status of laws in terms of their mythical status, re-enacted through constant rituals, and also to Freud. Psychoanalytic theory offers an account which is neither *a priori* nor contingent, but grounded in human emotional development, arguing that the necessary internalization of the symbolic Father, and the consequent development of the superego and a sense of guilt, accounts for the human apprehension of law as transcendent,[6] even though the content of particular rules or laws differs widely from one situation to another, and particular laws or rules may be a very imperfect approximation to that absolute concept of Value or Law. Most people have probably experienced themselves as 'outside the law' in this transcendent sense, and some fruitful avenues of feminist analysis have argued that the problematic status of femininity derives from its ambiguous relationship with the 'Law of the Father' or the 'Symbolic Order' in the version of Lacan (Mitchell 1982).

A characteristic means by which Law in the absolute sense can be identified is that it is protected by divine or supernatural sanctions. As such, it is removed from the sphere of mundane and sectional interests, from the ebb and flow of historical change and contingency.

However, it would be a mistake to try to universalize the religious function. It is clear that cosmological systems vary widely in the sorts of powers they attribute to fate, in the inevitability of sanctions and punishments, and in the degree of flexibility and negotiability to be found in the supernatural agents and embodiments of Value and Law. This was long ago recognized by Fortes for African cosmologies (1959). Even within the Judaeo-Christian tradition, this variation is evident, with the Catholic tradition emphasizing the perfectibility of human beings, the all-loving and forgiving nature of the Godhead, and hence the possibility of bending the law. Jewish and Protestant faiths by contrast tend to view Law as absolute and intransigent, and correspondingly have a more tragic and inexorable view.

The state of law

While anthropologists have been at pains to point out that the functional equivalent of law exists in societies not organized within forms of the state, it remains the case that modern state forms – as opposed to monarchical states – are closely identified with the principle of law. Most legal philosophers identify legal systems with the modern state. This remains the case regardless of what theory of the state is invoked, whether liberal arguing that the state and its laws exist to protect the freedom of the individual, or Marxist arguing that the state and its laws exist to protect particular class interests, or Weberian, focusing on the rational-administrative structure of the state, or Durkheimian, on the consensual aspect of the state and its laws. Foucault in turn emphasizes the spectacular nature of the state, and ritualized aspects of law-enforcement. These are manifested both through court procedures and through punishment, as Sanadjian's finely honed account of the spectacle of flogging in south-west Iran chillingly describes (Chapter 8). Merry has noted that anthropologists have paid little attention to punishment strategies (1992: 370), and as such Sanadjian's account is to be welcomed.

The integral connection between modern state and law leaves open, of course, what is the source of those laws that the state enacts, and this is another dimension of ambiguity. In nationalist thought, the laws of each people are the expression of their character and particularity. At the EASA panel in Oslo, Joan Bestard's paper explored this issue in the context of Catalan nationalism, and argued that late nineteenth-century legal theorists, focusing on the peculiarities of Catalan family structure, were an important influence in the

early development of Catalan nationalism.[7] However, as the work of
E.P.Thompson and others has emphasized, the customs of the people
and their moral rules can often be at variance with those of their
rulers.[8] In this volume, Manuchehr Sanadjian explores local forms of
resistance against repressive state law.

Law is an important aspect of state hegemony: 'law as an ideology
contributes to the social construction of the world as fair and just, and
at the same time provides a language and forums for resisting that
order' (Merry 1992: 360). None the less, it would be romantic to
idealize local, customary morality and demonize state law. As
Abrahams's suggestive overview indicates, vigilantism as a phenomenon is implicitly or explicitly a criticism of the inadequacies of state
law, or of the state's failure to enact its own laws, but vigilantism has its
ambiguous, even brutal side, illustrated in his chapter by the punishment of those suspected of witchcraft in Tanzania, and the treatment
meted out to black people in the USA (Chapter 3).[9] In such
circumstances, state law is the only defence of subordinate groups
or individuals who transgress local moral norms and values, as
Stephan Palmié's account of the Cuban Santeros defence of their
religious practices in the US Supreme Court against local opposition
vividly documents (Chapter 9). The 'rule of law' becomes a defence
against tyranny, as in classical and liberal political theory. Law in this
context represents the idea of an orderly state, in contrast to the
'chaotic state' which is the reality of many people's experience.

Custom, then, is ambiguous: on the one hand it represents the
possibility of acts of violence against women, against ethnic minorities, against those whose actions have offended the local power-
holders; on the other hand it invokes local values against an alien and
imposing state, illustrated here by Sanadjian's analysis of the conflict
between Luri and Islamic attitudes to gambling (Chapter 8), and
Gulbrandsen's discussion of Tswana courts (Chapter 7).

The move from custom to law involves, as we have noted above, a
move from argument and fluidity rooted in the past, to an attempt at
fixity. Palmié discusses this shift and its consequences for Santero
religious practice, characterized by informality and lack of agreement
regarding the nature of its 'laws', when it becomes recognized by the
US Supreme Court (Chapter 9). However, as those who have studied
legal systems in the periphery have been at pains to point out, those
systems are at best only partially based on indigenous customs.
Mono-ethnic states are rare, so that state legal systems are bound to
abstract from local practice in order to cover a wide variety of

populations and cultural forms. Moreover, legal systems have been part of cultural globalization, so that the English-speaking world generally follows the principles of English common law, while elsewhere, the Napoleonic Code has been favoured. In Latin America, it is still the basis of criminal and civil law, and only recently have Latin American countries begun to develop a distinctive corpus of laws relating to social issues. In practice, for example in Bolivia when a new law is to be drafted, common practice is to start by studying related laws of neighbouring countries. This is a far cry from the idea that the laws of a particular nation-state are the unique expression of its people.[10]

In such circumstances, the relationship between law and practice may be rather indirect. Laws may come to be the simulacrum of an ideal world, which the state is unable to enforce (Abrahams, Chapter 3). Post-revolutionary states are especially prone to enacting laws of high ideals which come up against an intractable reality. This is the background of Fleming's account of land law in Mozambique, where both local practice, and the limitations of the state bureaucracy, and the interests of former colonial settlers and transnational companies such as Lonrho, all militate against the spirit of the law (Chapter 4). It also underlies Sanadjian's analysis of a public flogging in post-revolutionary Iran (Chapter 8).

Human Rights law operates at the level of the international, rather than the national, community, as Dembour demonstrates (Chapter 2). Here we see levels of conflict not so much between the local and the state, as between the state and a political discourse of rights that operates beyond the frontiers of the state, as a means of putting pressure on particular states that are considered to have violated this code. But of course, while Human Rights may stand as an instrument to be used by lobbies and politicians to put pressure on particular governments to improve their treatment of their citizens, there is no institution with power to enforce human rights law worldwide. It is individual states which have the power to enforce their laws, if they are willing.

John Comaroff has referred to the 'inherently contradictory character of the colonial discourse of rights' (1995). In the South African context, he points to the irony of the missionaries' encouragement of individual rights and a 'healthy individualism' while the colonial administrators favoured the primacy of 'custom' for example in land rights. What is certain is that colonialism has created hybrid spaces, where the inconsistencies between law and practice, between local custom and state legislation, between ideal and reality, are more pronounced than in the core countries, as illustrated for example in the chapters by Bouysse-Cassagne (Chapter 6), Gulbrandsen (Chapter 7) and Fleming (Chapter 4). There is much that anthropology can contribute to the developing literature on the way that people understand, represent and contest the state(s) in which they live. A focus on law provides a fruitful way into this field of enquiry, since it is through the workings of the law that most people are brought into direct contact with the state and its operations.

The uncertainties of exclusion

As Charles Dickens demonstrated in his devastating novel of the lawsuit between Jarndyce and Jarndyce (*Bleak House*), legal processes can easily take on a life of their own, in a nightmare of papers, procedures and authorizations. The Peruvian economist Hernando de Soto made a study of the time involved for street hawkers in Lima to gain official authorization for building a market. It turned out to be over 14 years (1989). Fleming hints at some of this in her spare but telling description of the intricacies and imponderables of Mozambican land law (Chapter 4).

In such environments, what is known as 'corruption' flourishes. However, it is important to spell out the ambiguities of corruption. To receive or offer money or other resources in return for facilitating a legal process is strictly against the law, but those involved would usually deny that they are acting illegally. It is because they are poorly paid, it is because the law is unworkable anyway, it is because they wish to be helpful, or owe a favour to X or Y... Thus in many contexts, at the very point of operation of the law, there is uncertainty as to whether those involved are inside or outside.

In underfunded state sectors, the bewildering proliferation of legal documents is closely connected to the need to generate income. As more and more documents become necessary in order to remain inside the law, more and more people correspondingly become excluded. Identity depends on having one's papers in order, and if you fail to take the necessary steps you risk never having a legal identity at all.[11]

Social identity is in the first instance inscribed at birth, and the regulation of sexuality, particularly female sexuality, is a nodal point at which absolute and contingent notions of law interact. It is at the heart of Freudian notions of prohibition,[12] and of the regulation of sexuality and the implications for identity and property-inheritance that flow from it. It is no accident that to describe a person as 'illegitimate' without further qualification refers to the circumstances of their birth 'outside of wedlock', and it is also no accident that 'bastard' or its equivalent in other languages is a primordial insult imputing low moral status.

The regulation of women's sexuality has powerful implications for the drawing and maintaining of group boundaries, and one context where such boundaries assume a particular salience is the space of colonial rule. To cross these boundaries through 'mixed' unions is a form of subversion (Cooper and Stoler 1989; Stoler 1989). This is the theme of Thérèse Bouysse-Cassagne's vivid study of *mestizaje* – the mixing of races – in the colonial Viceroyalty of Peru (Chapter 6). The children of mixed unions were doubly 'illegitimate': firstly in the sense that they were often born out of wedlock, and secondly because early colonial legislation was formulated in terms of 'two republics' – that of the Spanish and that of the Indians – and did not plan for the existence of a rapidly increasing group of mestizos. The mestizos were thus anomalous in Mary Douglas's usage: they were assumed to be of low moral standing, and their mothers were symbolically defined as outside of civilization. And yet they survived and over the centuries prospered in the interstices of colonial law.

Alternative moralities

Bouysse-Cassagne suggests that in many instances Indian women sought European partners in spite of existing prohibitions, in order to provide a better life for their children in terms of the new criteria brought by the Spanish. That is, while they were acting outside the law, they were simultaneously responding to other sets of values within the same colonial society.

This theme is developed by Sophie Day in her thought-provoking study of prostitutes in contemporary London (Chapter 5). They see themselves first and foremost as independent businesswomen, in a morally neutral market rather than in an ambiguous relationship to the law. The law excludes and criminalizes them, and they perceive the state and its agents as punitive and arbitrary; however, the market includes them, encouraging them to make money through servicing an existing demand. In this sense they are admirable exponents of the 'enterprise culture' of Britain today. While there is some demand for the legalization of prostitution, they recognize that were this to happen their earnings would diminish. To bring them 'inside the law' would solve one problem, but at the same time create another. They therefore prefer to exploit the ambiguity of their situation, while being at the same time indignant at how they are viewed and treated in the eyes of the law.

Confrontations between law and market as alternative values take us back to the opposed views of Radcliffe-Brown and Malinowski as to the nature of society and social action. They also echo two of the most fundamental symbols of the power of law: on the one hand the State, on the other Contract. Day's analysis of the fallibility and vulnerability of state law in the face of sexual desire and the alternative 'law of the market' reveals the London prostitutes to be enacting the old liberal dilemma of how much law is good, and when it becomes too much.

The uncertainties of religious law

If secular law is beset by ambiguities, religious law at first sight might seem less so, as one of the possible bases for natural law theory, and as one of the manifestations of paternal prohibition in Freudian theory. But as several chapters in this volume argue eloquently, religious law is never entirely separate from the domain of mundane interests, even where attempts have been made to enforce a rigid demarcation between Church and State, between religion and politics. The chapters by Gulbrandsen, Sanadjian and Palmié each offer a particular insight on the complex of possible relationships between religious authority and law.

Gulbrandsen addresses a *locus classicus* of the anthropology of law – the Tswana, site of Schapera's magisterial studies (Chapter 7). He demonstrates that in spite of a century of colonial rule and conversion to Christianity the ancestors still hold sway in Tswana legal decisions, operating through the hierarchy of lineage authorities. What is particularly noteworthy is the capacity of the ancestors to change with the times. In contrast to the view of 'ancestor worship' as a practice orientated towards the past, Gulbrandsen shows that it provides an effective means of harnessing the power of the past to the needs of the present, and of providing continuity of values and of procedures in the face of dramatic changes. In the case of the Tswana, then, history has permitted the ancestors to adapt, and thus retain, their authority as symbols of a distinctive Tswana practice, by offering sound advice to their descendants.

Sanadjian's study of the operation of Islamic law in post-revolutionary Iran reveals a stark contrast (Chapter 8). Here again we see the operation of religious principles in every area of life, but as a return of theocracy in a nation-state that had previously operated a demarcation between religious and secular law.

Palmié's case-study of the Cuban Santeros in Miami situates us in a context where the US Constitution has made every effort to maintain the demarcation between religious and secular law, while respecting the freedom of religious worship for all (Chapter 9). He details for us the aporia of universal principles designed to respect and protect minorities, where the practices of those minorities infringe the universal principles. The Santero use of animal sacrifice, and the ambitions of a particular religious leader, lead to the High Court, where the judge is forced into a discourse which implicitly acknowledges the existence of divinities about which we can assume he was highly sceptical.

A central preoccupation of all these three chapters is the conflict between the customs or laws of a minority group and those of the encompassing nation-state. In the case of the Iranian Lurs, they are seen as imperfect Muslims, defying, through their nomadic lifestyle and relaxed attitudes, the law as interpreted by the Muslim jurists. Perhaps Palmié offers an important key to locating the uncertainties of religious law: the concept of religion as found in the US Constitution is essentially derived from the highly legalistic Semitic religions – Judaism, Christianity and Islam – which have all been subject to centuries of codification and legal dispute. By contrast, Santero religious practice operates in a domain of constant negotiation, where truth is relative to the situation. Gulbrandsen is explicit for the Tswana: in contrast to the absolute status of natural law concepts is the Tswana idea of law as an ongoing process of constant *dialogue* with the ancestors – the source of moral authority. This image of dialogue with the past, with the source of authority and rules, could perhaps usefully be applied in the context of current debates about social action and the mutability of norms and traditions.

NOTES

1   Due to circumstances beyond my control, this Introduction was written without access to a library, relying only on limited notes. As a result I have necessarily kept bibliographic references to a minimum. However,

over time I have consulted more sources than I have been able to cite directly.

2   Chris Fuller has recently argued the need for the reinvigoration of dialogue between Anthropology and Law (1994).

3   It should be noted that in practice the sub-field of 'the anthropology of law' after Radcliffe-Brown and Pospisil moved away from a concern with rules to study law as *process*, typified by Llewellyn and Hoebel's and Gluckman's emphasis on dispute-settlement (Roberts 1979: 197).

4   However, as Gulbrandsen argues (Chapter 7), the colonial impact on legal systems was far from uniform.

5   Though paradoxically, once the codes were in force, it was considered illegitimate to have further recourse to natural law, since the Code in principle contained all the resources necessary for resolving particular cases! (Fasso 1981–2).

6   Peter Fitzpatrick's recent work is an eloquent exposition of this perspective (1992)

7   Unfortunately Dr Bestard was not able to include his paper in this volume. This point is also argued by Fitzpatrick with relation to how the mythic power of the nation reinforces the authority of law (Chapter 4).

8   This theme is touched on in much of Thompson's historical writing. See especially 'The moral economy of the English crowd' (1991a) and *Whigs and Hunters* (1977).

9   E. P. Thompson's essay on local sexual moralities shows how those found guilty could experience rough justice at the hands of the male majority (1991b).

10 However, Rossanna Barragan in a recent analysis of early Bolivian legal codes has argued that while they are closely derived from the Napoleonic codes, there are none the less minor 'differences which make a difference' and which identify them as the Bolivian, rather than the Spanish or Venezuelan, versions of the same code (1996).

11 In a war-torn country like Peru, the difficulties of obtaining the basic documentation for an identity card are often daunting – an issue currently being researched by Sarah Skar of the University of Oslo. In recent local elections in Bolivia, a peasant who won a clear majority was unable to take office because his parents had never obtained a birth certificate for him.

12 In her account of the constitutive exclusion of women from the law, Carol Smart cites Freud on the lesser moral sense of women: 'I cannot evade the notion . . . that for women the level of what is ethically normal is different from what it is in men. Their super-ego is never so inexorable, so impersonal, so independent of its emotional origins as we require it to be in men . . . they show less sense of justice than men . . . ' (1989: 72–3).

REFERENCES

Barragan, R. (1996) 'The spirit of Bolivian modernity: citizenship, infamy and patriarchal hierarchy'. Unpublished paper.

Benveniste, E. (1969) *Le vocabulaire des institutions indo-européennes*, Vol. 2, Paris: Editions du Minuit.

Bourdieu, P. (1977) *Outline of a Theory of Practice*, Cambridge: Cambridge University Press.

—— (1990a) 'From rules to strategies' in *In other words*, Oxford: Polity Press, 59–75.

—— (1990b) 'Codification' in *In other words*, Oxford: Polity Press, 76–86.

Clifford, J. (1987) 'Identity in Mashpee' in *The predicament of Culture*, Berkeley: University of California Press.

Comaroff, J. (1995) *Legality, Modernity and Ethnicity in Colonial South Africa: an Excursion in the Historical Anthropology of Law*, LSE Centenary Lecture in Law and Society, London.

Cooper, F. and Stoler, A. (1989) 'Tensions of empire: colonial control and visions of rule' *Amer Ethnol* 16: 609–21.

Fasso, G. (1981–2) 'Lusnaturalismo' in N. Bobbio, N. Matteucci, G. Pasquino (eds) *Diccionario de politica* Mexico: Siglo XXI.

Fitzpatrick, P. (1983) 'Law, plurality and underdevelopment' in D. Sugarman (ed.) *Legality, Ideology and the State*, London: Academic Press, 159–83.

—— (1992) *The Mythology of Modern Law*, London: Routledge.

Fortes, M. (1959) *Oedipus and Job in West African Religion*, Cambridge: Cambridge University Press.

Fuller, C. (1994) 'Legal anthropology, legal pluralism and legal thought', *Anthropology Today*, 10 (3): 9–12, June.

Griffiths, J. (1986) 'What is legal pluralism?', *J Legal Plural*, 24: 1–56.

Kuper, A. (1988) *The Invention of Primitive Society*, London: Routledge.

Merry, S.E. (1992) 'Anthropology, law and transnational processes', *Ann Rev Anthropol*, 21: 357–79.

Mitchell, J. (1982) 'Introduction – I' in J. Mitchel and J. Rose (eds) *Feminine Sexuality: Jacques Lacan and the Ecole Freudienne*, New York: Pantheon Books.

Raz, J. (1979) *The Authority of Law. Essays on Law and Morality*, Oxford: Oxford University Press.

Roberts, S. (1979) *Order and Dispute. An Introduction to Legal Anthropology*, London: Penguin Books.

Rosaldo, R. (1991) *Culture and Truth*, Stanford: Stanford University Press.

Scarre, G. (1987) *Witchcraft and Magic in 16th and 17th Century Europe*.

Smart, C. (1989) *Feminism and the Power of Law*, London: Routledge.

Soto, H. de (1989) *The Other Path. The Invisible Revolution in the Third World*, London: I.B. Tauris.

Stoler, A. (1989) 'Making empire respectable: the politics of race and sexual morality in 20th century colonial cultures' *Amer Ethnol* 16: 634–61.

Thompson, E. P. (1977) *Whigs and Hunters. The Origin of the Black Acts*, London: Peregrine Books.

—— (1991a) 'The moral economy of the English crowd' in *Customs in Common*, London: Merlin Books.

—— (1991b) 'Rough music' in *Customs in Common*, London: Merlin Books.

Unger, R. (1977) *Law in Modern Society*, New York: Free Press.

Part I

The state and its attributes

Chapter 2

Human rights talk and anthropological ambivalence
The particular contexts of universal claims

Marie-Bénédicte Dembour

It is hardly possible today to open a newspaper without coming across a reference to human rights. We hear almost daily about abominable violations of human rights taking place around the world and occasionally of cases being brought before the European Court of Human Rights. Additional references to human rights demonstrate how pregnant this discourse has become. For example, as I was writing this chapter, an article appeared in the *Guardian* about a bank in Bangladesh which only lends to the poor (report by Clive Wood-cock, 16 May 1994: 16). It explained that the average loan of the Grameen Bank does not exceed the equivalent of £50 over 12 months and enables the borrower (who has no experience of handling money) to start a small business (for instance through the purchase of a second-hand sewing machine) and, thus, to get out of the poverty trap in which he, but more often she, has found herself. What interests me is not so much the unusual conditions under which the Grameen Bank works (borrowers have to be in groups of five and they participate in decision-making for the bank's operations) as the fact that the man behind it, Professor Muhammad Yunus, uses the language of human rights to describe the idea behind the successful project. He is quoted as saying that the Bank thinks that credit should not be the privilege of the fortunate few, and that it sees credit as a human right. Referring to human rights in this particular context makes sense. As I shall argue below, human rights are first and foremost political aspirations. They embody claims for a more egalitarian world, and these claims draw their strength and legitimacy precisely from the fact that they are cast in the language of 'human rights'. The last proposition is somewhat tautological. Why this should be so is the question which has driven me to write this chapter. I shall not tackle it directly, however. Instead I shall invite anthropologists to replace their original (and persisting) ambivalence about human rights with analysis.

After having outlined the reasons for this ambivalent attitude, I shall remark on the recurrent, but in my opinion false, debate on the universality of human rights. With reference to legal material, I shall seek to clarify different usages of the term, which is important as it is generally used as if what it was meant to cover was clear, while in fact it is full of ambiguities. This discussion will also highlight a number of paradoxes central to human rights talk. We shall see that the effectiveness of human rights at an individual level depends on the person belonging to the 'right' national state even though they derive from a universal concept of the human being, that their practice excludes whole classes of people even though they rest on an ideal which emphasizes individual freedom and brotherhood, that they represent the language of not-yet-realized – and ever-to-be re-identified – political claims at the same time as they are phrased in terms of eternal truth, in other words that the reality of their discourse is highly contingent even though the concept presents itself as absolute and value free. Anthropologists' wariness towards such a concept is understandable. None the less even they occasionally refer to human rights. Although on the whole they do so to denounce the intolerable rather than to declare rights, the fact that they do so points to the pervasive and inescapable place of human rights talk in current political discourse. The reasons for its 'success' should be part of the anthropological research agenda. Without exploring it here in any detail, I shall merely observe that the reification of the concept can be politically valuable, even though it is not intellectually tenable.

ANTHROPOLOGY'S AMBIVALENCE OVER HUMAN RIGHTS

In any discussion of human rights, one document always assumes a particular importance: the Universal Declaration of Human Rights.[1] Its signing in 1948 by the United Nations is invariably taken to mark the true start of the international protection of human rights. Not that it is suggested that nothing 'of the kind' existed before: a variety of documents, which had all served to limit the power of the modern Western state, are proclaimed as its predecessors. These include the French *Déclaration des droits de l'homme et du citoyen* of 1789, the Bill of Rights added to the US Constitution in 1791 (following the model of the Virginia Bill of Rights), and occasionally even the

Magna Carta. The signing of the UN Declaration, however, is presented as a breakthrough in the history of human rights, because of its (supposedly) universal application. To quote Antonio Cassesse, a lawyer of international repute: 'Since 1948 ... all countries in the world ... have at their disposal an international code, to decide how to conduct themselves and how to judge others' (Cassesse 1990: 1).[2]

Laws are enacted in reaction to particular situations. In this case, the atrocities committed during World War II were the impetus behind the Declaration; a genocide had been needed for human rights legislation to start developing. The late lawyer Paul Sieghart saw it as no little irony that

> today, we have to thank Hitler and Stalin for the installation of the new international code of human rights law – for, without them, the modern secular world might never have rediscovered the need ... for a set of universal standards, superior to the sovereign will of any Prince or state, which can place external constraints on their relationships with their own subjects.
>
> (Sieghart 1985: 38)

The trend among lawyers since the mid-nineteenth century has been a move away from 'natural law' and towards a legal positivism which understood law to be constituted by that which society, i.e. government, posited as such, irrespective of moral content. The events of the 1940s clearly indicated to lawyers that not all laws were acceptable.

Anthropologists must also have realized that not everything was acceptable; at the same time they were wary of the establishment of universal standards. In 1947 the Executive Board of the American Anthropological Association submitted a statement on human rights to the UN Commission on Human Rights. It identified the main problem in the drawing up of the Declaration as follows: 'How can the proposed Declaration be applicable to all human beings, and not be a statement of rights conceived only in terms of the values prevalent in the countries of western Europe and America?', and made three 'scientific' propositions. The first called for respect for cultural differences; the second asserted the impossibility of evaluating cultures; the last concluded that a Declaration could never apply to mankind as a whole. The author was none other than Melville Herskovits (1947). His strong cultural relativism can hardly have been of help to the UN drafting commission,[3] which nevertheless proceeded with its work and issued a document.

While the resulting Declaration did not allude to the right to credit with which I began this chapter,[4] it recognized the rights to presumed innocence, nationality, property, social security, education, and others of a vein which implied a particular type of society and could only confirm the ambivalence of anthropologists about the vocabulary of 'universal human rights'. Although anthropologists do sometimes protest as a professional body against 'the intolerable', which they are then ready to identify in terms of human rights violations (see below), on the whole, it is fair to say that they have avoided employing the language of human rights (Cohen 1989: 1015).

Significantly, the few reviews of the literature on 'anthropology and human rights' tend either to include pieces of work which have not been produced by anthropologists and/or to state that anthropologists are in fact contributing to the human rights debate, but without using such a label (Downing and Kushner 1988; Messer 1993). The reasons why anthropologists have distanced themselves from this particular language are understandable. The concept of 'human rights' is generally presented as a given – if not necessarily God-given – then none the less as something which exists independently of human or legal – i.e. social – recognition, whereas anthropologists would be quick to point to its socially constructed nature. This will be the standpoint of this chapter. My contention is that human rights only exist because they are talked about. Contrary to most philosophers working in this field (e.g. Pennock and Chapman 1981), I shall not attempt to elucidate the 'true' concept of human rights, but shall accept that the expression can cover different things and be used in different ways by different people or in different contexts.

THE UNIVERSALITY OF HUMAN RIGHTS – A FALSE PROBLEM

A recurrent issue in debates on human rights concerns the question of their universality. However, if we accept that human rights exist when they are talked about, their universality ceases to be a problematic issue.

The problem is generally framed around the fact that human rights originated in the West, which raises the question of the legitimacy or illegitimacy of their 'exportation' to non-Western societies. While some authors do not hesitate to speak of this 'exportation' as a form of imperialism (e.g. Pollis and Schwab 1980), others point out that to deny the relevance of human rights for the Third World only benefits the ruling classes by exempting them from obligations towards the people they rule (e.g. Donnelly 1989). In the latter group, many scholars argue that 'traditional' societies already had before European penetration, and still have, their own concept of human rights. Typical of this approach is the way Abdullahi An-Na'im and Francis Deng present the aim of a book which they edited:

> We sought [to reinforce and promote universal respect for and protection of human rights] by countervailing the conventional view that the concept of human rights is peculiar to the West and therefore inherently alien to non-Western traditions of third world countries to which it is now being extended. Our policy concern was that this conventional approach ... deprives [the concept] of the substantive enrichment from the variety of cultural values underlying the diverse notions of human rights around the world.
> (An-Na'im and Deng 1990: xi)

The anthropological contribution to 'human rights' is generally envisaged from this kind of perspective. For instance, Theodore Downing invites students doing fieldwork to take up the following questions (selected from within a longer list): What social groups hold human rights propositions? What rights do they protect? To whom do they apply? What institutions define and maintain these codes of conduct? (Downing 1988: 17–18).

Did human rights exist in traditional societies? More importantly, is this an interesting question? My feeling is that it is no more fruitful a line of inquiry than asking, as legal anthropology used to do, whether law did or did not exist in pre-colonial non-Western societies. The answer to the first question obviously depends on the perspective adopted. From a functional point of view, it is safe to assume that all societies have some kind of mechanism to restrain the power of their rulers. In this sense, all societies may well have 'human rights'. Basically this is the point of view adopted by Ronald Cohen (1993: especially 7 and 10) and Timothy Fernyhough (1993: especially 50) in arguments which, far from reifying the concept, insist that rights are not given but are fought for, and that they change over time. While I agree with the latter approach, I tend to align myself with the sociologist Rhoda Howard, who forcefully argues that 'most known societies did not and do not have conceptions of human rights' (Howard 1992: 81). She expands: 'Human rights are a modern concept now universally applicable in principle because of the social evolution of the entire world toward state societies' (ibid.; see also

Donnelly 1989: 50ff.). It cannot be denied that, from a formal point of view, human rights, *as we talk about them today*, did not formally exist in, say, pre-colonial Africa. Why, then, this insistence by most authors to discover 'human rights' in 'traditional' societies?

The aim is obviously to counteract the argument that the concept of human rights is alien to the non-Western world and is thus neither applicable nor even relevant to it. But why take this particular route to defend the applicability of (some) human rights throughout the world today? After all, no one would question the relevance of nationalism in the 'Third World' today, despite its clearly Western origin. Perhaps the variation in treatment comes from the fact that human rights, with their inescapable natural law connotations, tend to present themselves as eternal and universal truth, rather than as evolving matter, while nationalism is more obviously socially bound and more readily seen as adapting itself to particular social circumstances. However, this misses the point. What needs to be asserted is that both nationalism and human rights emanate from an individualistic ideology, that they both imply a certain homogenization, and that they are both linked to a particular form of political government, i.e. the modern state. This has been discussed in respect to nationalism (Anderson 1983; also Dumont 1986: 10). Anthropologists, I contend, should also undertake an analysis along these lines with respect to human rights. In particular, such an analysis would help explain the strength which the language of human rights has assumed in our modern 'global' world – something the present approaches in the literature cannot do.

As a preliminary step to this analysis, I shall use legal material to examine what the expression is meant to cover. I shall defend the view that it fundamentally serves to articulate political claims in a way which clothes them with an aura of incontestable legitimacy.

CLAIMS AGAINST THE STATE, BUT ALSO ASPIRATIONS FOR A BETTER WORLD

As I hinted above, human rights developed as a means to set limits to the power of the state *vis-à-vis* its citizens. The fact that a relationship between 'state' and 'civil society' (two concepts which cannot be taken rigidly to describe social reality) is involved is particularly clear when one looks at the European Convention of Human Rights. This document is arguably one of the most, and historically certainly the first, efficient pieces of international legislation on human rights. One feature of the Convention (adopted by the Council of Europe in 1950) is that cases can be brought before a Commission and a Court for alleged infringement of its provisions. These cases are *always* brought against a State, signatory to the Convention. In fact, no other defendant is imaginable. For example, if I am murdered in the street by someone who is after my money, there is no violation of human rights and no case to be brought to Strasbourg, as long as the state acts correctly, for instance by investigating the murder irrespective of the colour of my skin. By contrast, a violation of human rights would occur if I were killed in the street by a death squad which the government in power directly or indirectly supported. In other words, according to the best legal view, it is states, as opposed to private persons, that are ultimately responsible for violations of human rights.

The International Convention Against Torture (adopted by the UN in 1984) applies this point in its definition of torture as:

> any act by which severe pain or suffering... is intentionally inflicted on a person for such purposes as... obtaining information..., punishing... or intimidating... when [and this is the important passage for our present discussion] such pain or suffering is inflicted by or at the instigation of or with the consent or acquiescence of a public official or other person acting in an official capacity.
>
> (Article 1 of the International Convention Against Torture)

In this light, the imaginary example chosen by the lawyer Sieghart to illustrate one argument seems odd. He writes: 'Suppose... I am tortured... by my sadistic uncle...' (Sieghart 1985: 90). Presumably, the 'sadistic uncle', who is not further qualified, does not 'represent' a state; he is 'just' another individual. Strictly speaking, his behaviour, however physically damaging and reprehensible, is an example neither of torture nor of a human rights violation. Or is it? Why otherwise would an excellent lawyer make such a simple mistake? The answer lays in the fact that human rights discourse embodies claims not only against governmental abuses but also aspirations for a better, 'civil', world.

Jack Donnelly, a political scientist praised by many for having provided one of the most useful accounts of the concept of human rights, thus argues that these rights are held against 'all other persons and institutions' (Donnelly 1989: 1). He asserts this while recognizing that 'human rights came to be articulated primarily as claims of any individual against the state' (Donnelly 1989: 70, see also 266–9). In fact, because human rights were a reaction against the development of the modern state, he says that 'the West can perhaps be *blamed*, rather than praised, for inventing (or, rather, having been forced to invent) human rights' (Donnelly 1989: 65, original emphasis). None the less, when he states that human rights rest on 'a constructive interaction between the individual and society', the phrase 'especially the state' which immediately follows is in brackets (Donnelly 1989: 18). As the quotation at the beginning of this paragraph reveals, Donnelly sees human rights as governing relationships between individuals too. In this sense, then, being tortured by 'my sadistic uncle' violates my human right to physical and psychological integrity.

Human rights are not commonly regarded by those unfamiliar with the relevant literature as governing the relationship between state and citizens, but are more normally defined as those rights which everybody has by virtue of being human, a definition which does not say anything about who the holder of the duty corresponding to the right(s) is. The person of the duty-holder does not appear to be of particular importance to such definition of the concept. This silence is not a simple omission. Outside the sphere of human rights specialists, what is stressed is that every human being should be able to live a life of dignity, free from fear and from want (to adapt the terms used by F.D. Roosevelt in 1941), i.e. a life where his or her human rights are respected.[5] To go back to the example of the Grameen Bank, readers of the *Guardian*'s article probably did not think of explaining the lack of general credit facilities for the poor as a failing of the state's responsibilities. It is 'society' which is seen as responsible.

In a short and illuminating article on the nature of human rights, the Dutch diplomat J. Herman Burgers distinguishes between the 'vertical' and the 'horizontal' significance of human rights: although human rights standards are primarily set to govern the relationship between the individual and the state ('vertical' significance), they also necessarily govern relations among individuals ('horizontal' significance) and in some cases this may well be their main significance. He gives the example of Article 16, 2 of the Universal Declaration, which reads: 'Marriage shall be entered into only with the free and full consent of the intending spouses' (Burgers 1990: 66).[6] One could add that the Declaration speaks in its first article of the 'spirit of brotherhood', in accordance with which all human beings are invited to act. This last phrase renders perfectly the way in which human rights are held to be horizontally applicable. It also points to their 'lack of teeth' as anybody's responsibility becomes no one's respon-sibility, and to their utopian quality as they rest on a certain image of a beautiful, peaceful, inclusive world.

EXCLUSIONARY PRACTICES

The ideology of human rights stresses equality between human beings. In the words of the Universal Declaration: 'Everyone is entitled to all the rights and freedoms set forth in this Declaration, without distinction of any kind, such as race, colour, sex, language, religion, political or other opinion, national or social origin, property, birth or other status' (Article 2). Human rights talk is not conceptual-ized in terms of classes. It conceptualizes human persons as being of equal value. It is a manifestation of individualism in that it attributes value to the individual *qua* individual. According to the ideology, all human beings without exception should have their human rights protected.

However, this ideology masks a different reality. In practice, not everyone receives protection against violations of his or her human rights; in fact, huge classes of people are excluded from protection. Refugees are a good case in point. As is well known, the law makes a distinction between political and economic refugees. It does not specifically concern itself with the latter, who are those persons who seek to travel to another place in order to improve their material conditions of life – or to survive. Legally, they are treated like any other aliens. By contrast, international provisions exist for political refugees, who are legally defined as persons who

> owing to well-founded fear of being persecuted for reasons of race, religion, nationality, membership of a particular social group or political opinion, [are] outside the country of [their] nationality and [are] . . . unwilling to avail [themselves] of the protection of that country.
>
> (Article 1 of the 1951 Geneva Convention on the Status of
> Refugees)

Despite a common assumption, international legislation on political refugees does not make it an obligation for signatory states to grant asylum. The obligation which it lays down is one of *non-refoulement*, which means that a state who is party to the Convention cannot send back a political refugee who is already in its territory. If he or she is not yet in, the state is under no obligation to grant entry.

Thus, legal obligations only arise for the state when political refugees are within its sphere of influence: in such a situation the state must abstain from sending them back and it must also grant them various rights which make it possible for them to live in its territory (Goodwin-Gill 1983).

Such rules are obviously contrary to the ideology of human rights. For a start, the distinction between economic and political refugees does not make sense in the light of the declared aim of human rights to provide a decent living for everyone, irrespective of their status. Is it really much less sinister to die from hunger and/or in a civil war than to die as a result of torture inflicted because of one's personal opinion? In 1991, the European Court of Human Rights none the less declared lawful the deportation from the UK to Sri Lanka of Tamil former torture victims who were not, so the Court reasoned, in a situation dissimilar to that of other young male Tamils, and so did not qualify as political refugees (*Vilvarajah and Others*). To explain the distinction between economic and political refugees, one must turn to the history of human rights, which were originally conceived as those political and civil rights secured against the state. Economic and social rights were only thought about later. Pragmatic considerations help to maintain the distinction between these two 'generations' of human rights. It is much safer, because less threatening to the economic interests of the members of a relatively affluent society, to undertake to accept a limited number of politically persecuted individuals within its borders than to accept obligations towards fellow human beings across the board. One may well like to care for a limited number of fellow humans, but not for all of them.

Economic refugees are outside the realm of international law. Political refugees may be slightly more fortunate in that they come within its ambit, but their lot is not particularly secure. Apart from the dire difficulties of proving that one is actually a refugee, and the often penitentiary-like conditions reserved for the asylum-seekers who have arrived in a 'host' state (for the UK, see Amnesty International 1994), it remains true that the international community is ready to accept only very limited duties deriving from the concept of *non-refoulement*. Such a position, at odds with the generous ideology of human rights, can be traced to the main purpose of human rights, i.e. the successful articulation of claims against the state. From this perspective, it is possible to understand why no claims can be made outside an established relationship with a particular state. When the refugee has not entered a state, they are 'logically' left out of human rights protection: the prospective host state has nothing to do with them.

I have referred to the predicament of refugees. I could have talked of many other cases, such as those who are deemed to be outside the realm of many rights because national law classifies them as 'illegal aliens' (Weaver 1988), or those whose governments allow killings to take place in a climate of national and international impunity (see, for instance, de Waal 1994; Zur 1994; Werbner 1995). For these people, who ultimately fail to qualify for protection because they are nationals of the 'wrong' state, human rights talk does not offer much comfort. In other words, although the ideology of human rights does away with the concept of the state to concentrate on the equal value of all human beings, its practice relies on the way in which individuals are classified in relation to a state. The lack of fit between theory and practice is thus at the core of the human rights concept, which depends for its existence and application on a state organization. It is not just that practice does not (yet) reflect the principle, but that the principle is such that practice cannot match it.[7]

HUMAN RIGHTS AS ENFORCEABLE LEGAL RIGHTS – SOMETIMES

Clearly appalled by the treatment given to refugees, Art Hansen syllogistically argues in a contribution to an anthropological volume on human rights: '[H]uman rights must by definition apply to all humans. Unfortunately, refugees are not legally considered human. If they were, then they would be awarded rights already recognized as universal' (Hansen 1993: 141). The Universal Declaration indeed states: 'Everyone has the right to seek and enjoy in other countries asylum from persecution' (Article 14). Hansen also has in mind other rights listed in the Declaration, including the rights to change nationality and to leave one's country and thus, according to one interpretation, to seek economic opportunities wherever one wishes to do so. His syllogism is arguably faulty, however, in that if refugees are denied the exercise of these rights, it is not so much because they are 'not legally considered human' as because the rights contained in the UN document are not 'legal' ones.[8]

As its name indicates, the UN Declaration is only a declaration; it is not binding in law. Rather, it sets 'a common standard of achievement for all peoples and all nations' (Preamble), but without attaching any sanction to failure to reach these standards, and without even really defining the standards to be achieved. Take, for example, Article 3: 'Everyone has the right to life, liberty and security of person'. Its equivalent in the European Convention of Human Rights runs over more than one article. Let us examine Article 2, which deals with the right to life. It begins:

> Everyone's right to life shall be protected by law. No one shall be deprived of his life intentionally save in the execution of a sentence of a court following his conviction of a crime for which this penalty is provided by law.[9]

It goes on to list three situations, i.e. legitimate defence, arrest and social trouble, where deprivation of life shall not be regarded as inflicted in contravention of the Convention. The European Convention uses more precise language than the UN Declaration because it intends to make the rights it confers judicial. It also sets up a mechanism for the enforcement of the Convention through the creation of a Commission and a Court.

The European Convention, then, provides enforceable legal rights, while the UN Declaration (generally) does not. In terms of breadth, however, the Universal Declaration is much more encompassing than the Convention. It lists more than twenty-five rights covering both 'political and civil' and 'economic and social' categories. By contrast, the European Convention included about ten rights at the time of its inception. Although rights have been added through the adoption of Protocols, it is still the case that the rights conferred by the Convention can be said to belong to the 'political and civil' category. The Council of Europe produced a European Social Charter in 1961 (not to be confused with the EC legislation of the same name), but without providing for any mechanism of enforcement. It is not particularly difficult to see why governments have not wished to tie their hands in this respect. They wanted to distinguish problems of, say, unemployment and homelessness from violations of human rights (against any individual within their jurisdiction, whether one of their own nationals or not) for which they could be held legally responsible.

In human rights law, a rather strong dichotomy thus exists between civil and political rights on the one hand and social and economic ones on the other. International law privileges the former against the latter. But are human rights primarily about political freedoms? Organizations such as Amnesty International may well give this impression by presenting their work as if it is concerned with human rights *per se*, while it is arguably only concerned with a small fraction of them (Alston 1990). If one equates human rights with rights enforceable through application of human rights legislation, the assumption that 'true' human rights consist in political rights may hold – at least at present (cf. Cranston 1964). It miserably breaks down, however, if one embraces a larger definition of human rights (Donnelly and Howard 1988). Does the fact that economic and social rights are not, on the whole, the subject of enforceable international legislation, make them less of a human rights issue? The same question can be asked in respect of so-called collective rights which include, among others, the right to self-determination and the more recently 'discovered' right to a clean environment.

HUMAN RIGHTS AS EXTRALEGAL CLAIMS

When the member-states of the United Nations adopted the Universal Declaration in 1948 (with three abstentions),[10] they did not sign a document which was meant to produce legal effects such that someone could rely on rights contained in it before a court. This is more or less what happened, however, in the *Filartiga* case, when a ex-member of the Paraguayan police who was living in North America found himself in a US Court responding to charges of torture, after the family of a man who had been kidnapped and tortured to death in 1976 in Paraguay recognized him as the torturer of their relative. The father and sister of the victim, then asylum-seekers in the US, brought a case before a US Court. The latter had to decide whether it was competent to deal with a case which involved foreigners in a foreign country and, if so, which law it was going to apply. The Court of Appeals (Second Circuit) decided on 30 June 1980 that the right to be free from torture 'has become part of customary international law, as evidenced and defined by the Universal Declaration of Human Rights'. It found that 'official torture is now prohibited by the law of nations' and that 'the prohibition is clear and unambiguous, and admits of no distinction between treatment of aliens and citizens'. As a result, it felt confident that 'the dictum ... to the effect that "violations of international law do not occur when the aggrieved parties are nationals of the acting state" is clearly out of tune with the current usage and practice of international law'. As for the claim that 'even if the tort alleged is a violation of modern international law, federal jurisdiction may not be exercised [considering the case involved acts committed by aliens on alien ground]', the Court dismissed it on the grounds that the American Alien Tort statute indicated that 'a state or a nation has a legitimate interest in the orderly resolution of disputes among those within its borders'.

Although not strictly binding in law, it is clear that the Declaration is recognized as being part of international customary law and has acquired a highly persuasive authority. Needless to say, however, not all the rights it lists would lead to such 'adventurous' judgments as the *Filartiga* one. The kind of argument which the American Court pursued in this instance is not imaginable in respect of other human rights, such as the right to seek asylum or the right to 'a standard of living adequate for the health and well-being of [everyone], including food, clothing, housing and medical care and necessary social services' (Article 25 of the Universal Declaration).

The expression 'human rights' is thus ambiguous with regard to the meaning of the term 'right' which it contains. Although it sometimes refers to enforceable legal rights, it arguably refers more often to moral rights which have not yet found their way in legally binding provisions, but hopefully will. As Jack Donnelly remarks, human rights claims mainly serve 'to challenge or change existing institutions, practices, or norms, especially legal institutions'; they are 'essentially extralegal' (Donnelly 1989: 14). He goes on to argue that 'giving legal force to these rights [through international law, national constitution, or 'simple' national law] is the ultimate aim of the struggle for human rights' (Donnelly 1989: 14). He sees this as creating a 'possession paradox', for it is when one does not need to say that one has human rights (because one has legal rights) that one's human rights are best protected:

> To the extent that human rights claims are politically effective, the needs to make such claims are reduced or eliminated. One claims a human right in the hope of ultimately creating a society in [which] such claims will no longer be necessary. Where human rights are effectively protected, we continue to *have* human rights, but there is no need or occasion to *use* them.
>
> (Donnelly 1989: 14, original emphasis)

I cannot object to the statement that I have just quoted for, as it is phrased, it provides a correct analysis of the situation. At the same time, there is something in it and in the work of Donnelly generally, as well as of other scholars working on human rights, which leaves me uncomfortable: the firm commitment to the idea of human rights and the impression of a belief in some kind of definite, universal, human rights. To quote Donnelly once more:

> Human rights claims do imply a claim that one *ought* to have a *legal* right to the object in question. But in contrast to other grounds on which legal rights might be demanded – for example, justice, utility, self-interest, or beneficence – human rights-based demands for legal rights involve a moral *entitlement* to the rights in question.
>
> (Donnelly 1989: 15, original emphasis)

Where does this emphasized 'entitlement' come from, especially in view of the fact that it is distinguished from a concern for justice? Donnelly answers: 'human nature' (Donnelly 1989:16–19). Such answer is not anthropologically convincing – although one's own religion or values may incline one to adopt it.

In my view, human rights are (predominantly) extralegal not because they correspond to 'natural' moral rights but because they serve to articulate political claims which make sense in a particular social context – as illustrated by Professor Yunus's reference to the human right to credit or by the human right to a clean environment which begins to find its way into new national constitutions.[11]

FROM ANTHROPOLOGICAL AMBIVALENCE TO POLITICAL COMMITMENT

This is not the most common view, and the pretension to conceptual (rather than contingent) universality which pertains to human rights talk explains why anthropologists have refused to accept the concept of human rights at face value. Nevertheless, every so often, they refer to it. For instance, major anthropological conferences commonly proceed to adopt a number of resolutions written in the name of human rights. 'Anthropologists Against Ethnic Violence' included the following words in their statement against ethnic cleansing in Bosnia: 'We wish to re-assert our professional vision of the oneness of humanity, of the importance of understanding and respecting ethnic and cultural differences without allowing them to become a rationalization for violations of human rights' (BASAPP 1993: 24). Let us note that the expression 'human rights' is not defined in such statements, but used as if what it refers to is clear. Of course it is not – or not wholly. If pressed, the authors of such statements would probably find it difficult to circumscribe what exactly, in their view, human rights are. If they inadvertently escape the difficulty, it is because they speak in terms of human rights *violations*, rather than prescriptions. They express protest rather than declare rights.

Gabriel Gosselin remarks that cultural relativism is itself relative. He cites Louis Dumont: 'Such relativism is not absolute. The oneness of humankind ... sets limits to the variation.' The quotation continues: 'Each society is thus marked by this universal model. Such a mark is negative ... we cannot derive from it a prescription, but it represents the opposite of the prescription, or its limitation' (Gosselin 1989: 565, my translation).[12] To apply this idea to our present subject, anthropologists in their statements on human rights are ready to say beyond which limits the world should not have gone, but not to contribute to a positive definition of human rights. Their aim is not to draft international conventions but to denounce the intolerable.[13] Such a 'negative' task is more easily achieved than its opposite, which would be to define the 'tolerable', i.e. what can be done or, going one step further, what *should* be done. This does not mean that the intolerable is always easily identified, as the polemic surrounding the caning of an American citizen in Singapore recently reminded us (see for instance Janet Daley in *The Times*, 28 April 1994: 18; also Falk 1992: 50). Nevertheless, to give a contrasted extreme, few would refuse to accept that the massacres in Rwanda which followed the death of the President on 6 April 1994 are beyond the limits of the tolerable.[14]

By having recourse in their political engagement to the language of human rights despite their wariness towards conventions of human rights, be it the Universal Declaration, the 1989 UN Convention on the Rights of the Child, or other legislative documents, anthropologists show two things. The first is that the kind of cultural relativism towards which they are inclined does not need to entail a tolerance towards all that 'cultures' produce; Alison Renteln in fact beautifully argues that cultural relativism and tolerance are two separate theoretical positions (1988). The second is that the language of human rights has become both pervasive and persuasive. Even anthropologists use it, and, by doing so, they strike a chord. In fact, they need say no more, for violations of human rights are today by definition unacceptable.

HUMAN RIGHTS AND POLITICAL EXPEDIENCY

References to human rights may sound politically correct. What they cover, however, cannot be taken for granted. They are constantly evolving, and never beyond dispute.[15] Ultimately, human rights only exist because they are talked about. We may choose to use such language, but we should be clear about the reasons why we do so.

Donnelly asserts: '... human rights put one in a position to mount a particularly powerful moral attack on rights-abusive institutions. This is why having even an [legally] unenforced right is so important' (Donnelly 1989: 15). I cannot help feeling, as an anthropologist, that the truth of such a statement is part of what needs to be explained rather than posited/reported. Human rights claims carry with them an enormous legitimacy in the late twentieth century – even though they do not bring immediate changes in governance. But why do they achieve this, and why are they expressed in such a form? I do not have a definite answer to these questions, but I think anthropologists should address them. Individualism, globalization and legalism (i.e. the tendency to put rules and assumptions into legal terms) would no doubt be key words in the analysis, and political expediency would also need to be part of it.[16]

I have argued above that the generous ideology upon which human rights rest, based upon a conception of equality between human beings, conflicts with a practice which cannot avoid discriminating between human beings. At the same time, it must be recognized that human rights talk has helped to bring about revolutionary changes and to improve the lot of groups and individuals – albeit not all of them indiscriminately (Stammers 1993). This is so because human rights talk at times successfully manages to articulate (evolving) political claims. It is presumably because Professor Yunus, and the journalist who reported his ideas, found the phrase powerful that the former used it, and the latter quoted it, in respect of the activities of the Grameen Bank which tries to improve the predicament of the poor in Bangladesh.

Being engaged with one's world requires an engagement with the debates arising in this world; it may then also require adopting its vocabulary. Ironically, encouraging my readers to use the language of human rights is probably also inviting them to reify the concept. Political claims are at their best when they are essentialized. It is then that they appear to be unchallengeable, that they can hope to receive a legitimacy which is not contestable. How powerful would a demand to extend the human right of credit to the poor be, if the malleable nature of 'human rights' were put to the fore? To be persuasive, the demand needs to invoke something bigger and more permanent than social accident. It is therefore not surprising that the Universal Declaration is often invoked without referring to its precise content:

the vagueness which surrounds it is what gives it its strength. The expression 'human rights' is used as if it was clear, could stand by itself, and need not be substantiated. But it is not, for human rights claims can never be divorced from the particular context in which they are raised.

Most human rights activists (including academics working in this field) probably start from the assumption, and firmly believe, that human rights exist independently from social recognition, and need to be put into practice. I have argued by contrast that human rights only exist because they are talked about. I have also noted that such language has become unavoidable on the political scene (cf. Fox 1992: 13; Godelier as cited by Skalnik 1994: 23). As such, the phenomenon should be part of the anthropological research agenda. As to the question of political engagement, it is for anthropologists personally to decide whether they wish to use such language, which certainly can be beneficial. If they decide to do so, they should be aware of the limitations of the concept.

ACKNOWLEDGEMENTS

I wish to thank Richard Wilson, Rhoda Howard and especially Olivia Harris for perceptive and stimulating comments on an earlier draft. I also express my gratitude to the European University Institute (Florence) which granted me a Jean Monnet Fellowship in 1995 to work on a project about 'The idea of human rights', during which I prepared the final version of this chapter.

NOTES

1   There are many edited volumes which reproduce international law material, including the Universal Declaration and the other international law documents mentioned in this chapter for example Brownlie (1992).
2   This sentence gives the impression, in line with the mythological pretences of Western law, of a legal code which is coherent, complete (gapless) and just (cf. Lenoble and Ost 1980).
3   It was also criticized by other anthropologists, as the debates in the columns of the *American Anthropologist* after its publication demonstrate.
4   Rhoda Howard draws my attention to the fact that the 1979 UN Convention on the elimination of all forms of discrimination against women mentions credit. Article 23 provides that credit must be granted

to men and women on an equal footing. It does not, however, make credit a right as such.

5   It should be noted that dignity and human rights are conflated in this statement. Such confusion is the source of much sloppiness in the existing literature on human rights.

6   The provision on marriage, which rests on a certain idea of individual freedom, autonomy and determination, offers yet another illustration of the peculiar conception which underlies the formulation of rights in the Universal Declaration. It obviously raises the question of the pertinence of such a model outside its original (Western and state-oriented) context. Perhaps more importantly, it shows that human rights talk articulates dreams for the realization of a beautiful and problem-free world (based on the 'full' realization of the individual potential) in which human rights would 'simply' be respected, in this case in the sense that all men and women would 'freely' and 'fully' consent to their marriage – and live happy ever afterwards? Two remarks are in order. One is that 'happiness' and 'well-being' are indeed recurrent words in philosophical discussions on human rights (e.g. Pennock 1981: 12), revealing human rights as a utopia. The second, related to the first, is that a world respectful of human rights is an untenable hypothesis as soon as one accepts to take human rights seriously, i.e. at face-value, for what they present them-selves to be.

7   For a different view, denouncing the 'fallacy of confusing practice and principle', see Howard 1993: 318.

8   This is not to deny that some violations of human rights, particularly genocide, generally involve 'dehumanizing' processes, but rather to suggest that 'dehumanization' need not apply in the case of refugees, who are 'just not thought about'.

9   But see Protocol 6, adopted in 1984, concerning the abolition of the death penalty.

10   By Saudi Arabia, South Africa and the USSR.

11   For example the Belgian and the South African constitutions enacted in 1994. It is noteworthy that both these constitutions also specifically guarantee economic and social rights.

12   Original French text: 'Il ne s'agit pas d'un relativisme absolu. L'unité de l'humanité... met des limites à la variation... Il y a ainsi dans toute société l'empreinte de ce modèle universel... c'est une empreinte néga-tive... nous ne pouvons pas dériver de cette empreinte une prescription, mais elle représente le revers de la prescription, ou sa limite'.

13   Interestingly the word 'intolerable' appears more than once in a con-tribution by Richard Falk (1992).

14   Even this, however, is an 'external' view which is unlikely to be shared by those directly involved in the massacres: a friend of mine working for the Red Cross was 'coolly' made to understand by a Rwandese friend of hers that he had organized the killings of a village.

15   This is true even within a fairly homogeneous judicial space such as the Council of Europe where the European Commission and Court of Human Rights, and individuals within them, not uncommonly dis-agree on whether facts submitted to them for examination constitute

or not violations of human rights guaranteed by the European
Convention.
16   Richard Wilson is presently thinking about exactly this type of question
in his anthropological analysis of human rights. Although Kevin Dwyer
has not pursued this particular line of inquiry, his work (1991) is
noteworthy in that it seeks to document how human rights are talked
about in particular societies.

REFERENCES

Alston, P. (1990) 'The fortieth anniversary of the Universal Declaration of
Human Rights: a time more for reflection than for celebration', in J.
Berting, P.R. Baehr, J.H. Burgers, C. Flinterman, B. de Klerk, R. Kroes,
C.A. van Minnen and K. Wanderwal (eds) *Human Rights in a Pluralist
World: Individuals and Collectivities*, Westport: Meckler.
Amnesty International (1994) *Prisoners Without a Voice*, London: Amnesty
International.
An-Na'im, A.A. and Deng, F. M. (eds) (1990) *Human Rights in Africa: Cross-
Cultural Perspectives*, Washington, D.C.: Brookings Institution.
Anderson, B. (1983) *Imagined Communities: Reflections on the Origin and
Spread of Nationalism*, London: Verso.
BASAPP (1993) 'Anthropologists against ethnic violence: a statement',
Anthropology in Action 16: 24.
Brownlie, I. (1992) *Basic Documents on Human Rights*, Oxford: Clarendon
Press.
Burgers, J. H. (1990) 'The function of human rights as individual and
collective rights', in J. Berting *et al.* (eds) *Human Rights in a Pluralist
World: Individuals and Collectivities*, Westport: Meckler.
Cassesse, A. (1990) *Human Rights in a Changing World*, Cambridge: Polity
Press.
Cohen, R. (1989) 'Human rights and cultural relativism: the need for a new
approach', *American Anthropologist* 91: 1014–16.
—— (1993) 'Endless teardrops: prolegomena to the study of human rights in
Africa', in R. Cohen, G. Hyden and W. P. Nagan (eds) *Human Rights and
Governance in Africa*, Gainesville: University Press of Florida.
Cranston, M. (1964) *What Are Human Rights?*, New York: Basic Books.
Donnelly, J. (1989) *Universal Human Rights in Theory and Practice*, Ithaca:
Cornell University Press.
Donnelly J. and Howard, R.E. (1988) 'Assessing national human rights
performance: a theoretical framework', *Human Rights Quarterly* 10:
215–48.
Downing, T.E. (1988) 'Human rights research: the challenge for anthropo-
logists', in T.E. Downing and G. Kushner (eds) *Human Rights and
Anthropology*, Cambridge, MA: Cultural Survival.
Downing, T.E. and Kushner, G. (eds) (1988) *Human Rights and Anthropology*,
Cambridge, MA: Cultural Survival.

Dumont, L. (1986) *Essays on Individualism. Modern Ideology in Anthro-pological Perspective*, Chicago: The University of Chicago Press.

Dwyer, K. (1991) *Arab Voices: The Human Rights Debate in the Middle East*, London: Routledge.

Falk, R. (1992) 'Cultural foundations for the international protection of human rights', in A.A. An-Na'im (ed.) *Human Rights in Cross-Cultural Perspectives. A Quest for Consensus*, Philadelphia: University of Pennsylvania Press.

Fernyhough, T. (1993) 'Human rights and pre-colonial Africa', in R. Cohen, G. Hyden and W.P. Nagan (eds) *Human Rights and Governance in Africa*, Gainesville: University Press of Florida.

Fox, R. (1992) 'Comment: twice-told tales from India', *Anthropology Today* 8 (1): 11–13.

Goodwin-Gill, G.S. (1983) *The Refugee in International Law*, Cambridge: Cambridge University Press.

Gosselin, G. (1989) 'Sommes-nous tous des romantiques allemands? (Pour une socio-anthropologie des droits de l'homme)', *Bibliothèque des Cahiers de l'Institut de Linguistique de Louvain* 44 (2): 559–66.

Hansen, H. (1993) 'African refugees: defining and defending their human rights', in R. Cohen, G. Hyden and W.P. Nagan (eds) *Human Rights and Governance in Africa*, Gainesville: University Press of Florida.

Herskovits, M. (1947) 'Statement on human rights', *American Anthropologist* 49: 539–43.

Howard, R.E. (1992) 'Dignity, community, and human rights', in A.A. An-Na'im (ed.) *Human Rights in Cross-Cultural Perspectives. A Quest for Consensus*, Philadelphia: University of Pennsylvania Press.

—— (1993) 'Cultural absolutism and the nostalgia for community', *Human Rights Quarterly* 15: 315–38.

Lenoble, J. and Ost, F. (1980) *Droit, mythe et raison. Essai sur la dérive mytho-logique de la rationalité juridique*, Brussels: Facultés Universitaires Saint-Louis.

Messer, E. (1993) 'Anthropology and human rights', *Annual Review of Anthropology* 22: 221–49.

Pennock, J.R. (1981) 'Rights, natural rights, and human rights – a general view', in J.R. Pennock and J.W. Chapman (eds) *Human Rights*, Nomos XXIII, New York: New York University Press.

Pennock, J.R. and Chapman, J.W. (1981) *Human Rights*, Nomos XXIII, New York: New York University Press.

Pollis, A. and Schwab, P. (eds) (1980) *Human Rights: Cultural and Ideological Perspectives*, New York: Praeger.

Renteln, A.D. (1988) 'Relativism and the search for human rights', *American Anthropologist* 90: 56–72.

Sieghart, P. (1985) *The Lawful Rights of Mankind. An Introduction to the International Legal Code of Human Rights*, Oxford: Oxford University Press.

Skalnik, P. (1994) 'Mexico 1993: there is a bright future for anthropology', *Anthropology Today* 10(2): 22–3.

Stammers, N. (1993) 'Human rights and power', *Political Studies* XVI(1): 70–82.

Waal, A. de (1994) 'Genocide in Rwanda', *Anthropology Today* 10(3): 12.

Weaver, T. (1988) 'The human rights of undocumented workers in the United States–Mexico border region', in T.E. Downing and G. Kushner (eds) *Human Rights and Anthropology*, Cambridge, MA: Cultural Survival.

Werbner, R. (1995) 'Human rights and moral knowledge: arguments of accountability in Zimbabwe', in M. Strathern (ed.) *Shifting Contexts*, London: Routledge.

Zur, J. (1994) 'The psychological impact of impunity', *Anthropology Today* 10 (3): 12–17.

Chapter 3

Vigilantism
Order and disorder on the frontiers of the state

Ray Abrahams

INTRODUCTION

This chapter is a preliminary attempt at a general discussion of some
of the main characteristics of vigilantism. It follows some of my earlier
work on the subject, which was mainly focused upon recent developments in Tanzania where so-called Sungusungu vigilante groups
emerged in the early 1980s to combat cattle theft and other
criminality, as well as some more locally defined offences such as
witchcraft.[1]

Like many other Britons of my generation, I first became aware of
vigilantes as a teenage cinema-goer. I remember seeing a large number
of B Westerns on the silver screen of what we called 'the local' – in my
case a small building in North Manchester known as the MIP, which
was an acronym for the much grander 'Moston Imperial Palace'. The
place is now an indoor market, but its earlier glories return to my mind
when I read historical accounts of the Montana Vigilantes of the
1860s and the evil Sheriff Plummer whom I recognize almost as an old
acquaintance with a face uncannily like that of a minor 1940s actor.
My next conscious encounters with the subject were East African,
first when I noticed that night-watchmen in Kampala were available
through a self-styled 'vigilante' company, and later through preliminary reports of Suzette Heald's work in Bugisu. Then in the early
1980s, I first heard about local groups called Sungusungu which had
arisen among the Nyamwezi and Sukuma in west-central Tanzania at
that time, and which I labelled 'vigilantes' in my discussions of them.
    I mention all this for more than just the sake of reminiscence. For
the term 'vigilante' tends to conjure up emotive reactions of one sort
or another. Often they are negative, and this has been partly

influenced in recent years by the conflict between ANC-supporting 'comrades' and regime-supporting 'vigilantes' in South Africa. But there are also sometimes older deeper roots. Many fear vigilantism's disturbing implications for the authority of the police and courts and other formal instruments of state power, an aspect nicely brought out by the criminologist Les Johnston's recent (1992) characterization of vigilantism under the heading 'autonomous' as contrasted to 're-sponsible' citizenship. Beyond this, too, the term often smacks of violent 'mob rule' and the Captain Lynches of this world, in contrast to 'the rule of law' and respect for due process. Also, in addition to reactions to such threats to the established system, there is a common opposition from the left. For in spite of its potential for subversion, vigilantism commonly displays a non-revolutionary and even reac-tionary character, and one of its chief analysts, Richard Maxwell Brown (1975), interestingly uses the term 'conservative mob' when discussing its practitioners.[2] Rather than reject the state, vigilantism commonly thrives on the idea that the state's legitimacy at any point in time depends on its ability to provide citizens with the levels of law and order they demand. Its emergence is often more a vote of no confidence in state efficiency than in the concept of the state itself. Lastly, there is sometimes an assumption, which is correct for some cases but not others, that vigilantism is an elitist weapon dressed in populist clothing.

Vigilantism clearly highlights several ambiguities in relations between people and the state, and it is not surprising if my own reactions to it are ambivalent. My main research experience of it has been at Tanzanian village level, where fieldwork has tended – as with many anthropologists – to generate a sympathy for 'ordinary' villagers. For such villagers, situated on the edge of the state and at the bottom of the political heap, vigilantism has been part of their efforts to make sense of their lives and maintain some sort of order in their world in the face of increased cattle theft and other crime, and the state's apparent inability to deal effectively with this. At the same time, however, I am well aware of the warts on the face of villages and other small communities, and the sometimes oppressive social control which membership of such a 'caring' group may entail. I am also conscious that such communities are not simply homogeneous, and that elements within them and outside them may exploit 'community' institutions for their own ends.

WHAT'S IN A NAME?

I have used the terms 'vigilante' and 'vigilantism' in this and other contexts partly because of, and partly in spite of, these mixed qualities. In using them, I have wanted neither to overemphasize nor underplay their positive or negative connotations, and at the same time I have wished to recognize that what they represent are multifaceted, emotionally highly charged and changeable phenomena. The terms themselves create fewer problems for dealing with material from Tanzania, than from some other places, because the word 'vigilante' does not appear to have been as regular a part of Tanzanian vocabulary as it has been in some African and other countries; and even in Kenya and Zambia, where it is more common, it has been used relatively neutrally to designate small local groups of special constables and other keepers of the peace. Originally, the word was a Spanish one, which is of course related closely to the English 'vigil', 'vigilant' and 'vigilance', and it was first used in America in the nineteenth century. A similar term used there was 'vigilance committee', which was also found in South African townships around the turn of the century, though with an apparently different significance more akin to that of 'board of guardians'. The idea of 'neighbourhood watch', which has been much in vogue in Britain, is of course also closely related, despite the fact that it is often strongly contrasted there with vigilantism. Other early terms used in America were 'regulators' and 'moderators' as well as many other more specific titles. The different shades of meaning of such terms reflect the variety of forms which the phenomena in question may display, and the wide range of attitudes they may elicit from different people and at different times.

As all this implies, it is probably mistaken to attempt to define vigilantism in a simple, unambiguous way, though one can cope with the concept if one proceeds with caution and keeps certain points in mind. Firstly, vigilantism is not so much a thing in itself as a fundamentally relational or structural phenomenon. In this respect it is part of a broad zone in the world of law and politics which is comparable to the 'informal sector' in economics, or to the idea of civil society; and it is also rather like the concepts of a 'village' and of 'villagers' or 'peasants' generally which do not make much sense except in relation to – and often enough in contrast with – a wider setting.

Secondly, the unofficial nature of vigilantism tends to make it rather labile. It exists in an awkward borderland between law and illegality, in what I have elsewhere (Abrahams 1987) called 'the shadows rather than the bright lights of legitimacy and consensus', and it is always capable of slipping and sliding in one direction or another. As such, any definition *must* be treated as an 'ideal type' to which the phenomena which one investigates may interestingly approximate to some degree.

Despite some modern cinematic images of Charles Bronson or Clint Eastwood wreaking havoc in the city or on the High Plains, vigilantism is usually a group phenomenon both in America and elsewhere. It presumes the existence of the state, and of formal legal procedures over which the state normally claims a monopoly, and it is a form of self-help which is activated, *instead of* such formal procedures, against those whom the actors perceive as 'public enemies'. It is not self-help of the oppositional segmentary kind that operates between structurally equal groups. It may tend in this direction, and there may be argument about the extent to which it does so, but it moves away from the ideal type to the extent that it really has this quality. Its relation to the state is bound to be awkward. It typically emerges in zones where the state is viewed as ineffective or corrupt, and it often constitutes a criticism of state failure to meet the felt needs of those who resort to it.

ON THE FRONTIER OF THE STATE

Connected with all this is the more general idea of vigilantism as essentially a frontier phenomenon. Sometimes the frontier is simply a spatial one, with vigilantism operating on and beyond the literally distant edges of effective state control. This was clearly the case with many of the late eighteenth- and nineteenth-century American examples. Sometimes, it is the frontier of the urban no-go area or the underworld, which often enough exist in close spatial proximity to the governmental heartland. Sometimes too, there is additionally a kind of cultural frontier. In such cases state and vigilante often differ in their definition and/or recognition of a public enemy. In the Tanzanian case, both state and villagers agree that cattle rustlers are criminals, but there is much less accord between them on the question of witches which have also been a major focus of some groups' activities. Comparably, despite horrific exceptions, those who set out to control and harass minority and immigrant groups, or members of other races or religions, are not usually given explicit state support, though officials may find it convenient to turn a blind eye to such harassment.

As this last point suggests, and as Leach (1977) noted for other boundaries of the state, the frontier between formal law and vigilantism is commonly a fuzzy one. An important issue here is how clearly and effectively the division of labour between state activities and others is defined and maintained. An extreme case of blurred boundaries and ambiguity in this context is the 'death squad' variant of vigilantism, in which the officers of the state are also the vigilantes, and less violent forms of such role combination may arguably occur where police fabricate confessions and tamper with evidence in order to obtain convictions. Engagement in such activities commonly involves a disillusion with the state on the part of its own personnel, rather than simply on the part of those who are, or who would like to be, on the receiving end of its services. But such behaviour can of course also reflect a much wider range of political and economic motives.

Other broadly comparable areas of fuzziness are implicit in the distinction mentioned earlier between autonomous and responsible citizenship. The latter involves forms of community crime control which are sponsored and sanctioned by the state. Some early Chinese forms of local vigilance were of this sort as too are more modern Red Guard patterns. The official Tanzanian 'ten-house cell' system, of sets of households with an elected leader and a set of local responsibilities for maintaining co-operation and good social order within party guidelines, appears to have been derived from similar Chinese patterns. It is perhaps worth noting that a comparable ten-house system was established in early medieval London under Athelstan to combat cattle theft and other crime. Neighbourhood watch – to the extent that it collaborates with the police – is a common modern form of such responsible citizen activity, though it has a partly grass roots origin. Slippage may, however, take place across the boundary between autonomy and state control. Some groups may behave more autonomously than they were intended to, and the state may also try to take control of groups which began life as autonomous grass roots creations, as in fact happened in the case of Tanzanian Sungusungu groups in the late 1980s (cf. Abrahams 1987: 191).

Uncertainty and permeability are also characteristic of other boundaries surrounding vigilantism. Thus the distinction between vigilante action against crime and crime itself is both conceptually complex and pragmatically quite easily crossed. Vigilante groups, which have begun fairly straightforwardly as mechanisms of crime control, have often turned to crime. The possibility of robbing a few stage coaches for oneself, and blaming these offences on the bandits one was supposed to hunt down, had a natural attraction for some American groups, and others overstepped their initial terms of reference in other ways. The creation of groups of 'Regulators' to control crime, and the subsequent creation of groups of 'Moderators' to control the Regulators, bears clear testimony to such tendencies.

A WIDESPREAD PHENOMENON

Vigilantism, as I have just outlined it, has arisen under one name or another at many different times in many different areas of the world. I have already mentioned a few of many possible African and North American contexts, and there is also evidence of many cases from Latin America, the Philippines, and China where a long stream of vigilante activity dates back several thousand years.[3] As one might expect, I find that what I have learned in Tanzania is both enlightened by comparative study – of American historical and current cases for example – and enlightening when looking at developments elsewhere.

This brings me to a second, partly related point that, despite its widespread distribution, vigilantism has been relatively little studied. There are a few notable exceptions, such as Rosenbaum and Sederberg's (1976) collection, *Vigilante Politics*, and Richard Maxwell Brown's work on America (1975), but detailed case studies are rare and very little has been done by anthropologists.[4]

It could be said that, to a small extent, this is a question of descriptive terminology rather than neglect. In my own Tanzanian work, I have only used the word 'vigilantes' in my study of Sungusungu, whereas it is arguable, as I have noted elsewhere (Abrahams 1989), that somewhat similar things were going on in the same area at earlier times – things which I have described in other terms such as neighbourhood co-operation, threshing groups and neighbourhood courts. When Sukuma villagers provoked a showdown with their chiefs at the turn of the century by sorting out violent conflicts between neighbours, this had many of the ingredients of vigilantism, as did the fining of people by their neighbours at the end of the colonial period for breaking boycotts or failing to attend political meetings. Again, the classical segmentary state pattern analysed by Southall (1956), in which villagers on the edge of chiefdoms resorted to self-help rather than the chief for their resolution of their grievances, also had some things in common with vigilante activity.

But this is far from the whole story, and anthropologists have certainly paid less attention to vigilantism under any name than they have to other features of the informal political sector such as banditry and clientage. I am uncertain why this should be so. It is arguable that banditry was in a similar position until Hobsbawm's provocative studies inspired a body of further work aimed at revealing or denying the existence of 'social bandits'.[5] In that case, moreover, much of the discussion was concerned with incipient or other forms of class struggle, and it may be that the common propensity of vigilantes to protect rather than redistribute property has made them less attractive to some scholars. Yet, it is also surprising that the challenge which vigilantes have posed for the state has not attracted more attention from both anthropological friends and enemies of that institution.

In the case of clientage, the original stimulus for study came from several specific directions. First, there were apparent, though somewhat contradictory, links between African clientage and European feudalism and bureaucracy, and this was combined with a flight away from ascriptive structures and the search for individual actors playing a major role in political change. From both perspectives, clientage appeared as one of the dynamics of such change and as a sort of stepping stone along the road from status to contract, though it was later – in a European context – to appear as a step *backwards* from the modern bureaucratic state. And if such African studies can be seen as echoing Leach's (1954) call for more Weber and less Durkheim in political anthropology, subsequent work in a Mediterranean context also partly corresponded with a comparable call for more Marx and less Weber.

In addition to such considerations, it is of course also arguable that vigilantism is, like totemism, a false category. But banditry and clientage seem equally vulnerable to such a charge, and it is in any case unusual for such categories to be deconstructed before a large amount of work has been devoted to them. None the less, whatever the cause, it will be clear by now that I consider the anthropological neglect of vigilantes to be regrettable. They sharply illuminate a number of central issues in political anthropology and sociology, and they deserve their own space in our conceptual frameworks.

CRIME AND CRIME CONTROL

Law has sometimes been defined as a double system. At least in principle – since reality tends to be much less clear cut than theory – there are rules governing behaviour, and there are then rules about the rules. This second system sets out how issues relating to the first set of rules are handled, and sub-groups of these meta-rules can be at least analytically distinguished. Firstly, some of them define *who* has the say when creating such rules and when dealing with alleged breaches of them, that is who shall legislate, who may arrest and prosecute, and who has jurisdiction. Then there is the question of procedural rules, of *how* and in what settings cases should be dealt with. This includes questions of the way in which offences can be legally investigated, the rights of those accused to particular forms of defence, the definition of legitimate evidence, and so on. Deliberate breaches of these various meta-rules are, of course, also legal offences, and even accidental breaches seriously affect the validity of any legal action.

As I have already noted, vigilantes often share broad areas of agreement with the state about the definition of crime involving breaches of the first set of rules. Theft, drug peddling, vandalism and the like are offences for both vigilantes and the state. On the other hand, the vigilante definition of a 'public enemy' may also differ somewhat from that of the state, as I have said. It is well known that some American groups have, contrary to legal stipulations, defined being black and operating in particular contexts and locations as an offence, and have reacted violently to individuals who breach this 'rule' or encourage others to do so. Or individuals may be harassed for holding to particular political positions deemed locally offensive. Sometimes other breaches of morality, which may be generally disliked but which are not illegal, may become the focus of vigilante activity. The American 'White Caps', who seem to have borrowed their ideas about headgear from the early Ku Klux Klan at the end of the last century, were an example of this kind of thing. A contemporary newspaper article (*Cambridge Daily News*, 24 December 1888) describes their activities as follows.

> For several weeks the State of Ohio, which has been regarded as a civilised and highly developed region, has been the scene of a succession of serious outrages which the officers of the law have thus far found themselves powerless to check. The northern part of the State is inhabited by the descendants of the old Puritan stock. They have kept up many of the traditions of their ancestors... and

are now carrying into practical effects the antiquated Puritan ideas of regulating the morals of their neighbours.

The article goes on to relate how people who are unkind to their wives, or given to drink, or who are 'indolent and vagabondish', are seized at night by men disguised with white caps, and are given a thorough beating. Those individuals who tried to oppose the movement themselves were also threatened and sometimes beaten.

A somewhat comparable example in the case of Tanzanian Sungusungu groups is their reaction to alleged witches. This is a complicated issue, but it is perhaps worth exploration because of the boundary definition problems it involves. The first formal laws on witchcraft for the country as a whole were, of course, colonial, and modern law derives from a series of British colonial Ordinances. The main thrust of these laws, as in other British colonial territories, was directed not so much against alleged witchcraft itself as against witchcraft accusations. The reality of witchcraft activity itself was not totally discounted, but it was carefully circumscribed, largely in terms of the proven possession or use of *materia medica* or the witnessed threat of causing harm to others. False or ill-supported accusation was strongly discouraged by the threat of heavy penalties. As a result the definition of witchcraft as an offence was closely linked to the prescribed procedures for its prosecution.

As elsewhere in colonial and post-colonial Africa, this legislation has been a contentious issue in Tanzania. Villagers are typically firmly convinced of the reality of witchcraft, and they have often complained that the legislation exists to protect witches rather than their victims. Opinion in other sections of Tanzanian society appears to be more mixed. Many highly educated Tanzanians also recognize witchcraft as a real threat to their well-being, while others would deny that it exists. Many are ambivalent about the problem. They are not convinced that witchcraft is illusory, but they know that it is not a widely recognized reality in the 'modern western world', and they are aware that public acknowledgement of its power and threat might prove embarrassing in international contexts. Others again have argued that the legislation should be changed to make the detection and prosecution of witches more straightforward.[6]

Meanwhile, witchcraft has been dealt with in a range of different ways at village level.[7] In the Nyamwezi and Sukuma area during the colonial period, divination was commonly used, as it were behind the government's back. Often little further was done after this unless the problem recurred. This then sometimes led to an identified witch being actively or constructively driven from the community, but a more usual reaction was for the victim's family to depart and set up home elsewhere in the region. After independence, rumours appear to have spread in the Sukuma area that the new government approved of killing witches, and some suspects were murdered by crowds in the later 1960s. Later, a more intensive outbreak of witch killing erupted, in which a common pattern was said to involve the private hiring of assassins to kill the alleged witch. This led to an attempted governmental crackdown on these killings, which badly misfired when several suspects died in police custody. When Sungusungu vigilante groups emerged in the early 1980s, some of their activities were also devoted to the identification and banishment, and sometimes the killing, of witches especially in more remote parts of the area. In order to avoid clashes with the government, such activities are usually described and discussed locally in other terms which disguise their true nature.[8]

Although vigilantes and the state may not wholly agree on the definition of the 'criminal', they are both typically anxious to control crime by adopting both preventive and reactive measures against it. This shared aim is, however, the main locus of the opposition between them. In the context of jurisdiction as elsewhere, the state is not a notoriously good power sharer. Also, in the realm of due process, the state's judicial authorities tend, at least officially, to deplore procedures which flout their own complex rules. In Tanzania, as in Britain, those in authority express hostility to 'rough justice', in which thieves or others may not be handed over to the police and courts, but may be badly beaten and even killed by vigilante groups. This kind of reaction is again to some degree a variable matter. Maxwell Brown (1975) notes the existence of considerable support for vigilantism among some late nineteenth- and early twentieth-century lawyers, and he argues that in North America several factors have conspired to make vigilantism more acceptable than it has often been elsewhere. The revolution, he suggests, fostered an attitude to the state which tends to sympathize with private, and if necessary violent, action if the state fails properly to serve its citizens. In addition, the fact of 'the frontier', and the accompanying failure of the state to penetrate into more remote parts of the wide open spaces of the West, has clearly been particularly conducive to the development of alternative forms of crime control. Thirdly, in ways somewhat reminiscent of witchcraft law in Tanzania, the fact that much post-revolutionary law in North America remained paradoxically in an English mould, and was as such developed in a quite different socio-political environment, appears to have helped to give some lawyers and others a less enthusiastic commitment to it than it has received at home where it belongs.

A further source of conflict in this context is the fact that vigilantism typically emerges when the state fails to achieve a locally satisfactory level of crime control. In the case of Sungusungu, a main focus of this dissatisfaction was an apparent increase in the incidence of theft. Armed cattle theft in particular seems to have caused a great deal of anxiety among villagers in the Nyamwezi and Sukuma area, and there were also fears about other forms of rural theft and brigandage including highway robbery. It is possible that the situation at the beginning of the 1980s was exacerbated by the return of personnel, and possibly an increased availability of firearms, after the Ugandan War, but the situation also has to be understood against a general background of increasing worry about law and order in both rural areas and in the towns. In my own and others' conversations with villagers about the rise of Sungusungu, great stress was typically laid upon these issues of security and the failure of government and police to combat crime effectively. Some comments were relatively charitable to the police, acknowledging the shortages of the vehicles and fuel which are essential for dealing from an urban base with mobile rural criminals. But others were more critical, and ranged from suggestions that the police were uninterested in dealing with offences to insinuations and assertions that some police were in league with the criminals. Similar accusations were also levelled at some local level officials. Not surprisingly, the establishment of the groups appeared to constitute a vote of no confidence in official instruments of crime control, and this and the success of the groups in this context gave local and higher level officials much to ponder over. The groups became, and remain, very influential in the villages, and mark a clear example of the failure of the state to 'capture', as Hyden (1980) put it, the rural areas politically.

COMMUNITIES AND DIVISIONS

The article I quoted earlier about the 'White Caps' ends with the comment that ' . . . the strangest part of the history of this system of outrages is the fact that the popular sentiment in the community actually vindicates their outrageous proceedings. Local officials are in consequence powerless.' Such local support for vigilante activity in the face of official disapproval and hostility is quite commonplace. Tanzanian villagers' complaints about the interests of 'the victim' are often echoed with approval elsewhere in a vigilante context. The law, as there, may be deemed ineffective for one reason or another in the pursuit of criminals, and arguments may also be voiced, as in contemporary Britain, that the law does not deal harshly enough with them if they are caught. Due process is often seen as the chief culprit here, not least by some of the police themselves who consider they are badly hindered by some of the current rules. 'Undue' concern for the criminals' rights as opposed to the rights of those they harm, and of the community more generally, is often cited as a problem. Vigilantes are, in contrast, often seen as representing local fears and concerns, and getting their priorities right. They are seen to represent ideas of justice in contrast to those of strict legality.

Although such arguments can easily appear attractive, especially when the focus is on local interests as against those of the state, we have of course long since learned to treat the idea of community itself with some suspicion. Such local groups are rarely as homogeneous as we may be tempted to assume, and such homogeneity must in any case be treated as a variable. Compared with many local groups elsewhere, Nyamwezi villages and their Sungusungu groups are relatively uniform. They do not display either the class divisions or the divided ethnic interests which have been significant in some American and other cases. None the less they show a leaning, which is not uncommon among such societies, towards the definition of community interests along lines laid down by middle-aged and older men rather than by women or the young. Sungusungu groups are typically male groups, and although I encountered a Sungusungu women's wing in some Nyamwezi villages in the late 1980s, this appears to be a rarer phenomenon than I assumed at that time. Moreover, older women appear to be the usual victims of witchcraft accusation, and the return of wayward younger ones to their husbands is currently seen as one of the groups' standard functions. Keeping discipline among younger men has also been seen by more senior villagers as a useful aspect of the groups' activities.

Other differences between communities may also be significant for the functioning of vigilantism within them. In many modern urban and some rural communities, the heterogeneity of members' interests may be exacerbated by a high rate of residential mobility, and the absence of any long-established patterns of collaboration between groups of neighbours. In such areas, people know relatively little about each other's character and background, and they have no well-worn paths of co-operative organization which they can adapt to vigilante purposes. Reciprocal control over each other's actions seems likely to be more difficult in such circumstances, and the dynamics of power relations may be harder to control. Serious errors of judgement are possibly more easily made, and mechanisms for damage restriction in the wake of such errors may be limited or altogether lacking. All this appears to mark an interesting difference between some *ad hoc* spontaneous eruptions of vigilantism (as in parts of contemporary Britain) and its emergence within Nyamwezi and Sukuma villages where villagers share a well-developed package of experience of collaboratively organizing local affairs for themselves.

VIGILANTES, BANDITS, MAFIOSI

As Heald (1986) has noted, vigilantes are in some degree reminiscent of bandits and mafiosi, at least as these have been described by Hobsbawm (1956). I have expressed some scepticism elsewhere (1987) on the usefulness of such direct comparison. Hobsbawm was especially interested in 'social' bandits and the 'early' mafia, whose historical status has been subjected to close scrutiny by Blok and others. Both groups – at least as they are more generally perceived – seem more likely to be enemies of vigilantes than their fellow agents or competitors.

At the same time, it is perhaps worthwhile to comment further on the similarities and differences between them. At a general level, all three typically involve groups which operate *within* society and which provide an, often enough violent, alternative to the institutions of the formal political and economic sectors. All three are also commonly engaged, either among themselves or more widely, in one or other form of social control, and they all lay claim to some constituency of support. Also, the differences between them are not always clear in practice, because they all share the 'labile' tendencies which I earlier outlined for vigilantism, and this is also true of other groups such as guerrillas. The activities of all of them, whatever their starting point, may fairly easily degenerate into a lowest common denominator of less discriminating criminality.

But this does not mean that ideal type starting points cannot be usefully distinguished, and the main terms of such distinctions are, it seems, relatively simple. Firstly, the distinction which I noted earlier between breaches of first and second order rules is relevant. Bandits and mafiosi, to the extent that their main purpose is the pursuit of gain through activities like robbery, drug dealing and corruption, tend to be more openly in breach of first order rules than vigilantes. These, as I have suggested, are archetypically interested in the control of first order crime, rather than its commission – though they may also disagree with the state about some first order rules – and this focus leads them mainly into breaches of the second order rules of jurisdiction and due process. Secondly, some insight into differences between the ideal types involved here can be gained through almost everyday distinctions between law, politics and economics, though once again the slippiness of actual activities can blur this in practice. In these terms, vigilantes are especially interested in legal issues of crime control, while bandits' activities are more clearly focused upon economic gain. This is also true of mafias, but these additionally appear to have characteristically strong interests in the development of political power either directly at a local level or through the infiltration and corruption of the formal political system at the centre. However blurred these distinctions may be in reality, they appear to be worth maintaining analytically as points of reference against which shifts and extensions of actual behaviour can be measured.

NOTES

1 Cf. Abrahams (1987, 1989) and Abrahams and Bukurura (1993).
2 I have found Brown's work extremely helpful both for its detailed discussion of vigilantism in North America and for his more general comments on the subject.
3 Cf. Huggins (1991), Kowalewski (1991), Kuhn (1970) and Schurmann (1968: chapter 7).
4 A notable exception among anthropologists is the work of Heald (1986), and Peters' paper (1972) on the control of moral ambiguities is also worth noting here. This, in turn, is reminiscent of work by Thompson (1971) and Ingram (1984) on 'rough music' and charivari as popular forms of criticism and punishment of local miscreants.
5 Cf. Blok (1974) and Crummey (1986).
6 See Fisiy and Geschiere (1990) which suggests that such legislation may help elite rather than ordinary villagers.
7 For accounts of some such ways see the papers in Abrahams (ed.) (1994).
8 See Bukurura (1994) for discussion of such behaviour.

REFERENCES

Abrahams, R. (1987) 'Sungusungu: village vigilante groups in Tanzania', *African Affairs* 86: 179–96.
—— (1989) 'Law and order and the state in the Nyamwezi and Sukuma area of Tanzania', *Africa* 59(3): 354–68.
—— (ed.) (1994) *Witchcraft in Contemporary Tanzania*, Cambridge: African Studies Centre.
Abrahams, R. and Bukurura, S. (1993) 'Party, bureaucracy and grass roots initiatives in a socialist state: the case of Sungusungu vigilantes in Tanzania', in C. Hann (ed.) *Socialism: Ideals, Ideologies and Local Practices*, London: Routledge.
Blok, A. (1974) *The Mafia of a Sicilian Village*, Oxford: Blackwell.
Brown, R. M. (1975) *Strain of Violence*, Oxford: Oxford University Press.
Bukurura, S. (1994) *Sungusungu: Vigilantes in West-Central Tanzania*, unpublished Ph.D. Dissertation, University of Cambridge.
Crummey, D. (ed.) (1986) *Banditry, Rebellion and Social Process in Africa*, London: James Currey.
Fisiy, C. and Geschiere, P. (1990) 'Judges and witches, or how is the state to deal with witchcraft?', *Cahiers d'Études Africaines* 118: XXX–2.
Heald, S. (1986) 'Mafias in Africa: the rise of drinking companies and vigilante groups in Bugisu, Uganda', *Africa* 56: 446–67.
Hobsbawm, E. (1956) *Primitive Rebels*, Manchester: Manchester University Press.
Huggins, M. (1991) *Vigilantism and the State in Modern Latin America*, New York and London: Praeger.
Hyden, G. (1980) *Beyond Ujamaa in Tanzania: Underdevelopment and an Uncaptured Peasantry*, London: Heinemann.
Ingram, M. (1984) 'Ridings, rough music and the "reform of popular cuture" in early modern England', *Past and Present*, 105, 79–113.
Johnston, L. (1992) *The Rebirth of Private Policing*, London: Routledge.
Kowalewski, D. (1991) 'Cultism, insurgency and vigilantism in the Philippines', *Sociological Analysis* 52(3): 241–53.
Kuhn, P. (1970) *Rebellion and its Enemies in Late Imperial China*, Cambridge: Harvard University Press.
Leach, E. (1954) *Political Systems of Highland Burma: a Study of Kachin Social Structure*, London: G. Bell & Sons.
—— (1977) *Custom, Law and Terrorist Violence*, Edinburgh.
Peters, E. (1972) 'Aspects on the control of moral ambiguities: a comparative analysis of two culturally disparate modes of social control', in M. Gluckman (ed.) *The Allocation of Responsibility*, Manchester: Manchester University Press, 109–62.
Rosenbaum, H. and Sederberg, P. (eds) (1976) *Vigilante Politics*, Philadelphia: University of Pennsylvania Press.
Schurmann, F. (1968) *Ideology and Organization in Communist China*, Berkeley: University of California Press.
Southall, A. (1956) *Alur Society*, Cambridge: W. Heffer and Sons.
Thompson, E.P. (1971) ' "Rough music": *le charivari anglais*', *Annales*, E.S.C., xxvii, 285–312.

Chapter 4

Trading in ambiguity
Law, rights and realities in the distribution of land in northern Mozambique

Sue Fleming

It was 1989, in the Green Zone, the safe area on the periphery of Mozambique's capital city Maputo. Inside the three-metre-high gates lay the fertile valley, constantly fed by water in summer and winter, rainy season or dry, water stored by the imposing dam that blocked its free passage. The land was cultivated by Lonhro, and the peasant farmers who had once used it had been pushed outside the high perimeter fence onto marginal and barely usable land while armed guards protected Lonhro's interests.

By 1993 there were more of such stories. In Malema, Nampula province, there were reports of peasant farmers being told either to grow tobacco or move. They had been farming since the demise of the tobacco companies and the new owners had arrived. Myers reports that

> [i]n Chokwe District, Gaza Province, several hundred families have recently been displaced from their land by 'new' private interests and by the expansion of a joint venture enterprise...LOMACO has either acquired new land, or begun to exploit previously acquired land, in the district that was occupied and farmed by smallholders (family sector)....In Angonia and Tsangane Districts, Tete Province, it has been reported that private interests have reactivated holdings formerly belonging to the company CAIA...[which] once totalled more than 20,000 hectares. Smallholder families returning from refugee camps in Malawi have reportedly returned to Malawi due to land shortages and disputes in this area.
>
> (Myers 1993: 1)

Organizations such as the World Bank talk of 'inconsistencies of policy, laws and practices'. The World Bank reports that 'large farms have sometimes been given concessions or titles to tracts of land which include areas currently occupied by smallholders. This raises the possibility of future evictions, and some have already occurred' (Binswanger 1993: 2). At the same time agricultural land policies favour smallholder and subsistence sectors in land allocation and use. The land laws protect the existing users of the land, the majority being smallholders. While policy and laws favour peasant farmers, the practice is different, and it is evident that these intentions are not being realized on the ground.

Ambiguity in law and policy is being manipulated, and is allowing the exploitation and acquisition of land by people in power. This chapter tries to match local, global realities and relationships of interests to understand the processes of this appropriation. The differing moralities, of land as personal and social identity, as nation-building for the socialist state, as economic resource in a free market, do not necessarily interconnect into common understandings. The framework and intentions of the law are subservient to macro-policy, and policy ambiguities disguise the contradictions in objectives.

Actions outside of the law are legitimated by their echoed references to colonial experiences. The constantly shifting concepts and values of the state are mediated through a bureaucratic and administrative structure that provides its own smokescreens and sets of meanings. The dominance of free market ideology and the opportunity it provides for international capital leaves little space for local and national level frameworks of reference and action.

CONCEPTS OF LAND AND PEOPLE

Concepts of land are multiple and shifting, opening the way for ambiguities in interpretation. The newly independent government of 1975 linked land with liberation. The 1979 land law states

> [t]he present law is a fundamental instrument for the consolidation of the great revolutionary victory consisting of the liberation of the land and the people on it achieved by the war of the People of Mozambique against Portuguese colonialism and against imperialism.
>
> (Sachs 1981: 17)

For Sachs '[i]n its symbolic function, the [land] law was like a flag of liberty that flew over soil reconquered, a soil that had been drenched with the blood and with the sweat of generations of slaves and forced labourers'(Sachs 1981: 3).

Unity was a rallying cry for Frelimo both in the fight for independence and in consolidating the newly independent nation. This unity was provided by the state, and the relationship between people as citizens of the state. The constitution, approved by the Central Committee of Frelimo just before independence, defined this citizenship: 'all citizens enjoy the same rights and are subject to the same duties' (Article 26), this equality involves the elimination of 'colonial and traditional structures of oppression and exploitation' (MAGIC 1979: 21).

People's identity was as workers and peasants. As defined by the 1975 constitution, 'power belongs to the workers and peasants' and was labelled 'People's Power' (MAGIC 1979: 21). Representations of people in the symbolism of the flag reflected this identity: the hoe symbolized the peasantry and a cog wheel the working class. The Third Congress of Frelimo in 1977 elaborated the unity between worker and peasant. They were constituted as 'the working masses' or 'labouring classes'; while their primary identity was as producers, they were defined by their suffering under 'feudal as well as capitalist' systems of exploitation (MAGIC 1977: 22).

Land was the great unifier. In the 1975 Constitution land became the property of the state, linking worker and peasant in common ownership. People's relationship with land was essential to the socialist transformation. Land was the 'fundamental means of production' (MAGIC 1977: 22) that linked the exploitation in the past with development for the future, and the state assumed responsibility and control over how it was to be developed and used. As stated by the Third Congress, 'the abolition of private property in land was the first basic step in transforming the social relations of production in our country' (MAGIC 1977: 24).

The development of the peasant sector after independence implied a very different set of social and economic relationships in the rural areas. In 1977 the Third Congress, consolidating the experiences of the liberated areas during the fight for independence, promoted communal villages, collective production as well as peasant co-operatives and state farms. While these developments have a clear economic function, with perceived economies of scale allowing 'advanced' technology and the beginnings of rural industrialization, they go far beyond this. It is the 'socialization of the countryside' that allows the revolutionary capacity of the peasantry to develop. The communal villages are 'the fundamental lever for liberating the people in the rural areas' (MAGIC 1977: 43). They are 'the battleground on which the reactionary ideas of colonialism and traditional society would be vanquished' (Isaacman and Isaacman 1983: 153).

The policy of communal villages and collective farms did not recognize a direct personal relationship between peoples and land. Within this relationship, land may be seen as social wealth. According to Tiago from Itoculo 'land is valuable, riches. It is the social property of a group. It cannot be abandoned in whatever manner.' Land has a value beyond its potential or actual economic use, making nonsense of the concepts of 'unproductive' or 'empty' land (Loforte 1993; Carrilho 1993b). There are lands that are sacred, that house important ancestors, or that are traditional religious and healing sites.

The ambiguity in the socialist state's attitude to the peasantry relates to different sets of values associated with land. The peasantry are valorized as labouring classes, the oppressed, and as agents (with workers) of people's power. At the same time peasant identity, their direct relationship with land, is denied. The policy of communal villages, co-operatives and state farms shifts personal relations between people and land, rooted in ancestry, tradition and identity, to social relations contextualized by class and history, and linked to building the nation-state.

The separation of peasantry and land in the socialist ideology provides, in a sense, a continuity with the colonial past. Drinkwater (1991) cites a continuity between socialist and capitalist experiences in Zimbabwe, as in both cases the 'modernization' of society views the peasant as inferior, objects of policy, colonizing local understandings and rationalities. While this may in one sense be true for Mozambique, with its centralist state, it ignores the fundamental difference in morality that lies behind the colonial, socialist and capitalist regimes. For the socialist state, this morality intertwines people, the state and land with concepts of equality and liberation as opposed to exploitation, promoting systems of economic production for social, not only economic, ends.

There are also practical attempts by Frelimo to reconcile the local and socialist approaches to people and land. Isaacman and Isaacman talk of the dynamizing groups, the rural party activists, trying

> to relieve peasant anxieties about giving up their private holdings, to overcome their confusion about the organization and operation

of these collective ventures, and to assure them that participation was voluntary and would not jeopardize the right to maintain a small private plot for their own use.

(Isaacman and Isaacman 1983: 119)

The active encouragement of communal villages was subsequently stopped in 1984.

The 1979 land law elaborates on the 1975 constitutional law and gives priority to peasant rather than private access to land. The peasantry – or 'family sector' – is given preferential treatment, along with the party and party organizations, state institutions and co-operatives, as non-paying users of land (Sachs 1981). Paid licences are needed for commercial use by both individuals and private companies. At the same time notions of personal or private property are not attached to land. Individuals and organizations can only own property affixed to the land, or the value-added they have contributed through transforming the land, such as clearing the land, planting trees, and crops in the ground (Sachs 1981).

THE WORLD BANK AND THE IMF – THE MARKET ECONOMY

Ambiguities in the land law arise from the changing policy environment brought about by the economic reforms from 1987 onwards. These stabilization and structural adjustment measures have been in effect to greater or lesser degrees since that time. The recent Policy Framework Paper for 1994–6, worked out by the IMF, the World Bank and the Government of Mozambique, aims to reduce the government's internal debt and the external current account deficit (International Monetary Fund 1994). The market is the key to the future: 'The Government will promote conditions for private sector expansion by allowing market forces to allocate resources efficiently through increased competition' (International Monetary Fund 1994). These policies involve privatization and liberalizing of trade and prices.

Within the free-market philosophy, the concept of land shifts, from questions of identity and nation-building, to becoming an economic resource. For the World Bank land is for making money and 'the objective of land policy is broad-based sustainable growth' (Binswanger 1993). The World Bank proposes the buying and selling of both private and custom-managed land. Communities, through consensus or majority vote, should be able to trade in land and sell community-based land (Binswanger 1993).

Changes in the land law were needed to match the changing economic policy. Regulations amending the law came out in 1987. These regulations focused on commercial use and environmental protection (Government of Mozambique 1988). The time limit for commercial use by individuals and private companies was extended from five to fifteen years to up to fifty years. Joint-venture companies, involving state and usually foreign investment, are licensed for the life of the company. The regulations detail the steps for land registration. To give some protection to the peasantry, the 1987 Regulations also clearly state that licences could only be granted for empty land, that is *free* of people.

COMPETING POLICY INTERESTS

The aims and objectives of macro-economic policy and structural adjustment are not directly mirrored in sectoral policy. There is space for specific support to the smallholder. Agricultural policy gives priority to peasant food production (Ministério da Agricultura 1992). To ensure sustainable food security 'the family sector must have a right to the priority allocation of resources' (Ministério da Agricultura 1992: 4). Policy on poverty reduction also supports the development of peasant agriculture (Fleming 1995). At the same time these anti-poverty objectives are meant to parallel an agricultural and industrial policy of developing a 'strategy of efficient commercial farming' (Government of Mozambique 1992: 8) through promoting an 'emerging private sector' and attracting foreign investment for large-scale ventures.

The intention of the government to develop both the family sector and foreign-sponsored enterprises is problematic. How does the sectoral policy balance priority to smallholder farming with a growing private sector, and foreign investment in agriculture? How does it deal with both food and cash crop needs at both national and local levels, especially if the interests of the foreign investor are in production for export? The increasing attractiveness of Mozambique to outside interests is reflected in the activities of Malawi businessmen who flew to Malema to look at potential tobacco production, and of South Africans flying direct from Maputo to Monapo to check on opportunities in cotton and sisal.

THE PRIVATE SECTOR

In reality land is rapidly being transferred to private enterprise and private farmers. Land currently being claimed through the registration system in Nampula totals 215,461 hectares (ha). This leaves, according to the Provincial Department of Agriculture's estimates, only 100,000 ha of estimated arable land for peasant, smallholder farming. Large enterprises predominate: 1,770 ha are registered by Napula Province, while 3,088 ha are registered for larger holdings through Maputo. Land under the control of Maputo, the state farms/ joint venture or private companies, account for 39,713 ha.

The Ramiane Plantation land claim in Monapo District was being processed in 1994. According to its management, it has been bought from the previous owners by various foreign investors. The land is being farmed as if approval were a mere formality. The peasant farmers who have been using the land have been told they cannot continue and have to move out for the 1994/5 season. The land was certainly not empty.

Today external claims to land are coming from previous colonial owners (*colons*), who fled at Independence. The 1987 Regulations were accompanied by a one year grace period for claims on state enterprises and a three year period for private farmers and co-operatives. These grace periods have now expired but it is still possible for old owners to register their lands. As the survey department in Maputo said, 'we are taking each case on its own merit'.

More cautious *colons* are testing the waters. Several of the Portuguese UN Peacekeeping troops reported that they had deliberately come to Mozambique, where they were born, to check out the viability of returning to their family's previous lands. Others are aggressively asserting what they regard as their rights. There are witnesses to the forcible removal of displaced people from land in Mutuanha Piloto as the previous Portuguese owner is claiming it back. UN troops have apparently been 'assisting', by providing transport. As one of the UN Peacekeeping troops told me, 'the UN trucks are standing by'.

The encouragement of foreign investment has also generated large-scale private transnational and joint venture enterprises with rights over concessionary areas. The distinction between concessionary rights and land rights is not always clear in practice, and creates ambiguities around the existing land law. Concessionary areas give these large production enterprises the right to carry out extension work/seasonal inputs for a particular cash crop, and the monopoly right to buy this product from the peasant producers.

The pressure from traditional authorities and government structures can mean *de facto* control over peasant land by these companies, especially as companies borrow working practices and a sense of legitimacy from the colonial past. In Muelege and Itoculo, Monapo District, land could easily be obtained for cotton growing through the local Party/Government structures and through SAMO, the joint venture cotton company that has a monopoly on marketing. Land is demarcated by the village authorities along with the company overseer 'in the same way as colonial times'. The traditional authorities, the *regulos* as they were known and chosen by the Portuguese, would help with land allocation and organize labour.

Why, despite the law and the agriculture policy, is there a bias towards commercial and private farming? The law is being interpreted in the light of current economic policy. According to the Provincial Survey Department in Nampula, commercial land use, especially for export production, has highest priority. The presence of infrastructure for the growing and processing of cash crops outweighs other considerations, such as the presence of displaced or local people on the land. Ramiane Plantation has a sisal factory, so the land has another value; this means the peasant farmers have to leave, so the land can be used for what it is intended for. You cannot destroy a large area with commercial export value for people who are only producing food.

BUREAUCRATIC POWERS AND ADMINISTRATIVE HOLES

Ambiguities in the law have been created by the actions of the bureaucratic structures set up to implement it, and benefit the private over the family sector. The administrators are applying what Gledhill labels the 'insidious strategies of power' (1994: 147). His call for the study of 'how the actors in political systems exercise power' (1994: 94) obviously applies also to bureaucratic systems of government.

The 1987 Land Regulations in Mozambique gave a scale of responsibilities to different levels of government; provincial government acquired powers to give licences for up to 250 ha of agricultural land, 500 ha of land for livestock and 1,000 ha for forestry. The Ministry of Agriculture in Maputo could allocate up to 2,500 ha of agricultural land, 5,000 ha for livestock and 10,000 ha for forestry.

Beyond this, licence requests have to be passed by the Council of Ministers (Government of Mozambique 1988). These responsibilities are manipulated, and favoured applicants are advised to break their application into appropriately sized plots.

The process of dealing with large estates, including the privatizing of state farms, involves more than the Ministry of Agriculture and its policy and practical interests. Joint-venture companies come through the Maputo Office for the Promotion of Foreign Investment, and agreements require the signature of the Prime Minister. The main Ministries concerned are Finance and Commerce, not the Ministry of Agriculture which houses the Survey Department concerned with land registration. Policy priorities of these Ministries are more likely to be export- rather than food-orientated, and seek to attract foreign investment rather than secure land for resource poor farmers.

The *de facto* procedures for dealing with land claims, especially for the larger holdings, are outside local control. The district and sub-district stations in Monapo complained about being left out of decision-making on land. According to the District Director of Agriculture, local government should be involved in giving a technical and financial analysis of each land claim. They should check the land is empty, and that the applicant is capable of using the land. Similar experiences were noted at a NGO seminar on land and small-scale farmers:

> The district and local level are frequently not involved at the moments when they should be according to the law, for the purpose of providing information on available land and to present their opinion in concrete cases. . . . The consequence of such practice in some cases has been distribution of land to individual persons or to entities where this land is already occupied by small-scale farmers.
> (LINK 1993: 3)

The state clearly lacks the capacity to implement the law (Macamo 1993). Lack of basic information is characteristic at all levels of government. The districts have very little data on the registration of land in their area. There are attempts to address this by basing survey department staff in the districts, but it is unlikely to solve the basic problem, that the confusion in land status suits too many interests.

There are various official versions. The map of the Department of Physical Planning of the Provincial Planning Commission is not consistent with the registration information: various land titles are omitted and areas without title are included. In fact the legality of the registered land is questionable, as at the time of fieldwork in December 1993, none had appeared in the Bulletin de Republica, as is required by law.

The procedures are being manipulated as essential information on previous land allocations disappears. Of the 251,461 ha currently claimed through the registration system in Nampula up to December 1993, 4,747 ha of claims were 'lost' and not mapped. The most sought-after maps of Monapo District suddenly could not be found. Information is being shelved; for the district of Monapo alone, 1,463 ha of requests have not moved beyond district to provincial level.

The bureaucracy is rent-seeking. False documentation is sold that has no legal basis. A man arrived in the Survey Department asking about his piece of land, but a search through the files came up with nothing. The man then asked for a new map and documentation, drawing an outline of the area with his thumbnail. The technician obliged, made a rough copy which he handed over to the client who left happy, having given sufficient thanks. What is that paper worth? Who recognizes it as legitimate? Will its existence be enough to ensure the eviction of the peasant farmers?

PEASANT EXPERIENCES

There is, *de facto*, a dual system in the administration of land and natural resources. LINK distinguish the formal distribution system from 'actual, informal' land allocation (LINK 1993). Macamo (1993) cites the legal existence of community tribunals, who make decisions on land based on local/customary law, as proof of the state's acceptance of this duality.

The customary law in Monapo District is that of the Makhuwa people. Makhuwa practise matrilineal inheritance and uxorilocal residence. Land-use rights pass from mother's brother to sister's son, and a man has special responsibility to his sister and her children. Generally the *mwene*, the head of the lineage, answerable to the Council of Elders, is regarded as the guardian of the land, and the *humu* – representative and head of the sub-lineage – allocates it (Loforte 1993).

The concentration of population through settlement policies and war means that there is more than one *humu* in each location. The degree of population movement was such in Muelege, where I carried out fieldwork, there were two *mwene*. The village was situated on the boundary of their respective areas, and each had jurisdiction over about half the village and lands beyond, the *shosherona*.

Recent trends, attributed to a more market-oriented peasant society, are towards virilocality and patrilineal inheritance (Loforte 1993). This is not uncommon. Moore and Vaughan (1994) have noted a similar trend in their work in Zambia, 'that some men are looking for ways to exclude matrilineal kin from inheriting valuable property after their death...[implying] that the value of land, particularly cleared land, is changing and that a market in land may start to emerge' (Moore and Vaughan 1994: 213). Yet the 'choice' of the market and price of land is not the only factor influencing residence and property patterns. In Mozambique, according to Isaacman and Isaacman, '[t]here were also indications that in matrilineal areas, especially in Nampula Province, men joined newly-formed communal villages to break the control exerted by their wives' lineages over family matters' (Isaacman and Isaacman 1983: 153).

Access to land in Muelege and Itoculo was obtained through many channels, and indicates the flexibility of the current local customary system. Kanihosa Mpita obtained land through her brother as did Ajira Irisi. Faridei Misse had land through her mother. But Handia Joanea in Itoculo was farming land given by a neighbour, acting as a *de facto* 'brother-in-law'. Cristina Sulimane was farming her husband's ancestral lands. Cristina Oscar, married to the assistant village secretary, was working on land allocated through the government structures, but had recently cleared a plot on her father-in-law's land.

A market in customary/local land rights is beginning. Victor had bought one of his plots, justifying payment as it had been planted with sugar cane (value-added) and included a water source: 'I bought the land from the previous owner in front of the Secretario, and the Chef de Zona [the village government authorities]'. This satisfied Victor that it was a 'legitimate' transaction, even though land sales as such are forbidden.

The choice of land access does not extend to land registration. While the intention of the 1979 land law favours smallholders, registration made possible through the 1987 Regulations has inverted this aim. Registered land is almost exclusively accessed by private sector farmers and transnational or joint venture enterprises. Peasant access to registration is either through co-operative membership, or through the rare issuing of 'certificates'. But as pointed out by the Maputo-based NGO co-ordinating unit, LINK, holders of '[c]ertificates are likely to lose in a conflict with someone holding a title' (LINK 1993: 3).

The complexity of the law, a general lack of awareness of its contents and the cost of registration separate the law from peasant farmers (Macamo 1993). On the other hand, it is possible that the flexibility in the customary system of land allocation is still sufficient to absorb the impact of land evictions, making the need for protecting rights to land appear less urgent. In Monapo District the villagers and farmers of Muelege and Itoculo say there is plenty of land. Some also say they have been moved off land by private enterprise. But the general opinion is not one of concern. A survey by Eduardo Mondlane University and the Ministry of Agriculture in 1993 stated that 'the level of land conflicts is not significant. Peasants have stated that there are no land problems or that the numbers [of problems] have decreased' (Freire *et al*. 1994: 24).

Local awareness of land shortages depends on the pace at which new owners take up their claims or rights. Land claims are being taken as *de facto* land rights, and claims to land are regarded as sufficient for eviction of peasant farmers. Ramiane Plantation managers evicted people in 1994, other actual, assumed, or future owners have not yet gone so far. In Monapo District most smallholder farmers have not yet realized the significance of their situation. There is clearly a general lack of knowledge about land titles by peasant farmers (Freire *et al*. 1994). Similar to Moore and Vaughan's (1994) experience in Northern Zambia, local people are not aware of the impact of registration, because they have not yet seen the consequences of it.

FUTURE DIRECTIONS

The procedures for dealing with land are clearly not achieving the spirit or text of the law. Appropriate to this, discussion of a new land law concentrates on the need for a different range of institutional arrangements for dealing with land. Guidelines produced by the *ad hoc* Land Commission argue for gradual legal changes based on existing law and that these should not have priority.

Proposals for improved institutional arrangements attempt to link the local with state traditions, interests and structures. For Carrilho (1993a, 1993b) and Garvey (1994) the favoured decentralized system involves local authorities, for Myers (1993), it includes civil society. Martins (1994), rejecting the law as 'unusable', asks for greater recognition of the role of customary chiefs in land distribution, paralleled with a strengthening of state bodies. Alexander (1994) also sees the importance of the role of the state in providing an institutional and legal framework for resolving land disputes, but local involvement needs 'a more complex and subtle solution than a re-emergent alliance between official and traditional authority' (Alexander 1994: 92).

Decentralized systems for land allocation and use could provide a break with the continuity of centralist colonial, capitalist and socialist approaches. Such systems could prevent the separation of people from their own understandings and specific knowledges of their land. As in Zimbabwe 'policy actions have been carried out in ignorance of the local environmental knowledge peasant farmers possess and utilize in their production systems' (Drinkwater 1991: 13).

The complexity of relationships and understandings of state and customary land law, and the administration of these laws, is becoming more generally realized, and this bodes well for the future, especially as these demands are coming from development practice, as well as academics and policy-makers. Mozambican civil society, through the NGO co-ordination unit, LINK, have asked for a 'profound knowledge of local conditions and practices' so the formal and informal distribution systems can be integrated 'in a just manner' (LINK 1993). Anthropologists, although slow in bringing together the local and global, have an important role in informing this debate.

At the same time the influence of global markets, and push for markets in land, too easily segregate land from people, their identities and self and social worth. Land becomes a commodity, where people relate as classes of buyers and sellers. The experience in Mozambique demonstrates the ease with which international capital and powerful national interests can appropriate land despite the legal framework protecting peasants. What changes are needed in structures and understandings to ensure actions stay inside the law? Is the force of law able to command the necessary economic policies and controls that ensure it can be put into effect?

The technical approach to land in the land-use planning of the Ministry of Agriculture further alienates land from people. While the *ad hoc* Land Commission aims to address land-use planning needs at all levels across the range of government institutions, these needs and interests are in very different structural positions of power and will not necessarily talk with the same understandings, or have the same voice.

Community participation was proposed as one mechanism for defining land zoning and then land allocation (Government of

Mozambique/UNDP 1992). The other techniques – land cover
mapping, agricultural research and socio-economic statistics – treat
land as a production resource. These top–down techniques are
designed for extracting information according to the rationale of
national and international policy makers. Capital-intensive aerial
photography and cadastral mapping are being carried out to 'facilitate the allocation of sufficient and suitable land to the family
subsector' (World Bank 1992: 24).

Who decides on the weight given to the community voices? Which
sections of the community are heard? What morals are setting the
framework for this decision? How, with these technocratic and
economic concepts of land, can the emotional, sacred and personal
be given value? Rather than localizing power with the peasantry,
there is a danger that local participation becomes marginalized as
just another source of information for national and international
interests.

REFERENCES

Alexander, J. (1994) 'Land and political authority in post-war Mozambique:
   notes from Manica Province', in R. Weiss and G. Myers (eds) *Second
   National Land Conference in Mozambique; Briefing Book*, 25–27 May 1994,
   Maputo.
Binswanger, H.P. (1993) 'Suggestions for land policy in Mozambique', World
   Bank, July.
Carrilho, J. (1993a) 'Case studies on customary and formal administration of
   land and natural resources in Mozambique', prepared in the framework of
   FAO–UNDP TSS-1 MOZ/92/T02/A/02/12 Advisory policy on rural
   resettlement and land tenure. Food and Agriculture Organization, Ma-
   puto.
—— (1993b) 'Guidelines for the development of a framework geared to a
   gradual improvement of security of land and natural resources tenure',
   Food and Agricultural Organization.
Drinkwater, M. (1991) *The State and Agrarian Change in Zimbabwe's
   Communal Areas*, Basingstoke: Macmillan.
Fleming, S. (1995) 'Policy constraints on sustainable rural poverty reduction
   in Mozambique', report to the Overseas Development Administration,
   University of Manchester.
Freire, M., Raffi, L. and Fernandes, P. (1994) 'Land use, tenure and conflict in
   Monapo and Ribaue Districts in Nampula Province and in Montepuez in
   Cabo Delgado Province', in R.Weiss and G. Myers (eds) *Second National
   Land Conference in Mozambique; Briefing Book*, 25–27 May 1994,
   Maputo.
Frelimo (1987) 'Mozambique's economic recovery programme', Maputo.
Garvey, J. (1994) 'Mozambique's land law: contradictions within the

legislative framework', in R. Weiss and G. Myers (eds) *Second National Land Conference in Mozambique; Briefing Book*, 25–27 May 1994, Maputo.

Gledhill, J. (1994) *Power and its Disguises: Anthropological Perspectives on Politics*, London: Pluto Press.

Government of Mozambique (1988) 'Legislação sobre o uso e aproveitamento da terra'.

—— (1992) Mozambique policy framework paper 1992–1994, prepared by the Mozambican Government in collaboration with the staffs of the International Monetary Fund and the World Bank, October 1992.

Government of Mozambique/UNDP (1992) 'National family sector agricultural development programme – pre-programme', Maputo.

International Monetary Fund (1994) 'Republic of Mozambique, Enhanced Structural Adjustment Facility, Policy Framework Paper for 1994–1996', prepared by the Mozambican authorities in collaboration with the staffs of the International Monetary Fund and the World Bank, 11 May 1994.

Isaacman, A. and Isaacman, B. (1983) *Mozambique from Colonialism to Revolution 1900–1982*, Boulder, CO: Westview Press.

LINK (1993) 'Land tenure issues for small scale farmers in Mozambique', LINK NGO Co-ordinating Unit, Maputo, November 1993.

Loforte, A. (1993) 'Aspectos antropológicos a considerar na definição da política de terras em moçambique', TSS-1 MOZ/92/T02/A/08/12, advisory policy on rural resettlement and land policy, Food and Agriculture Organization, Maputo, May 1993.

Macamo, F. (1993) 'Quadro legal para a administração de terras e recursos naturais', TSS-1 MOZ/92/T02/A/08/12, advisory policy on rural resettlement and land policy, Food and Agriculture Organization, Maputo, July 1993.

MAGIC (1977) Central Committee Report to the Third Congress of Frelimo, 3–7 February 1977, Mozambique, Angola, and Guinea Bissau Information Centre, London.

—— (1979) 'Principles of revolutionary justice. The constitution'. Documents on law and state in the People's Republic of Mozambique. State papers and Party Proceedings Series 2 Number 2, Mozambique, Angola, and Guinea Bissau Information Centre, London.

Martins, M. (1994) 'Presentation to the national seminar on land in Mozambique organised by the Ministry of Agriculture and the Land Tenure Centre', in R. Weiss and G. Myers (eds) *Second National Land Conference in Mozambique; Briefing Book*, 25–27 May 1994, Maputo.

Ministério da Agricultura (1992) 'Bases para uma política agraria. Republica de Moçambique', September 1992.

Moore, H.L. and Vaughan, M. (1994) *Cutting Down Trees: Gender, Nutrition and Agricultural Change in the Northern Province of Zambia, 1890–1990*, Portsmouth: Heinemann.

Myers, G.W. (1993) *Confusion, Contradiction and Conflict: Land Access in Mozambique in the Post-Peace Period: Four Case Studies from Manica, Sofala, Gaza and Inhambane Provinces*, Land Tenure Center, University of Wisconsin-Madison.

Sachs, A. (1981) 'Introduction to Mozambique Land Law', Harvard University's Committee on African Studies.

World Bank (1992) 'Agricultural services rehabilitation and development project', Southern Africa Department, Agriculture Operations Division.

Part II

Sexuality and legitimacy

Chapter 5

The law and the market
Rhetorics of exclusion and inclusion among London prostitutes

Sophie Day

INTRODUCTION

London prostitutes present themselves as workers and business-women.[1] Indeed, women often suggest that they are in a good position to take advantage of market opportunities. At the same time, they say that their freedom to make money is constrained by the law and, in particular, its enforcement. In the UK, as in many countries, it is legal to *be*, but not to *work* as, a prostitute. Accordingly, London prostitutes consider themselves outside the law. Rhetorics of inclusion and exclusion associated with the market and the law are explored in this chapter.

Initially, it seems that prostitutes construct a simple division between a punitive state and a morally neutral market which they can work to their advantage. However, this contrast appears less straightforward in the context of legal reform. While London prostitutes universally agree that the laws and their execution are unfair, they are equivocal about possible reform. I suggest that one important factor accounting for their ambivalence concerns ideas about the market, for it seems that a position outside the law is, in fact, central to a sense of autonomy in an apparently free market. Although the laws are manifestly unjust, reform might compromise the precarious freedom that these women prize so highly in their business affairs. At the end of the chapter, I refer to campaigns by prostitute activists for legal reform, which suggest that our data may have more general relevance. The broader literature reveals a similar contrast between the law and the market, and a similar set of business values.

I should emphasize that this chapter is concerned with a very general point which, I hope, will not imply too much homogeneity among London prostitutes. The women described below are very different from each other and I have chosen to delineate common themes rather than equally prominent differences. Furthermore, campaigns for reform are described from the perspective of these ethnographic data and the account is, therefore, partial.

BUSINESS IN LONDON

Prostitution, we are often told, is only a specific expression of the universal 'prostitution' of the worker. Indeed, prostitutes are often presented as symbols of the degradation of wage labour in general: people alienate their body, sexuality or some essential part of themselves for mere money. There is a certain irony to this metaphor from the perspective of London prostitutes for, of course, the last thing they receive is a wage. Most prostitutes in London are self-employed, and intend to work for a short period so as to amass some money for their future lives. They consider themselves, first and foremost, as businesswomen.

Since it is legal to be a prostitute in the UK, women in London attempt to situate themselves in an informal, rather than illegal, economy. Sex work[2] in London is insecure and women make a precarious living in difficult circumstances. This does not necessarily mean that they are poor, but their earnings fluctuate in unpredictable ways. Conversations reflect this, as women share local knowledge about the market and about state interference in an attempt to increase their control over the supply of money. Some women consider prostitution as a job that is restricted to certain times and places, which will yield a predictable minimum 'wage'. But the majority, from diverse backgrounds and working in all sectors of prostitution, consider sex work as a freelance business. They continually try to maximize their earnings through a highly flexible approach to the market which includes a willingness to go where the money is. Women move to different sectors of prostitution,[3] they work abroad and they invest in alternative and often innovative schemes. Comments about particular work practices illustrate the importance of business.

Jane[4] generally worked in a private flat. However, every few months over the past eight years she has mentioned some new money-making scheme. For example, she had earned £5,000 from a trip to the Middle East, then lost money through an abortive visit to Asia. She had moved her work from central London to the suburbs in an attempt to decrease her overheads. She bought a house, and then planned a move to the Caribbean. She worked in saunas when she did not have enough money to finance a flat of her own. When Jane discussed her move to the suburbs in March 1991, she said that business was slow: 'A regular [a regular client] who would have come once a week now comes every two to three weeks'. Jane had thought of moving back to central London, 'to get a better class of clientele', and had carefully considered the costs and benefits of various alternatives. She decided against a move to the West End: '... your overheads go up. I still get passing trade where I am, you know, labourers... I keep my outgoings to a minimum and maximize my ingoings...'. She pondered the cheapest and most effective form of advertising. She had tried the local paper for two months, but had not got much business. Stickers [advertising cards placed in public places such as telephone boxes] were too expensive, so she used the local shop windows: 'When I have too many regulars, I think, the only way to get regulars is from new clients so I'll have to advertise again. It's like any business. I need an accountant though.'

Another woman worked primarily through escort agencies during the three years I knew her. She was saving for a mortgage and, when she had her own flat, she wanted to open an agency herself. While I knew her, she also worked on streets, in saunas and privately in an effort to earn more. She attempted to make money through 'chat lines' involving telephone sex and, in order to set up her own business, she registered for an exam at an International School of Beauticians.

In conversations such as these, women commonly talk in terms of 'making their money' (Day 1994). They glean an income through business acumen and not through wage labour. They take the market for granted and assume that money can be made if only they are sufficiently enterprising. London prostitutes are, after all, on the game as they say, not on the job.

Entrepreneurial activity is not confined to the process of gathering money but applies also to saving and investing. Many women speak of their earnings in terms of future businesses and they often mention freelance commercial careers – in tax advice, insurance work, property advice, rentals and sales. Small businesses are often established while a woman works as a prostitute, and business affairs may become complicated. For example, in the late 1980s, Doranne worked in prostitution, earned commission or rental from other women and worked as a mortgage broker. She had two London properties and had recently sold a third. In 1989, she planned to build a house and a shop in the Caribbean. She wanted to run a guest house. Later, she diversified her sex work even further, working as a maid for a friend and also abroad. In the past, she had been a make-up consultant. As she earned more or less, she retrieved goods from the pawn shop, resurrected her plans for moving to the Caribbean and pursued schemes for making money out of selling her house.

In one conversation, Nancy said in passing that she had saved £20,000. On the advice of a client, she had moved the money to Switzerland and then to Jersey. She complained that she did not know what to do with it. She could buy a house but it was so complicated. Where was she supposed to have got the money from? How was she to pay tax? She wanted her money in England: 'At least you can say you earned it abroad. He [that is, this particular client] said I should register a company abroad and have a subsidiary over here.' Nancy wanted to make this money productive, through some kind of business.

Another woman continued to see some clients privately through personal referral so as to consolidate her businesses. These included importing cars for resale, a video rental business and her newest venture, in which she offered training in word processing. This woman reflected: 'I've always wanted to go into business and I've been very successful. I used money from prostitution to get some of the capital assets.'

This idea of business is central to women in all sectors of prostitution, irrespective of their backgrounds. The most popular labels that London prostitutes use to refer to themselves continue to be 'business girl' or 'working girl'. Prostitution in London is associated with a radical individualism in which prostitutes assert that they can make their own lives through creatively accumulating, spending, saving and investing money. This rhetoric attributes a general personal autonomy to success in business and it is not confined to prostitution. References to the 'small business', to the 'self-made' businessman or woman, and to enterprise in general are common in the UK. Policies are developed for those who will get 'on their bikes' to hustle for any opportunity that presents itself. Free competition and liberty in economic life are currently promoted by government policies restricting the operation of a state that is conceived, by contrast, as a realm of coercion. It is expected that enterprise and initiative will flourish spontaneously if the power of the state is curbed (Heelas and Morris 1992).

However, London prostitutes also oppose their kind of business to 'straight lifestyles' and consider themselves outside mainstream society. For example, one woman said: 'I hate the word prostitute. Hustler is OK because we all have to hustle in this world.' Another valued her marginal position more explicitly:

> Every time I have to get up early in the morning to come down here [to the clinic where we were talking], and I [see] the straight geezers on the train going to work, then I know I'm going to stay with my work.

Prostitutes enjoy their opportunities to do business without the restrictions of fixed work hours, managerial interference and state inspection. Operating in an informal economy, they are invisible to the state bureaucracy that regulates business. But, since this informal economy is also illegal, they come into contact with another branch of the state, namely, the criminal justice system.

THE LAW AND ITS ENFORCEMENT IN THE UK

Strictly speaking, prostitutes can operate within the law so long as they work invisibly and alone: all other business is illegal. It is against the law to associate directly or indirectly with someone else, to advertise or solicit custom in other ways. In addition, the use of earnings is circumscribed by laws which prohibit other adults access to money from prostitution. Prosecution through specific prostitution laws is complemented by general laws, for example, on morality and public order. A woman working on the streets may be charged with causing obstruction of the highway. While some women may work legally, everyone I have met contravenes the law and is therefore open to prosecution.

The incongruity of these laws derives from an 'abolitionist' approach. Contemporary forms of abolitionism developed from nineteenth-century attempts to abolish slavery. Prostitutes were and are seen as slaves who should be rescued, not punished. In theory, it is only the other people involved in prostitution who have the status of criminals. Abolitionist approaches to prostitution in the nineteenth century were opposed, in particular, to any state attempts at regulation through registration, licensing or taxation. Such 'regulationism' has been largely displaced in the twentieth century by abolitionism all over the world.[5] However, at the same time, informal regulation operates in most countries through a range of state agencies, particularly the police.

While abolitionism is supposed to penalize businesses rather than prostitutes, individual sex workers are usually the ones who get prosecuted. In the UK, a pragmatic approach to law enforcement means that prostitution is recognized as part of contemporary life, to be controlled within acceptable limits which are dictated largely by the visibility of the trade, and according to changing perceptions of public order and nuisance. Prostitutes are prosecuted and thereby prevented from working. The state apparatus penalizes the sale of sexual services more than its purchase or management, and this pattern tends to coincide with a gender bias, so that women are criminalized more than men.[6]

Street workers are the prime target as they work most visibly. They are generally prosecuted under laws relating to soliciting. A first conviction as a 'common prostitute' requires the evidence of two police officers and two previous cautions. Thereafter, 'known' prostitutes can be prosecuted successfully through the evidence of a single officer. Thus, unlike other crimes, which can be committed by anyone, prostitution is a crime only when committed by a 'common prostitute'.[7]

The Criminal Justice Act of 1982 replaced imprisonment for soliciting with a fine. As a result, fines rose tenfold in some courts and prostitutes began to be imprisoned for non-payment. In London, the fines imposed by local courts still vary enormously. A scheme introduced in 1991 may have decreased the rate of imprisonment, as those convicted were allowed to pay their fines in instalments. However, it is not clear how many women are still imprisoned for prostitution offences as records are kept on the basis of non-payment of fines rather than the initial charge that was made.[8]

Street workers in central London deal routinely with police and courts, unlike women working indoors. Many are charged and fined once or twice a night. Since prostitutes are anxious not to alienate the police, and since they perceive difficulties in negotiating the legal system, most plead guilty to charges that are brought, and case law is consequently scant. Conversations with a single woman over a period of months illustrate the situation.

Karen visited us in April 1990. There had been five women at court that morning. The police were arresting everyone twice a night now. In consequence, she had only made £100 last night. She saw a client, got nicked [arrested], saw another client, got nicked and went home. In the past month, she had only been out twice without being arrested: 'The police ask me why I don't go to another beat [street area]. I'm not giving into them, that's why. It's ridiculous.'

In May, Karen dropped in with a friend, Sue. They were off to work a different area in the afternoon so as to avoid the 'tom squad' [special police or vice squad]. They would not work their normal beat at all that week. Two nights previously they had both been in a police cell all night, because they had been arrested twice. Sue had outstanding fines totalling £300. She had acquired another £30 that morning in Great Marlborough Street court: 'You have to do your work before you get nicked now. Because, once you've been nicked, you can't go out again.'

In June, the two dropped in after paying off most of their fines. Each had just £50 outstanding. Karen said that she'd been done twice the night before: 'I had to go home by twelve because they were going to do me a third time. They're driving us off the beat, closing it down. I'm not moving.' Karen said she'd been in a cell all night again: 'They pull you in more if they think you've got a ponce [an adult living off prostitutes' earnings] and they have seen me with Pete [her boy-friend].' In August, Karen chatted with friends in the project drop-in. One woman had appeared at Marylebone with outstanding fines. The magistrate had told her to bring a toothbrush next time, if she hadn't paid. Another woman had appeared with her, arrested in Edgware Road. She said she never worked there and had just gone to the 24-hour shop to get some cigarettes. She had no condoms with her. She said, 'I would have got off, only they shifted all the two o'clock appearances to ten and I got £100 for not appearing. They said I would have known if I'd been at the address I gave the police, but I had checked my mail.'

A few months later, Karen gave in to police pressure and began to work in a sauna. However, she soon left as she 'couldn't handle the hours'. She had worked a twelve-hour shift in the sauna, and complained that she could earn as much on the streets in three hours. She was not prepared to try other methods of work indoors. Neither flats nor agencies were safe enough. Indeed, Karen had begun to work on the streets after an attack from a client she had seen through an escort agency. As far as she was concerned, working with other women, either on streets or in saunas, provided the best guarantee of safety.

For these women, it makes a great deal of difference which court and which magistrate is involved. One police station routinely keeps women such as Karen in police cells overnight, by refusing bail. One magistrate is infamous for his very steep fines and for imprisoning women for non-payment:

I used to make very good money, £300 a night. Normally, you are fined £30 or £50 for a first offence. I was fined £330, on the Monday. I was picked up again on Wednesday when Judge M put me in prison for 30 days for non-payment, even though I couldn't possibly have paid [by then] ... I ended up serving 15 days of the 30, in an open prison. My boyfriend came and bailed me out, he must have bought me out or paid the fine or whatever.

When I've been in Paddington Green, I've had no access to a solicitor [legal representation] ... I haven't been able to make a phone call ... [That time] I was told by the police that I couldn't have a solicitor for that trial, that I couldn't be represented for soliciting [seeking clients], because 'you're a working girl'.

Even the police officer said I shouldn't have been inside.

When they hear that Judge M is on in Marylebone, it's very quiet [on the streets].

That's why I've stopped working on the streets even though the money's better. [This woman now worked through agencies.]

Many street workers face with resignation the prospect of nightly fines, as a 'tax' on working. This resignation turns to outrage when fines escalate in amount and/or frequency and, particularly, when they are charged for simply being on the streets.

Women who work off the streets are prosecuted far less often. The policing of women who work in private flats is variable but those known to the police are subject to close surveillance. Those who work in organized businesses seem to be prosecuted no more frequently than their managers or agents. Women who work privately, through personal referrals and through madams, are prosecuted least often. Our research with 192 women suggested different experiences of the law according to workplace. Some 42 per cent of women had been in prison or police cells overnight, including 86 per cent of women currently working on streets as compared, at the other extreme, to none of those working through a madam.

As with street work, the laws are generally less relevant than their arbitrary execution. In matters of vice, the police are allowed a good deal of discretion. Women consider themselves vulnerable to an apparently unlimited set of charges by the police, as illustrated by the following examples.

Mary was familiar with the law. She worked on her own and

advertised with some caution. At the end of 1988, she described a court case, set in motion by an erstwhile associate, who she used to pay for distributing 'stickers':

> When I sacked him, he said to me before he left that I would get what's coming to me and that was it.... He sent me up for the old bill. He made a report ... that I was disturbing the peace, never mind that he has been nicked about six times since then. The police have to react when they get a complaint like that. I got done, and bound over to keep the peace.

Ultimately, Mary said, she was charged with keeping a disorderly house. She had been told that this was because she had a cane in the flat: 'they said whether I had one cane or twenty canes, that was it'.[9]

Jane, who was quoted above, was worried about surveillance of her flat at around the same time. She thought that she was more likely to be charged if she worked with other people. Jane explained how she and her colleague took care to work shifts so that each operated alone. Her colleague had already checked the legality of this shift system with a solicitor. Jane appeared somewhat cynical about their efforts. She explained how she had been charged previously for controlling prostitutes in a sauna near London: 'We were under surveillance for ten months before we were all three busted. The R. vice have a huge umbrella, they did me for controlling prostitutes, for management, when I was just ... the receptionist.'

A final example illustrates the response of women to changes in policing. Lesley currently worked indoors, from a flat. She had worked on the streets in London some years ago, where she had been arrested often: 'The minute I came of age to go to jail, I left [the UK] and went to Germany because I had no intention of going to jail ... I went to avoid the police after so many arrests.' After a time in Germany, Lesley had returned to London to work primarily from flats. Currently, she minimized any possibility of police attention by working through a third party. She paid a contact, from previous escort work, to place her in a flat, to complete any legal negotiations and to advertise regularly. This form of work seems to be growing in popularity in parts of London because the police have been paying more attention to flat workers. In the late 1980s, women generally rented the flats they worked in themselves. Today, many rely on the 'protection' of a third party, who can move them from one flat to another and provide some camouflage.

The situation in the UK affects women's lives in general and not simply their working conditions. Any adult who shares a woman's income may be prosecuted. Men are charged with living off immoral earnings while women are generally prosecuted for controlling or managing prostitutes. Prostitutes often react more strongly to the criminalization of their private lives than their work. Laura, for example, had a boyfriend whom she supported financially. She commented:

> He makes his own money, which is like pocket money. I pay the bills so he could be charged for immoral earnings which doesn't seem fair. If I was working normally as a director and I was bringing in the money I am now, would he still be done for poncing [i.e. living off immoral earnings]? It isn't at all fair. He does make his contribution.

The women consider the state to be most oppressive in penalizing them for having a private life at all. In reaction to these laws, London prostitutes frequently possess at least two legal identities, using one as a private citizen and another for work. This manoeuvre enables them to segregate their working affairs from other state records. Without it, they encounter acute problems when they want to buy a house, pay tax or register with the state for some other purpose. A criminal record can make it hard to travel abroad, and known prostitutes may find it difficult to keep custody of their children. With two legal identities, they can juggle for a position inside the law as far as their family lives and children are concerned. Most also have a number of working names, partly so as to make record-keeping by the authorities more difficult.

When prostitutes talk about the iniquities of the law, they discuss arbitrary policing and the extreme isolation in which they are forced to work. They emphasize the absolute necessity of maintaining some quasi-legitimate front in certain dealings with the state, not just for business reasons but also so as to minimize state interference in their private lives. Perhaps the single most common complaint concerns the lack of safety. Prostitutes are exceedingly vulnerable to exploitation, robbery, assault, rape and murder, and they get virtually no protection from the state. The women we have met are in universal agreement that the laws and their enforcement are harsh and unfair; and that they have been turned into 'deviants' by an oppressive state.

It can be seen that business opportunities are highly restricted by the law. If prostitutes make their own lives through entrepreneurial activities, they do so in the interstices between the informal and the illegal. The relationships between these two domains may be clarified through a discussion of prostitutes' ideas about potential change through legal reform.

LEGAL REFORM

London prostitutes speak continually about the abuses of the law in concrete terms, with reference to their personal experiences. Some of their stories include general comments about possible reforms. One woman spoke of the lack of safety in her flat, where she had a dog and a boyfriend for security, and the hostility of the police: 'The police, they're spies. I got a conviction from the sauna. I lost my job even though I was on the desk and they couldn't prove I knew anything about the girls having sex.' She concluded a long tirade with the comment: 'The present system makes the court a ponce. It should be decriminalized'.

For Anna, 'Prostitution should be legalized and prostitutes should pay tax. Prostitution is necessary to society so that people like you [i.e. S. Day] can walk around [in safety].' While Anna emphasized the safety of other women with the truism that commercial sex reduces rape, others speak rather of their own safety: 'they should make it legal. We could have check-ups, we could be registered . . . it would be much safer.'

Prostitutes who had worked in other countries differed in their reactions. Where commercial sex is closely regulated by the state, some women claimed that they were safer and work conditions, including health care, were better. But others suggested that an illegal sector continued to operate and compromised the safety of all prostitutes. One woman, for example, said of a German city:

> The pimps were real pimps, not like the ones here. If it were legalized or decriminalized here, you would end up with pimps like that, who would kill you if you complained to the police. . . . There were places . . . that I would never go.

When I attempted to elicit fuller statements from scattered comments such as these, women presented conflicting ideas about reform. Laura thought the laws victimizing her boyfriend should be repealed, but she supported the criminalization of street work. She worked indoors and said that, where she lived, 'It's not safe to walk out at night – I have to take a car.'

Despite great antipathy to the criminal justice system, many women supported the *status quo*. One noted, 'if you made laws, there would be too many girls doing it'. This woman was discussing the many risks associated with sex work and suggested that there was a trade-off between safety and earnings: prostitution was lucrative because it was dangerous. Should conditions improve, more and more women would be attracted into the business and so earnings would decline.[10]

Advocacy for the *status quo*, or for legalization and for decriminalization, suggest differences that are more apparent than real. Women were rather vague about the implications of these terms, so the precise meanings associated with public campaigns for reform cannot necessarily be applied to their comments. However, it seems to me that the lack of discussion and widespread confusion about reform point to a general dilemma. Prostitutes in London find it difficult to imagine reforms that would increase equity and safety without compromising business. They were also wary of any reforms that might make their identities as prostitutes more public.

RELATIONSHIPS BETWEEN THE MARKET AND THE STATE

Initially, it seemed to me that London prostitutes took advantage of the market despite the law. But these comments about legal reform suggest that prostitutes recognize connections between the law and the market, and that they are more concerned about the potential threat to business from reform, than about current oppression by the state. This reading depends upon situating the comments about reform in relation to the comments on business.

Two aspects of the law are important. Currently, business is either illegal or invisible. Activities which are illegal carry specific sanctions that, I suggest, in fact foster enterprise. Prostitutes value their skills as entrepreneurs who are constantly poised to make the perfect deal, and who avoid the drudgery of wage labour. Equally, however, they are forced to work alone and to constantly diversify their work in response to changing patterns of law enforcement. They have to work opportunistically and secretly, through personal networks and the rapid appraisal of costs and benefits. They have to operate as self-made businesswomen and hustlers.

Secondly, activities which are invisible remain unregulated by the state. London prostitutes are unhampered by the business codes and regulations that apply to most entrepreneurs. They operate beyond as well as outside the law. It seems to me that generalizations can be made from comments such as the one suggesting an inverse association between safety and earnings. Positive features of the market are attributed to negative features of the law. Reform might enable the state to intrude into a previously 'free' market and to regulate businesses directly through demands for records, taxes and so forth. If independence in a 'free market' comes to stand for a general identity, as I have suggested, it is not surprising that prostitutes are concerned about any possible threat to their status as freelance businesswomen. What is perhaps more surprising is their extraordinary valorization of what looks like a precarious and limited autonomy.

It is the resilience of the rhetoric of freedom or inclusion that requires further explanation. Business values remain unquestioned and unchallenged. The characterization of free enterprise in London seems to involve a central ambiguity. Most women operate independently in their transactions with clients and generally deny that clients play an active role in the negotiations. Prostitutes basically represent the market as if it were theirs. It is they who select clients, negotiate the services for sale and fix the price. It is the prostitute rather than the client who is in charge of a commercial sexual encounter. While this rhetoric reflects accurately certain aspects of prostitution in London, it obscures others. It does not acknowledge any role to the clients who buy services, who are scarcely subject to legal sanction and who are sometimes hard to find. Of course, women do talk about difficulties with individual clients and also a general scarcity of work which they attribute to economic recession. But they continue to take a generalized market demand for granted. This generalized, indeed universal, demand is explained in terms of biological and economic differences. Men have a great need for sex or they have a greater buying power than women, and will continue to spend their surplus on pastimes which include recreational sex. This can be fuelled by a constant diversification in the types of sex and 'pretence' or 'illusion' offered for sale.

Prostitute women in London seem to have effected a fundamental ideological transformation by representing a site of dependency as one of freedom. In practice, they depend upon a market demand that is neither fixed nor universal, and individual clients who purchase services are as likely as prostitutes to consider themselves 'in charge' and, often, to have got the better bargain.[11] Equally, there are wide fluctuations in the prices that prostitutes are able to charge, according to economic conditions.

Yet, London prostitutes continue to represent themselves as entrepreneurs who simply avail themselves of rich pickings and take advantage of market opportunities. The compelling nature of this imagery must surely owe much to the experience of different kinds of domination. What might be glossed as market dependency remains distinct from state repression. The distinctions are not just an obvious fact of everyday life and state policy. They are also refashioned so that a condition of exclusion becomes the raw material out of which a particular kind of free market is fashioned, epitomized by the hustler. In turning their marginal position into the very hub of modern life, prostitutes achieve a remarkable sleight of hand. The freedom of the market comes to exist *sui generis*, before rather than after the law. Hustling is detached from its roots.

I have suggested that entrepreneurial independence is a fundamental value, and that positive views of the market lead London prostitutes into a general silence about legal reform despite the experience of oppressive laws and arbitrary policing. Londoners are not unique in this respect. In the final section of this chapter, I refer to a very different setting which is concerned primarily with legal reform. A closer reading reveals continuities with the London ethnography and, in particular, a similar idealization of business.

PROSTITUTE ACTIVISM

At first sight, the ambivalence about change among London prostitutes contrasts strongly with the platform developed by prostitute rights activists.[12] The partial emancipation of women in the 1960s, together with diversification in the sex industry, which led to increasing professionalization among some workers, contributed to the formation of prostitute organizations from the early 1970s to the present day. Self-help groups were established initially in North America and Europe[13] and exist today all over the world. The significance of prostitution for women's rights in general has been contested fiercely and the relationships between prostitute activists and other feminists are varied. Alliances between self-help groups have led to international bodies such as the International Committee for Prostitutes' Rights (ICPR), formed in 1985, and, more recently, the Network of Sex Projects. These act as umbrella organizations and important lobbyists for the decriminalization of prostitution.

Decriminalization, in this context, means the removal of all laws specific to prostitution. Prostitutes should not be seen as victims, as in abolitionist systems, where prostitution is usually suppressed. Nor should prostitutes be registered or licensed, as in various 'legalized' or 'regulated' systems. Prostitution is simply work or labour and, as such, can be controlled adequately through laws that govern other forms of work.

This goal has united diverse activists in the last twenty years. It is shared with many other groups who are opposed to laws for crimes without victims, which affect women more than men, and which fail to address the exploitation of prostitutes by managers and agents. For example, other feminists and non-governmental organizations such as the de Graaf Stichting in the Netherlands lobby for the recognition of prostitution as labour. While past campaigns for reform have characterized prostitution as a form of work,[14] contemporary efforts are led by political interest groups constituted largely on the basis of self-help.[15]

An example of the demands made by activists can be found in the manifesto agreed at the First World Whores' Congress which took place in 1985 in Amsterdam under the auspices of the ICPR (Phetersen 1989). The World Charter for Prostitutes' Rights demands the international decriminalization of prostitution so as to assure prostitutes of basic human rights, some control over work conditions, access to health care and other services and, finally, a means of influencing public opinion. Prostitution, it is argued, must be recognized as a legitimate occupation so that legal contracts can be made concerning immediate working conditions as well as general rights relating to insurance, taxation, freedom of movement and so forth.

This platform speaks to the abolitionist approach that characterizes national and international laws today. Activists question widespread assumptions that all prostitution is 'forced' or involuntary. They claim that women may freely choose to work as prostitutes and that they should have the same rights as any other worker. In this way, activists formulate a distinction between 'forced' and 'voluntary' prostitution. Voluntary prostitution includes economic aspirations related to poverty and the lack of reasonable alternatives, but excludes deception and physical coercion. Individuals under the age of consent for sexual activity are also excluded.

At one level, these different approaches to political emancipation present a simple contrast to material from London. Activists can be characterized as a political interest group coalescing around a single issue. The term prostitute acts as a badge of identity inside and outside the domain of work. Like many other communities that have emerged in the last thirty years, prostitute activists attempt to negotiate citizenship or inclusion within the state on the basis of a single feature (Weeks 1989). Women in our London research have no such unitary identity. The majority used the term 'prostitute' in a restricted fashion,[16] and maintained a radical separation between work and the rest of life (Day 1990). Few of them let anyone outside the industry know of their work. The difficulties of segregating some activities from others are associated with an important set of distinctions between the short and the long term. Most women in London conceived of sex work in the short term only and, in practice, few of the women we have known work for more than five years. Women work as prostitutes for the money and they hope to earn enough to launch themselves in an alternative career. They often wait until they have left sex work to set up their homes and families (Day 1994).

References to campaigns for reform show just how far prostitutes in London embrace a position outside the law as part and parcel of their position inside a free market. It would have been possible to refer to a range of other studies and reformist movements in order to make this point but I have focused on self-help groups in order to make a further point, about less obvious continuities.

I have indicated that London prostitutes embrace a general identity as businesswomen. Similarly, much of the activist literature implies that prostitution is not simply work, like any other, but business. In the charter for decriminalization, working conditions are presented thus: 'Prostitutes should have the freedom to choose their place of work and residence. It is essential that prostitutes can provide their services under conditions that are absolutely determined by themselves and no one else' (World Charter for Prostitutes' Rights 1985). The focus on self-determination and autonomy is similar to statements made by London prostitutes. There are many references to business in the literature. For example, the Red Thread self-help group in the Netherlands has argued, 'Prostitutes should also be able to set up businesses themselves' without being 'subjected to a whole lot of rules and regulations' (International Committee for Prostitutes' Rights 1988: 12). They want 'opportunities to start on one's own' (Verbeek 1987: 9).

In another example from Italy, a prostitute argues: 'Prostitution is my work but it's not like other work because I decide how and when to do it.' Her colleague agrees:

The freer we are from codification, the better we can do this work. Every person can then make her own rules. This work cannot be codified. It is tied to each person, to her sexuality, to her freedom. A prostitute can share costs with other prostitutes [in, for example, running a business] and pay for services, but should not share profits.

(International Committee for Prostitutes' Rights 1988: 11)

Activists and London prostitutes alike make reference to their professional skills in sex, therapy, entertainment and health. In both contexts, prostitution is seen primarily as a business service. At least some of the activist literature conceives of voluntary prostitution as a business of the self-employed, and argues that it should be controlled like other businesses, through a market mechanism complemented by local systems of licensing. Given the long history of oppression, and the 'special' services that are offered, business regulations should be applied sparingly.

These examples demonstrate some continuity between London prostitutes and prostitute activists. Not only do both groups oppose the iniquities of control but both describe prostitution as a business of the self-employed. Both present the wider political economy in two parts, contrasting the legal apparatus that excludes prostitutes from full citizenship to a morally neutral market in which they claim full membership as enterprising businesswomen.

However, the relationship between these two realms differs. The activist position implies that the removal of an oppressive state apparatus will enable business to flourish. The realm of autonomy enshrined in the market principle will automatically expand. People maintain this position despite anticipated problems and despite past experiences of reform.

Many of the groups cited in this chapter recognize potential difficulties with reform. The Red Thread has expressed concern about the inevitable expansion of an illegal circuit in the event of decriminalization, and about the role of established business interests (Verbeek 1987). These problems have also been recognized with hindsight. For example, an act of 1986 in Victoria (Australia) moved control of brothels to town planning. Local authorities seem to have refused to grant any new licences and there has been a trend towards large and luxurious brothels and other agencies, run by vested business interests. In this instance, reform has not enabled prostitutes to run legal businesses and those who work alone or in small groups continue to be prosecuted (Neave 1988: 211).

Such experiences challenge the values associated with freelance business. Responses by activists have focused on the loss of autonomy among prostitutes and the need to protect small business interests against monopoly capital. As in London, the focus remains on the independent operator.

Despite the differences between women 'getting by' in London and activists working for political emancipation, there is a shared idealization of the hustler. Even though activists campaign for civil rights, inside the law, the independent business reappears as a fixed ideal. This ideal may relate indirectly to the abolitionist policies which activists contest.

In the nineteenth century, moral arguments about abolitionism and the slavery of women occurred in the midst of extensive debates about the role of the state in the economy. Abolitionism had particular affinities with *laissez-faire* economics as it opposed state administrative or regulatory control, but prostitution had to be presented as a special case, since market principles were constrained by the moral imperative to combat slavery. The influence of *laissez-faire* economics can be seen in the limits that were proposed to state intervention. Individual adults were not prevented from selling and buying sexual services as long as they entered freely into 'contracts' that applied only to their own transactions.[17] In this way, restrictions were applied to the role of the state through ideas about an independent market which would regulate itself. Additional pragmatic considerations suggested limits to state intervention. The structure of the industry was changing and women were less willing to enter the regulated sector, where it existed. In France, for example, the end of the nineteenth century saw an increased supply of and demand for prostitutes. The traditional brothel structure was undermined by an influx of 'independent' women as well as occasional and street prostitutes. Corbin has argued that 'official prostitution' satisfied a sexual demand that existed 'outside' urban society among soldiers, students, immigrants and so forth while unregulated prostitution catered to individuals well integrated into society. These men had new erotic demands which did not fit into the brothel structure (Corbin 1990: 187).

The triumph of abolitionism, I suggest, owed as much to economic ideas and realities as to moral arguments. Widespread policies over the past 150 years have led to a paradoxical situation where prostitution is extensively controlled and suppressed by the state but remains associated with a 'free market' in another, invisible economy. Despite the views cited in this chapter, I would argue that abolitionism has not been associated exclusively with negative prohibitions. Abolitionism also seems to provide a positive exhortation to do business, usually independently and alone, in a market characterized simply by an impersonal pricing mechanism. General state policies can be seen, therefore, to have promoted a contrast between the oppression of the law – applied by the state within the formal economy – and the freedom of a market that exists 'beyond the state' and which regulates itself.

It seems likely that the activist literature reflects the personal experience of legal sanctions, similar to those reported by London prostitutes but differing in the details associated with particular national policies. But the literature is explicitly opposed to any abolitionist position, and I have tentatively suggested that views of independence in business may be related to a muted strand within abolitionism, where market freedom constitutes a positive value. Moreover, once abolitionism is seen as an economic strategy as much as a moral one, a series of other views of the economy become equally relevant. Contemporary neo-liberalism may further encourage prostitutes to identify notions of freedom with the market, as the economy becomes in general the major site of self-determination (see p. 75 above, on the UK context). Whatever the precise constellation of influences in different circumstances, London prostitutes and activists appear equally to recognize interconnections between the law and the market. Different ideas about reform speak to a common dilemma concerning the difficulties of achieving both civil rights and maximum independence. Individuals involved in prostitution may fear that reform will impinge on business or they may anticipate change eagerly because of the benefits it will bring to business. A consensus view of autonomy in a free market seems to prevail in the midst of these complex and conflicting views of legal reform.

CONCLUSION

While this chapter relates to prostitutes working in London, the wider discussion of legal reform is intended to show that Londoners are not unusual in the significance they attach to independence. The fixed and unquestioned nature of this value becomes even more striking when the political strategies of those involved in prostitution are taken into

account. Experience has shown that small-scale independent businesses cannot be realized simply through the market mechanism any
more than through the state, and in the context of an entrepreneurial
outlook, certain questions are simply not asked. It remains unknown
how individual prostitutes have reacted to changes in their working
conditions. For example, women in the brothels of Victoria, Australia
may consider themselves better off as workers inside the formal
economy and citizens of the state, than as 'hustlers'. Presumably,
many are not only safer but also enjoy the wider security that goes
with a wage, such as employment, union and benefit rights. London
prostitutes who have stopped working also seem to have stopped
looking for the perfect business. As prostitutes, many women aspired
to commercial freelance careers but, to judge from the few women
who have remained in contact with us when they leave prostitution,
they mainly take up salaried work in the public sector, as secretaries,
teachers, clerks and social workers.

The rhetorics of freedom and oppression outlined in this chapter
are both general and specific. They share much with a range of
contemporary neo-liberal attitudes and entrepreneurial practices, but
they are also situated within a long history of prostitution control. At
the local level which has provided the focus of this chapter, they relate
to specific experiences of sex work which have produced a rich
vocabulary and practice of hustling. Hustling, beyond the law and
beyond the state, offers prostitutes some control over their own work.
This limited freedom to do business has been elaborated into an
ideology, shared by prostitutes and activists alike, which conceals a
fundamental dependency as much as it reflects a precarious autonomy. One can only speculate whether deregulation would result very
generally in new rhetorics, where the state and the market would be
less clearly opposed and where the market would no longer connote
an undifferentiated realm of freedom.

NOTES

1   Data are drawn from research which was conducted largely between 1986
    and 1991 through the Praed Street Project that I established with Helen
    Ward at St Mary's Hospital Medical School, London. A cross-sectional
    study of 280 women based on single interviews was carried out between
    1989 and 1991 and a longitudinal study of 357 women was conducted
    between 1986 and 1991. Both studies involved research in different
    settings; in the hospital STD (sexually transmitted disease) clinic, a
    separate project office, and in areas where women worked or came into

contact with state agents (such as local courts). Field research focused on street work in parts of West and Central London but interviews with women using the Praed Street Project concerned experiences all over the country. These studies were supported by AVERT, North West Thames Health Authority, the Medical Research Council and the Jefferiss Trust. I should like to thank those who participated in the research, Praed Street Project staff and, in particular, Helen Ward, my colleague throughout this research. Thanks also to Olivia Harris for her editorial comments.

2   Sex work, prostitution and commercial sex are used as synonyms in this chapter.

3   Prostitution sectors are classified in various ways in the literature. For my purposes, women working independently are distinguished from those who depend upon third parties, whether as agents or employers. Among those working independently, the amount of investment involved tends to distinguish street workers from those working indoors.

4   Personal names are pseudonyms.

5   Abolitionism also dominates the international arena, for example in a number of documents adopted by the United Nations, such as the Universal Declaration of Human Rights (1948) and the Convention for the Suppression of the Traffic in Persons and of the Exploitation of the Prostitution of Others (1949). In the former, for example, it is stated that 'prostitution and ... traffic in persons are incompatible with the dignity and worth of the human person...'

6   Male prostitution is not discussed in this chapter. However, in the UK and other countries, the criminalization of male prostitution relates as much to laws on under-age sex and homosexuality as to prostitution. While UK law now criminalizes public soliciting on the part of clients as well as prostitutes, those who purchase sex are rarely prosecuted.

7   See English Collective of Prostitutes (1984). A first conviction can be completed within a single evening, according to reports to the Praed Street Project from West and Central London, so it should not be assumed that cautioning procedures necessarily protect against abuses.

8   Available data suggest that prostitutes continue to be imprisoned for non-payment (e.g. Leng 1992: 272).

9   Mary worked on her own largely so as to avoid breaking the common law offence of keeping a brothel. However, women working alone can be convicted for running a disorderly house, often on evidence relating exclusively to their working equipment.

10 No one explicitly told me that they were selling 'risk' to clients but it was clear that some men were attracted to prostitutes precisely because of the criminality. In a separate study, a number of clients made this point explicitly, speaking of the 'buzz' and 'excitement' of illegal sex.

11 During interviews, some clients explained how they shopped around to get the best deal. These men considered that consumer choice determined the shape of the market and the relatively strong position of the buyer.

12 This term refers to a range of interests associated with prostitutes' attempts to legitimize their work. I use the term activist, prostitute activist and prostitute rights activists interchangeably. See Bell 1994 on the differences between these and other prostitute movements.

13 COYOTE (Call off your old tired ethics) was formed in 1973 in California. A year or two later, several groups were formed in the UK and in France; Hydra was formed in Germany in 1980 and Pia Covre in Italy in 1982.

14 For example, a broad-based alliance which led to the repeal of the Contagious Diseases Acts in the UK in the 1880s included, initially, a recognition that poor women working as prostitutes were simply making a living as best they could, in an environment where few alternatives were available (Walkowitz 1980).

15 The emphasis on experience of prostitution and the degree to which this is made public varies. The English Collective of Prostitutes (ECP) does not define itself as a self-help group, largely because of possible discrimination through UK laws. Other groups are composed strictly on the basis of self-help, for example the Red Thread in the Netherlands. Different groups also have distinctive policies. For example, the ECP considers prostitution as one of many forms of gender inequality legitimized by the state and they campaign for the recognition and remuneration of all forms of female labour, including housework. In what follows, the comments on business apply to many groups, including the ICPR, but they do not apply to the ECP.

16 The London research included some activists and so there is a small overlap between the two settings.

17 Abolitionist policies in the UK permit the sale and purchase of sexual services (as noted above). This policy is common but not universal: in some countries, commercial sex is wholly prohibited and it is not legal to purchase or sell services.

REFERENCES

Bell, S. (1994) *Reading, Writing and Rewriting the Prostitute Body*, Bloomington and Indianapolis: Indiana University Press.

Corbin, A. (1990) *Women for Hire: Prostitution and Sexuality in France after 1850*, trans. A. Sheridan, Harvard: Harvard University Press.

Day, S. (1990) 'Prostitute women and the ideology of work in London', in D.A. Feldman (ed.) *AIDS and Culture: The Global Pandemic*, New York: Praeger.

—— (1994) 'L'argent et l'esprit d'entreprise chez les prostituées à Londres', *Terrain* 23: 99–114.

English Collective of Prostitutes (1984) 'Response to the Criminal Law Revision Committee's Working Paper on Offences relating to Prostitution and Allied Offences', unpublished.

Heelas, P. and Morris, P. (eds) (1992) *The Values of the Enterprise Culture: The Moral Debate*, London: Routledge.

International Committee for Prostitutes' Rights (1988) *World Wide Whore's News* 88(2).

Leng, R. (1992) 'Imprisonment for prostitutes', *New Law Journal*: 28 February: 270–2.

Neave, M. (1988) 'The failure of prostitution law reform', *ANZJ Crim* 21: 202–13.
Phetersen, G. (ed.) (1989) *A Vindication of the Rights of Whores*, Seattle: The Seal Press.
Verbeek, H. (1987) 'Priorities for a new prostitution policy', unpublished, The Red Thread, the Netherlands.
Walkowitz, J. (1980) *Prostitution and Victorian Society: Women, Class and the State*, Cambridge: Cambridge University Press.
Weeks, J. (1989) *Sex, Politics and Society: The Regulation of Sexuality since 1800*, London: Longman.

Chapter 6

In praise of bastards
The uncertainties of *mestizo* identity in the sixteenth- and seventeenth-century Andes

Thérèse Bouysse-Cassagne

Illegitimate birth, which we tend to think of as a fairly marginal social phenomenon, has long been so central a fact of life in post-Conquest Latin America that a consideration of it can lead us straight to the uncertain and ill-understood nature of one of the identities it engendered – that of the *mestizo*. Two sets of circumstances in particular bear directly on the shaping of Latin American *mestizaje*: the circumstances of its birth, since it quite literally issued from the Spanish conquest of Indian societies and the Spanish–Indian racial mixing that flowed from it; and the nature of the legal regime – divided rigidly between the 'republic of the Indians' and the 'republic of the Spaniards' (*república de Indios/república de Españoles*) – that presided over the society in which *mestizo* bastardy flourished. If there is cause for praise of bastards it is in part because many Indian mothers' preference for illegitimacy reveals itself as a strategy for enhancing the lives of their children.

The terms in which *mestizo* identity have so far been discussed reflect two dichotomies: the image of the Conquest as foreign conquistador versus indigenous victim – which is gross distortion of reality; and the dichotomous legal regime which was real enough, though it was not the whole of reality. This regime had no place for a category of people that belonged to neither of its two parts. The status of *mestizos* as moral persons was typically ambiguous: they were associated with all kinds of vice and perceived as a growing threat to the fabric of society. But as is often the case with law, the disadvantages of the *mestizos*' illegitimate status were outweighed by hopes of social betterment and the new choices available in the colonial order. Rather than merely reflecting the legal categories of the time, and the social attitudes that derived from them, we need to break down these dichotomies in a fresh analysis, and note in particular how the behaviour of Indian women themselves – not least via bastardy – eroded the dual regime. As we shall see, they created a space for *mestizos* not so much inside or outside the law as *between* the laws.

THE SILENCE OF THE MOTHERS, THE VOICE OF THE CONQUEROR

Stereotypes die hard. To this day the genesis of *mestizo* Latin America is typified in the caricature of the victorious conquistador and the violated or perfidious Indian woman – the archetype of this couple being Cortés and his Mexican mistress, La Malinche. It is plainly an image of male superiority: the Spanish man appears as conqueror in the full sense of the word – of the land as of the women.

In the case of the Andes, in contrast to Mexico, difficulties with the interpretation of surviving documents are exacerbated by the fact that there are no documents of Indian provenance relating to *mestizaje* that could act as a counterweight to the conquerors' point of view. It is the voice of the conquerors – the voice of the fathers of the *mestizo* children – that has come down to us. As for the 'victim': she allows us to project that conquering voice into the space of the silence in which we cannot hear her voice, even though hers is the only voice that is properly entitled to speak about the children whom, in the last resort, she and she alone has decided to bring into the world. The *mestizo* child – and this is invariably left out of the account – is fruit of the Indian mother's womb: often desired, sometimes just accepted, but rarely forced on her. Given that silence, Latin American *mestizaje* which, as we shall see, is nearly always the biological and social choice of the Indian women, is usually analysed on the basis of the legalistic and prohibitory discourse of the Spanish men.

The silence of the mothers, contrasting as it does with the voices of the conquerors, is additionally peopled with the voices of those other potential fathers, the Indian men, rushing to the rescue of their own and their children's privileges, and those of the Indian family caught up in the full flood of change. Neither the voices of the former nor the latter allow us to understand the reasons that moved a good number of women to give their children Spanish rather than Indian fathers. From the women's point of view, in contrast to the men's, the issue of *mestizaje* presented itself as an alternative and a choice: whether to reproduce Indian society under Spanish tutelage or to create, however precariously, a new *mestizo* society.

Hence the paradox that characterizes the genesis of *mestizaje*: the

mestizo children who often do not know their own father are only
known to us through their fathers.

FEMALE DESIRE AND THE BIRTH OF *MESTIZAJE*

With the capture of Atahualpa, the last Inca king, the Inca empire
foundered and the defeated warriors surrendered together with their
female companions who had been present at the battles. This moment
– the prelude to the formation of a new society – is described by Zarate
and Cieza de León in similar terms that are worth analysing.

> Atahualpa having been taken prisoner, the next morning they went
> to take his camp, it was a marvel to see so many gold and silver
> vessels... and more than 5,000 women who accompanied the
> nobility came towards the Spaniards with good will...
>
> (Zárate 1947[1555] cap. V)

> And among the nobility there were many *palla* women who, upon
> seeing the final day, and being much desired by the Spaniards, and
> they feeling the same love for them, were delighted to go into the
> service of such strong men.
>
> (Cieza de León 1979[1553]

It seems that the wives of the Inca nobility, the *pallas*, having become
war-booty, joyfully welcomed the fate that the conquerors had in store
for them, even desired it. Is this mere boastfulness on the part of the
Spaniards commemorating their military feats by presenting their
readers with the ultimate (and the most conventional) image of the
victorious soldier? Or does it bear witness to 'eternal female artful-
ness'? On either reading we find ourselves in the domain of seduction
– a posture that analyses of the Conquest do not generally take into
account.

Under the Incas it was a noblewoman's destiny to follow her spouse
into the grave. But the fate of noblemen who had been defeated in
battle was truly unenviable. They themselves were massacred, their
gods desecrated, their women raped; they were utterly destroyed.
Should we, then, interpret the attitude of the *pallas* towards the
Spaniards as a last – but realistic – welling up of the will to live?

In the above texts it might seem as though the fate of the *pallas* and
the Spaniards had been sealed from the first. We must, however,
differentiate between the women intended for the soldiery – whose lot
it was to accompany the Spanish soldiers throughout the Conquest –

and whom Indian leaders occasionally gave as gifts; and those whom the conquerors married.

According to Fernandez de Oviedo, Francisco Pizarro took from Atahualpa 'six hundred women and six hundred young men to be distributed among his people' as war-booty. According to the same source, the principal chieftain of Caxas gave Pizarro 'two hundred women' as a gift (Fernandez de Oviedo 1851[1549], vol. V: 137). What happened to the noblemen's wives, on the other hand, belongs not to the categories of war-booty or gift-giving but to that of alliance. These women quickly became the wives of the conquerors, in keeping with a custom that had existed also under the Incas. Thus, one of the Inca Huayna Capac's sisters married the Conquistador Molina el Almagrista and the Inca Amaru's sister married Baptista de Armero. These strategic marriage alliances continued, culminating in the 'exemplary' marriage of Captain Martin Garcia de Loyola, victor over the Inca Tupac Amaru, and the Princess Beatriz Coya, a marriage that linked the rising Jesuit order with the peaks of the Inca nobility – Coya Beatriz being the daughter of Don Cristobal Sayri Topa Inca, son of Manco Inca, and his wife Cusi Uarcaya Coya.

The status of the Indian noblewomen who married Spaniards remained firmly inscribed within the logic of indigenous strategies of alliance – albeit this time with a different conqueror. As for the conquerors, marriage with the Indian nobility gave them and their children a status they could never have hoped to attain in their native land.

Sayri Topa, Inca himself, married his own sister (on both his father's and his mother's side) thanks to a dispensation from the Pope and the mediation of the Archbishop of Cuzco. In this case of a family of royal blood, the Catholic Church was prepared to depart from the established rules prohibiting marriage between first-degree kin, and consent to the perpetuation of an Inca tradition – on condition that the princess become a Christian. The least we can say about this is that the rules of the nobility could be squared with the Almighty, while for its part the Church, at the price of a few departures from orthodoxy, bestowed indigenous legitimacy upon itself by recognizing the nobles and taking them in its embrace.

A generation of young *mestizos* also sprang up who were the children of conquerors who had neither titles of their own nor wives from the Indian nobility.

But this question of alliances, which lies at the core of *mestizaje*, was posed in a more novel form for the commoner Indian women, who conceived illegitimate children by the *encomendero*, the parish priest, the passing Spaniard, and later the *mestizo*, to the extent that this new world of little bastards very quickly became so large that it frightened its fathers. In polygamous Andean societies it was common for nobles, as well as lesser chieftains, to have several secondary wives. Trial marriage (*sirvinacuy*) existed as well at all levels of society, and does to this day. A tradition which, in contrast to the Spanish, treated tenuous relationships, as well as multiple simultaneous ones, as legitimate probably did much to facilitate concubinage with the conquering Spaniards, themselves unused to such freedom in their relations with the opposite sex.

The Spaniards' behaviour towards the women was far from irreproachable: they regarded force, deception and corruption as perfectly acceptable. The following passage, taken from one of the trite and anonymous collections of stories that the Jesuits used to show how an Indian woman's virtue might be proved, serves as an illustration.

> [A certain Indian woman] having been pursued by a Spaniard with gifts and entreaties, and she having resisted his annoying solicitations, this bad man, blinded by his vile intent, determined one night with one of his friends to enter her house and by suasion or force carry out his evil aim; past midnight and in execution of this plan they entered her dwelling and, not succeeding with soft words, using many threats and making other efforts, still they did not succeed in getting anything out of this good Indian woman but constancy and firmness and saintly responses. . . . Another case, no different from the preceding and ending in the same way, [concerns] another Spaniard returning to court a certain Indian woman, who brought her a load of maize at a time when she was in dire need, she threw it out into the street. Many other cases of the same kind have occurred, and several even nastier ones.[1]

This source seeks to show how quickly Christian morality proved its mettle, but ignores the mutuality of the attraction between the conquerors and some Indian women. Indian women, and then the first generation of *mestizo* women, very quickly became coveted sexual objects. And yet two centuries had to pass before colonial society – by then mainly *mestizo* – dared to acknowledge its sexual fantasies and to go so far as to represent them in paintings. From the sixteenth century onwards, Indian sexuality was mentioned only under the heading of sin – in the confessional; and as late as the second half of the eighteenth century the Christian public was shown *mestizo* women only as embodiments of lechery. A painting of the Cuzco School of Christ of the Earthquakes, now in La Paz cathedral, shows these women in the arms of demons and surrounded by serpents and toads, the symbols of lust.[2] This sexualized image of *mestizo* woman appears again in one of the drawings of Vicente Alban, the painter who in 1783 illustrated Celestino Mutis' botanical expedition. The woman is depicted with the following legend: 'Yapanga of Quito in the clothes worn by the class of women who seek to please'. In her hand she holds a *capuli*, similar to a passion fruit. The erotic symbolism attached to this fruit is illustrated by the lascivious saying 'to go to Urubamba to pick *capuli*'.

But let us leave these male representations aside and return to the women. Given the situation in which they found themselves, what did they expect, for themselves and for their children? Why did they prefer a Spaniard to an Indian? In what sorts of family structure would their children grow up?

The Spaniards legislated ceaselessly for this new society, whose shape they had not anticipated, but which they feared might become as hybrid as the society they had had in Spain, from which in the end they had expelled the Jews and Moriscos. The law towards Moriscos and Jews had been so harsh that – notwithstanding attempts at assimilation through intermarriage, royal pardons from Philip II for a few, and papal absolution from Clement VIII for a few more – they were socially marginalized, and viciously persecuted by the Inquisition. Assimilation had its limits in any case, because their 'blood' was not 'pure', and those of Saragossa, Teruel, Albarracin, and from the Jewish ghettos and Moorish quarters of the Kingdom of Valencia, continued to be discriminated as mere 'New Christians'. Barred from holding public office, forbidden to own horses, bear arms, or wear silken garments, they had no access to the distinguishing marks by which the 'honour' of Old Christians was recognized. Their women, on pain of punishment by the Inquisition, could wear neither jewels nor fine cloth, silks, pearls, gold nor silver.[3] Even the good Friar Alonso Chacon, who wrote to the King asking him to favour a policy of integration, suggested 'that the hats and caps and head-dresses of the Moriscos bear a distinguishing mark similar to that worn by the Jews of Rome'.[4]

To be sure, the differences by which in Spain one could tell at a glance the persons who were 'well born' from those who lacked 'honour' were of no effect in the Andes, and no law was passed regulating the appearance or dress of the future *mestizos*, save for a prohibition on bearing arms. And yet, though Indian women and men soon wore silks and gold and pearls, they were frequently compared to the 'New Christians' of the mother country. Indeed, in the Spaniards' minds, Spaniards and Indians inhabited two different and separate public domains – on one and the same territory. In harmony with the dichotomy conjured up by the Conquerors at the beginning, there was, for them, a *república de Españoles* and a *república de Indios*. This dichotomy in due course became a stereotype. And stereotypes die hard, because of the interest that people have in keeping them alive.

In the Andes it was above all the behaviour of the *mestizo* women, who did not strictly belong to either of these 'republics', that began to break this dichotomy down. In the Audience of Charcas, silk and taffeta from Granada, Priego and Jaen, stockings from Toledo, cloth from Seville, satin from Valencia and Cordoban Muria, fans from Madrid, all arrived in Lima to be shipped to Cuzco and Arequipa. (Though by law only Spaniards were permitted to deal in fabrics, a fair number of Indian nobles took up the trade as well, to provide themselves with the funds needed to pay the taxes owed by members of their communities who were absent by reason of death or flight.)[5] If they could afford them, Indian and then *mestizo* women seized on these fabrics, as we shall see, to break the old order down.

However, Indian men of noble rank had a different attitude towards dress from that of the women, especially the commoner women, and used outward garb not to break down the old order but to perpetuate it – indeed an even older order. Sixteenth- and seventeenth-century archives are filled with 'proofs of service and merit' (*probanzas de servicio y meritos*) in which the local chiefs make display of their indigenous titles, plainly with the aim of preserving their privileges within the colonial society. These distinctions translated into insignia and distinctive garb since these noblemen, as they claimed, had been at the time of the Inca, or 'since time immemorial in these parts', equivalent to the ranks of count or marquis in the kingdoms of Spain. In this way ancient legitimacy was used to secure recognition in colonial society, to defend privileges, and to preserve social status through adherence to the strict dress code for men.

A MATTER OF PETTICOATS

In contrast to the conservatism of the nobles, the commoner women's attitude to dress was so strikingly audacious that it can be taken as evidence of a will for change and a desire for social mobility. Very quickly, and without asking anyone's permission, they got hold of the ornaments and finery that in Spain distinguished ladies of honour from the rest. And so we see the Spaniards' Indian domestics (called *chinas* in the documents) getting themselves up with the elegance of the Inca princesses (*pallas*) from whom they copied some of their finery. What would not have been permitted in Inca times became possible in the new society.

It was above all in Potosí – the vast silver-mining city to which from the end of the sixteenth century Indian labourers, merchants and newcomers streamed – that this phenomenon flourished, thanks to the combination of the anonymity created by the cosmopolitan environment and the unparalleled wealth of the city. Garcilaso de la Vega (1960[1609]) tells a brief anecdote on this topic. A parrot in a street of Potosí calls out to a beautiful woman passer-by dressed to the nines trying to pass for a *palla*. But instead of uttering the expected compliment, the jeering bird hurls an insult at her – no doubt a just one: 'Huayro! Huayro!' it cries, and so with a single word relegates her to the category of Inca courtesans, and women of the lowest social class (Bouysse-Cassagne 1988: 72).

Salomon's (1988) study of wills left by women of Quito, a city of great mobility, shows that Indian women were wearing Chinese silks, the fine embroidery of European textiles, rustling taffeta and elaborate brocades, fashioned to their own taste. At the same time they continued to wear prestigious items of traditional Indian clothing, as well as choosing from the fashions of Cañar, Huancavelica and elsewhere – whatever pleased them most and best set off their looks. The jewellery that enhanced this jumbled new fashion best was a mixture of shell necklaces (*chakira*), corals, baroque pearls, gold and silver fibulas (*tupus*), chains and bells. In short, they wore anything they fancied, without worrying about either tradition or the emerging social order.

The beautiful Maria de Los Amores, twice married to Spaniards, mother of two *mestizo* children and two illegitimate ones, willed to her progeny thirty items of clothing and, in addition to her mirror – symbol of her femininity – jewellery that would not have put a Spanish coquette to shame. The intricacy of the silver and gold satin borders, of the Roman-style purple silk sashes, of the 'Chinese' silk shawls show how the Conquest had opened the floodgates to seduction: where hitherto clothing had exhibited social rank, now any and every woman potentially had access to elegant attire.

By creating new emblems out of old, the Indian women succeeded – as they do to the present day – in expanding the symbolic language of indigenous tradition beyond its existing boundaries, while at the same time the new insignia borrowed from Spanish culture attested to the novelty of their status. They were in fact, in Hobsbawm's sense of the term, inventing a tradition. These deliberate innovations were the first visible signs of the historic novelty of the *mestizo*'s entry into colonial society. We should not, therefore, analyse the *mestizo* phenomenon in terms of a dichotomy, but rather as a series of predominantly innovative exercises in social ingenuity that in practice tended to abolish the dichotomy between the *república de Indios* and the *república de Españoles*.

It was in the face of this upheaval in women's outward appearance that some men took stock (but much too late) of what they stood to lose by this sudden emergence of female freedom, and spoke up. The provincial nobleman Huaman Poma, champion of Indian men's privileges, frequently condemned women's behaviour in no uncertain terms. One consequence of women's abandoning of Indian garb for the new type of apparel was the unsettling disappearance of some of the most visible signposts governing social relations in the old society, among them the rules of female behaviour and their male corollary – rules about access to women.

Andean attire locates individuals within their social networks, their families, their communities. It is the signifier of coded space and time, a signpost, and thus a provider of reassurance. For example, to this day the red animals that adorn the over-skirts (*axsu*) of the women of Potolo distinguish them from the Macha women with their striped over-skirts; horses are found only on the garments worn by women from Candelaria. Men's clothing, too, is clearly differentiated between one group and another. So people can tell at once who are outsiders and who they are entitled to choose from. Things are in order because everything is classified, and desire is guided by the attire; for the rule is that people choose a spouse from their own group. The *chola*'s costume creates confusion because it removes familiar landmarks and codes and replaces them with a dangerous uniformity in the appearance of women from quite different places.

By escaping the dress code and becoming unrecognizable, women turned their backs on the communities of their birth and opened up for themselves new avenues. Henceforward alliance and desire were to be subject to individual rather than collective strategies, strategies that the men of their communities could not control, and that gave birth to the *mestizo*. By the same token, it was no doubt because *mestizo*, as opposed to Indian, social behaviour flowed from an ensemble of individual rather than collective strategies that it took as long as it did for *mestizos* to be recognized as a distinct social entity.

One can now understand why to Huaman Poma social disorder is at times a matter of skirts. 'The Indian women who have become prostitutes', he says, 'wear petticoats, blouses, fancy boots and stockings, and each of them drags along half-a-dozen *mestizos* and mulattos, *cholo sambahigos*. Being such great whores they no longer want to marry their Indian peers' (Huaman Poma 1980[1615]: 1115).

The word for prostitute in the Aymara and Quechua languages of the sixteenth century was *pampayruna*. In Inca society the *pampayr-una* were driven from the villages:

> They lived in miserable huts, each one by herself and not together, they were not allowed to enter the villages, so as not to commu-nicate with other women.... The men treated them with the greatest contempt. The women did not talk with them for fear of being given the same name and treated as infamous and, if they were married, of being rejected by their husbands.
>
> (Garcilaso 1960[1609] IV)

Pampa is a polysemic word that refers to anything that is uniform and continuous. It refers here to the space outside the village, the indifferent terrain beyond the reach of culture. And the people (*pampa runa*) who inhabit that space are not far removed from the primaeval human beings of the mythical universe at the dawn of the world, on which the sun did not shine, who lived 'without wisdom or prudence, just as they please, and subject to no one'. However, there may also be an implicit reference to the disregard for social codes expressed in their attire.

The *chola* (*mestizo* woman) whose clothes bear no traditional distinguishing marks confuses the male gaze. Like the primaeval *pampa runa* she stands outside the social codes and so threatens the established order. Perceived as a woman who belongs to no one, she potentially belongs to all: a prostitute.

Today, the difference between the social codes of femininity (and therefore of dress) for the Indian woman and for the *chola* turns on whether she wears western dress or the *pollera*, the heavy gathered skirt. No doubt – as in the sixteenth and seventeenth centuries – each attire arouses different expectations and addresses itself to different men.

Solorzano Pereira in the 1640s described the erosion of the strict rules separating Indian and Spanish society:

> The consequence of cohabitation is that many Indian women leave their Indian husbands and either hate or abandon the children they begot with them, and desire and love and shower with more gifts the ones they beget out of wedlock with Spaniards, because these children are free and exempt from the tribute.
>
> (Solorzano Pereira 1648)

If Indian women took the risk of leaving their community and all that was familiar to them, it was because by choosing Spanish partners they afforded advantages to their children. The *mestizo* child, unlike the child of an Indian man, was exempt from the tribute. The consequences that flowed from this fact for the demography of the Indian family, its structure, the status of women, and the movement towards a new society will probably never be sufficiently stressed.

Owing to the demographic decline caused by the epidemics of the sixteenth century, Indian society was much poorer at the beginning of the seventeenth century than it had been at the time of the Conquest. Entire populations, groups, villages, families had disappeared. To the calamity of death was added the burden of the colonial economy. By begetting children with non-Indians, the women were depriving their communities of the children that might have replaced those who had died. But was it really a matter of choice when the alternative – tribute – was equally painful, and condemned Indian society to a different set of problems and threats?

In 1603, Indian women's children not only with Spaniards, but also with blacks, mulattos, *zambahigos* (the offspring of an Indian and a black) and foreigners had reached such proportions that, in a memorandum sent to the President of the Council of the Indies, Father D. de Torres Bollo suggested that only the offspring of Spaniards be considered *mestizo*, to prevent all the rest from escaping Indian status and so from paying the tribute:[6]

> The taxes and tribute that the Indians pay are very high and since the daily wage given to them for their services is very low, they have reached a state of great poverty, and their burdens and work have

greatly diminished. This has caused two things to increase. Firstly, the Indian women, who loathe having Indian children obliged to bear such burdens, marry blacks, mulattos, *zambahigos* and foreigners, or cohabit with them, and consequently, on one hand, they defraud the community of children who would be required to help them if they were Indian, and on the other hand, being of the previously mentioned mixtures, they are a dangerous burden to the other Indians of the community. And one should remedy this matter by deciding that in the future the sons of such Indian women, unless born in wedlock with Spaniards, share the same burden and condition as their mother, as if they were pure Indians. The second obstacle to the Indians improving their situation and reproducing is that many Indians make themselves servants of the Spaniards from childhood, and wander from one place to the next without knowing the priest or the *encomendero* or helping the community. This also needs to be remedied, which can be done by means of a strict ordinance that Indians shall not be servants to the Spaniards, there being so many half-breeds who can serve them.

(*Monumenta Peruana* 1970)

THE MIRROR STAGE

Being the mother of a *mestizo* child was an altogether different proposition from being the mother of a tribute-paying Indian. It gave maternity a completely different aspect, as it did also when the father was a *mestizo* or black. It is in this context that the words Huaman Poma puts in the mouth of a priest speaking from the pulpit take on their full meaning:

The sermon preached by the priest says as follows:

If a *yana* [black man] rapes you, you will give birth to a bear.
If a mulatto rapes you, you will give birth to a monkey.
If a Spaniard rapes you, you will give birth to a very beautiful child.
If a *mestizo* rapes you, you will give birth to a *mitayo* [Indian labourer].
You are not multi-coloured, like a person asleep looking up and counting *yanas* in their dreams.

(Huaman Poma 1980[1615]: 610)

This brief homily allows us to see motherly love being influenced by the rules of a new social game which prompt the mother to appreciate her children according to a scale of values laid down by the dominant society but, by the same token, lead her to reflect on her own identity. What is she? Is she herself multi-coloured thanks to her capacity to give birth to such a range of different children?

It is in the intimacy of this mirror game played between the look of the mother and the dissimilar looks of her children that the *mestizo* condition was first really questioned. By reflecting back on their mother a multiple image of herself, weren't her children forcing her to see herself as no longer an Indian but transcending the cleavages of society and of race – as already a *mestizo* herself?

So greatly did these women desire freedom for their children that they often had recourse to tricks or deception in order to conceal the true identity of the fathers. With the occasional complicity of the actual fathers, where these were Indian, they would at the baptism declare their little ones to have been born to fathers unknown, to some passing muleteer, or to someone from far away. Thanks to such tricks mothers with a thought for the future hoped to see their boy children, when they turned fifteen or sixteen, able to evade the compulsory labour service of the *mita* (Potosí 1661, Archivo General de Indias, EC 868 A: 15–16). (Of course, these mothers trick us as well. For what can we get out of baptismal registers if we forget that the best-kept secret, that of paternity, in the last resort always stayed with the women; or that what these women did or did not want to reveal determined what became of the family and, in the final analysis, of the society?)

From the sixteenth century onwards the women used bastardy as a social weapon. If we want to understand *mestizo* reality in the Andes today, we must bear in mind that the term covers a wide variety of biological conditions. Whether her child was born to an Indian or a Spanish or, later on, to a *cholo* father, the only way an Indian or *mestizo* woman could protect it from the humiliations of Indian status was to declare it a bastard. Even so, it would not be protected from the misfortunes that awaited the *mestizo*.

And what of the father? How would he, be he the real or supposed father, look upon this 'carnival baby', as the little bastard, born of the desire or social choice of the mother, is called today? Would he acknowledge the child in his discourse, and, if so, how? And – the mother having wanted this child to have a different place from that of her Indian children – under which law would the father insert it into society?

BETWEEN FATHER AND MOTHER

It is not difficult to conceive how the attitude of the dominant society (and often of the Spanish father as well) differed radically from that of the Indian mother and allowed doubt to hover over the true identity of the father; it followed that the child, whether or not it was biologically *mestizo*, could become one socially.[7] The mother was in this way betting on the future of a society yet to be constructed, while her own status as the mother of a *mestizo* gave her, too, a new place in society, and launched her on a path towards an identity that did not yet exist.

As far as the father was concerned this child, which he could never even be sure was his, occupied a position in society that had not been foreseen by the colonial legislation, and was regulated from time to time (in a less repressive fashion, it seems to me, than in Mexico) as the number of *mestizos* grew.

Some of the young bastards were legitimated directly by the Crown in consideration of payment; occasionally the King even granted them substantial pensions. Such was the case of Gaspar Centeno and his sister Maria, the children of Captain Diego de Centeno, who had remained loyal to the Crown at the time of Gonzalo Pizarro's rebellion in 1544–48 (Lopez Martinez 1964). The 'original stain' of bastardy was in this way removed through a process of legitimation by grace and favour which made entry into the dominant society possible. Such changes of status could be very profitable for the Crown: according to a document of 1595 these proceedings had yielded the Crown 4,400 ducats, and two years later more than 9,000 pesos in assayed gold (Archivo General de Indias Cont. 1760 A). We can compare this highly selective legal process with the way changes were effected in the categories of assessed tribute in Indian society of the sixteenth century which, for example, allowed the lowest category called Uru to rise into the next category – the Aymara – through payment of a generous contribution. In the same vein there was redemption through military service, from which only the few *mestizos* benefited who had taken part in the conquest of Chile.

The two significant features of this road to legitimacy are, first, that although it was exceptional and expensive: it had nothing to do with any overall recognition of *mestizos* in law; and second, that the initiative always came from the *mestizo* offspring: in none of these cases was it an act of recognition on the part of the father.

All this puts a twist in the tail of the paradox we began with, the paradox that informs the very genesis of Latin American *mestizaje*, namely that thanks to the silence of the mothers, the *mestizo* children who often as not do not know their own fathers are known to us only through their fathers. With the small but significant exception of those fine Spanish gentlemen and those noble Indian ladies who actually got married, the strategies of the Indian mothers entailed that the Spanish fathers often as not also did not know – and generally did not even want to know – their own *mestizo* children. The voice of the fathers that has come down to us is less the personal, individual, caring voice of the real fathers than the impersonal, collective, domineering voice of the Spanish conqueror's state and church – the voice not so much of fathers as of the Father. As we inquire further we find that the strategies of the Indian mothers followed not only from their undoubted daring, their *joie-de-vivre*, their readiness to break with tradition in claiming their freedom, but also from an acute sense, quickly acquired, of what they could do for the future welfare of the children they brought into a world dominated by a regime besotted with the double dream of purity of blood and purity of faith.

That brings us to the second paradox, likewise intrinsic to the history of *mestizos*: the same Spaniards who, in pursuit of 'purity of blood' (*limpieza de sangre*) and of faith, had expelled Jews and Moors from the Peninsula, in the New World began to spawn a whole new population of the 'impure'. If, therefore, it was their lust for life and a feeling for the advantage that had prompted Indian women to seek Spanish fathers for their children, it was probably their innate good sense that made them protect their children as best they could from the racist Spanish Father.

It is clear enough that the Spanish Crown, in expelling Jews and Moors, was nurturing its dream of the territorial unification of the Peninsula together with the formation of a homogenous national identity based on 'purity of blood'. What is not so clear is what that Crown was thinking of when it sent its minions to conquer the New World. It cannot have supposed the Americas to be uninhabited; it is not likely to have intended that all the natives should simply be put to the sword; and it probably did not imagine all of its soldiers would be sworn to chastity. What, then, did it think would happen to 'purity of blood? The short answer seems to be that the Crown just did not think: as we have seen, colonial legislation for the Andes had not provided for the possibility that the new lands would in part be peopled – and very quickly at that – by offspring of mixed parentage. We can only surmise that the urge to conquer was in the end more powerful than the commitment to 'purity of blood'.

The simple fact is that, from the very first, Spaniards got together with Indian women to produce new hybrid human beings. Spanish women not being very plentiful in America – though they were not as rare as is sometimes supposed (Konetzke 1945) – there is nothing surprising in the fact that the conquerors turned to Indian women who, apart from anything else, had the attraction of novelty. It often happened that the men – having set off alone for the New World – forgot after a few years of living in the Americas about the wife and children they had left behind. Having left in order to get rich and having drawn a line under their lives at home, they often made new lives for themselves in the New World.

But though their new lives generally included the begetting of children, the Spanish fathers appear to have done little individually or collectively, to further the life-chances of their 'impure' offspring. The mixed races in the New World were initially treated in much the same way as New Christians, Jews and Moors had been in the Old World – in keeping, perhaps, with the principle that 'one only learns what one already knows'. These new human beings were tarred with the same brush of social prejudice as those who had been expelled from Spain; and that prejudice helped shape the laws of both church and state in the colonies.

Even if the *mestizo* child knew its father, indeed if that father had actually acknowledged it, the *mestizo* generally occupied the position in society of the mulatto or the New Christian. Once again, purity of blood was measured by religious faith. 'These people are foolhardy and have no God, in the same manner as the mulattos of Spain', wrote Father Lopez in 1569.[8] As for the Dominicans (who did not indulge in niceties), their position was even more radical. In barring *mestizos* from entering their Order they simply included them in the established Spanish categories upon which they had already imposed a veto. The sentence was almost like a curse upon descendants of Moriscos, Jews, *mestizos*, mulattos, up to and including the fourth generation.

The church was the only entity which decided from the outset to place *mestizos* in the same category as Jews, Moriscos and mulattos – excluded figures of the past. As a result, *mestizo* children were often drawn towards paganism, which reminded the church of the lack of orthodoxy of the Spanish infidels. To these faults, obviously 'inherited' from the mothers, were added a number of defects which had been 'borrowed' from the Spaniards. The end result was so unsatisfactory that Father Lopez cried out in dismay that all in all, things would have been better had the *mestizos* been left in the state of paganism.

How, in a castes society, could new elements be accepted without endangering the existing social status? When Father Lopez exclaimed that 'things would have been better', he acknowledged his power-lessness to deal with the situation, and at the same time expressed a feeling of regret that sounds somewhat peculiar coming from the clergy. In 1578, Philip II responded to Lopez's wish by sending a royal decree to the Archbishop of Lima, forbidding him to 'ordain *mestizos*, whatever the circumstances'.

Although the Conciles in Lima had not yet taken a position against *mestizo* ordination they had already legislated at length on the subject of marriage. They forbade any union without preliminary inquiry of a woman with an outsider (*forastero*), a stranger (*no conocido*) or a vagabond (*vagabundo*). *Mestizos* were considered to belong to these categories. They were regarded as outsiders in relation to the *originarios*, the Indians who supposedly had always lived in their community. To the *originarios*, the *mestizos* to some extent incarnated the external side of the *pampa runa*, who belonged to a world difficult to control, like the *pampa*, the space outside the village.

They became metaphorical, if not literal, vagabonds, since they were doomed by intentionally prohibitive legislation to wander between the gaps of society and occupy the intervening spaces. Indeed, by 1549 Charles V had prohibited the appointment of *mestizo* bastards to public office without their obtaining a royal licence. Thus they were excluded from a whole section of active colonial life. They were also forbidden to carry weapons or to hold the position of chieftain in the Indian villages.

But in truth, it was usually among their Indian brothers that the young *mestizos* sought refuge, because legislation made it difficult for them to integrate into Spanish society. Of the legitimate Creole son and the illegitimate *mestizo* only the former had the advantages of paternal filiation. That is probably why Alvaro, the *mestizo* son of the conquistador Francisco de Carvajal, killed his Creole brother, spurred to commit the crime by his father who had been filled with rage when his legitimate son set out to claim a share of his property. The crime accomplished, Alvaro naturally found refuge among his Indian relatives on his mother's side (Lopez Martinez 1964). This fratricidal act is a clear though extreme illustration of the differences at stake between Creole legitimacy and *mestizo* illegitimacy. Though at the time of the Viceroy Martín Enriquez (1581–1583) the *mestizos* were obliged to learn a trade and to cultivate the earth, they were always relegated to an inferior rank in society.

Nevertheless, regardless of ideology and of the different attempts to exclude *mestizos*, demographic reality prevailed. The rapid proliferation of *mestizos* was depicted as a huge breaker capable of sweeping the new colonial society away. Somehow, the flow had to be checked. This anticipated fear seems to have been justified, though the lack of reliable demographic information for the sixteenth and seventeenth centuries impedes an accurate estimate of the size of the *mestizo* population at the time. (Martín Enriquez was the first Viceroy to order a survey of the *mestizo* population.)

The Jesuit Acosta wrote directly to the King of Spain to express his concern:

> In this whole kingdom, there are many blacks, mulattos, *mestizos* and other mixtures of people and every day their number increases. And most of them are born out of wedlock and therefore many of them do not know their fathers. Some people are wary and fear that in time these people will be much more numerous than the children of the Spaniards who were born here and who are called Creoles. And they could easily revolt within a city, and with one revolt there would be no end to the number of Indians who would join them for they are all of one caste and they are all relatives and share the same way of thinking because they grew up together, especially if they were promised freedom; together, it would be easy for them to seize all of the cities in the kingdom one by one without encountering resistance, because the cities are so distant from one another that they would not able to save each other.[9]

Were the Indian women, as was sometimes said, truly more prolific with the Spaniards than with their Indian husbands? According to an eighteenth-century ecclesiastical source:

> the Indian women appear to be prolific who do not marry Indians but other men of superior positions: they multiply abundantly because their children are no longer Indians, they are no longer considered tributary, they improve in colour, in wealth, and are respected more than the Indians.

On the one hand, women probably found the most favourable psychological conditions for pregnancy when procreating with Spaniards; on the other hand, they might have resorted to abortion, a common practice in the days of the Incas as well as today, in order to do away with children who were destined to have the status of tributary Indian, which they rejected. Finally, the over-registration of 'bastards' in the baptismal registers shows, as we have noted, that the number of *mestizos* had been recklessly inflated.

THE *MESTIZO* BETWEEN APPEARANCE AND REALITY

Acosta's concern over the *mestizo* children's situation proceeded not only from the demographic reality or from the Creole society's sense of being in danger. Owing to the force of circumstances, *mestizos* would belong to families without a proper head – brotherhoods or female-headed households – and this new family order rooted itself in a new system of social relations, some of which have lasted to the present day.

It would be a mistake to think that during these centuries, the Spanish ideal of an open and welcoming family where legitimate and illegitimate children, Indians, Spaniards and Creoles lived in harmony with the master, the servants and the godparents, was realised in the Andes. At least two main categories of *mestizos* must be distinguished, corresponding to different forms of insertion in society and to two family types.

Among the Indians *mestizo* men, who spoke the same language and wore the same clothes, would be perceived by the Spaniards as dangerous agitators, all the more so because they were difficult to identify: physically they looked just like Indians (especially if they were biologically Indian and had deceitfully been declared *mestizo* at birth!). The Spaniards charged the *mestizos* with being idolatrous – as they had done with the mulattos in Spain – and with being the seat of social unrest. As Father Acosta wrote:

> These people are raised in great vice and freedom, they are unwilling to work and have no jobs, They are busy either with drink or sorcery. Not once throughout the year do they listen to mass or to a sermon, or only rarely, and subsequently they do not know the law of God, our creator, and no sign of it appears in them.
>
> (*Monumenta Peruana* 1964 Vol. V)

Already by 1575 *mestizos* had been strictly forbidden to live in the Indian villages (*pueblos de indios*). However, fifty years later in 1626, in a report drawn up by the Protector of the city of Guánuco on behalf of the Council of the Indies, the policy of segregating Indians and *mestizos* was clearly considered a failure.

Indeed, despite prohibitions, the *mestizos* had already woven their way into the social and economic space lying between the two separate worlds of the *república de Indios* and the *república de Españoles*. Apart from the vagabonds who were punishable by death and had found refuge among their own, other *mestizos* had settled in the Indian villages. They had either purchased land or acquired it through marriage, and the cities were supplied with their products. Some owned farms, textile workshops or cattle ranches.

In the documents of the period, this category of *mestizos* is referred to as '*mestizos en hábito de indios*' (*mestizos* in Indian clothes). Once again, for the Spaniards as well for Indians, clothing was regarded as the basis of social classification. Moreover, the 'improvement' of original skin colour through blood mixing, was extremely relative; for numerically the European population was never very high in the central and southern Andes with the exception of Potosí, the silver-mining centre. As for the first generation of *mestizo* men, access to European women was practically always barred, so they continued to marry Indian or *mestiza* women. Blood-mixing did then take place, but the initial mixing at the time of the Conquest was not a continuous biological process. This probably explains why, in the Andes, racial nomenclature never reached extreme degrees of complexity and, unlike Mexico, no large grids display the different degrees of blood-mixing.

An Andean *mestizo* was recognizable not by his skin colour but rather by his capacity of changing it. It was because clothing resembles a second skin (on a social level) that these social transformations became possible. The caste system was subverted by the *mestizos*' practice of varying their use of clothes, thereby demonstrating their consciousness of the importance of appearance in Andean life. But if clothing makes a person, it can also appear to be a disguise. The Spaniards, who followed strict codes of appearance, were not to be fooled. In classifying *mestizos* by their dress, the Spanish revealed their discomfort towards those whom they could only perceive as camouflaged (*en hábito de*) and who, the following day, might appear different. For want of a real social position (and a code of appearance), it was impossible to know whether *mestizos* were hiding under their clothing (whether Indian or Spanish) or whether they were consistent in their dress.

In urban society, which was essentially Spanish, the *mestizo*, like a chameleon, would no longer dress as an Indian. He would become a *'mestizo en hábito de español'* (a *mestizo* in Spanish clothing). If we bring together the adjectives used by the Spaniards to describe the first generation of *mestizos*, they are practically the same as those used in Spanish literature to portray the *pícaro*, a character who had no family or traditional social ties and lived in the criminal underworld. Just like the *pícaro*, the *mestizo* often had no job, lived in vice, and was free, daring, and without a god, halfway between drunkenness and sorcery, a stranger, a vagabond. Let us not forget that the most famous of the Spanish *pícaros*, 'El Buscón', spent the end of his days in America changing his life, searching in vain for a better world.

How far can the supposedly astute *cholo* be identified with the Spanish *pícaro*, always about to break the rules, living with his gang in the darkest intervals of urban society, creeping around to find his own space? The *pícaro* can be identified with the gutter while the *mestizo* can not. The latter, peasants' children, are newcomers in the developing urban society born like them at the Conquest. While the cities in Spain had lost their appeal and had already begun to decay, the cities of the Andes – especially since the founding of Potosí – were bursting with energy: the setting was most favourable for the independent and ambitious *mestizo*, who could find his own space often in the company of his mother.

> The Indian widows and single women leave their villages and provinces with their children and settle in the densely populated places (towns and cities) where they join new religious brotherhoods. . . . And the male children are given to the clergy who have them learn the trades of silk maker, tailor, shoemaker and thereby convert them to being free *yanaconas* [a less burdensome tribute category].
>
> (Archivo General de Indias, EC 868 A)

This is how, from the sixteenth century, the small world of artisans, merchants and urban religious brotherhoods (*confradías*) began to develop. New social bonds – free of old family burdens – were sealed, favouring personal preferences and co-operation: one could become a *compadre* regardless of being a bastard. Strangely enough, the parish priests patronized this dynamic – albeit religiously unorthodox – workforce, which they saw both as a means of strengthening their power and as a considerable source of wealth. Their role was far from negligible. Through education and community work, the clergy often replaced the absent father. The *mestizo*, who had become a mediator, found a place in society halfway between the Indian and the Spaniard. He was simultaneously the accomplice or the enemy of both, and at times he would remain uncontrollable by anyone.

This offers me the opportunity to underline the fundamentally ambiguous role of the church in the establishment of *mestizo* identity. Distrustful when it came to recruiting *mestizos* into its ranks, distrustful in matters of orthodoxy, the church nevertheless appreciated *mestizos* in the early colonial period, for he was the much-needed interpreter (*lenguaráz*). And it was the church – in this case the Jesuits – who encouraged the *mestizos* to address Pope Gregory XIII in 1583, thereby giving them for the first time the opportunity to think collectively about themselves in writing. This letter, the first manifesto of *mestizo* identity, is also the doing of a 'progressive' section of the church, which until the present day has sought alliance with the *cholos*.

> What sorts of cruelty are not performed against us? What enormous and atrocious calumnies have been whispered in King Philip's ear for him to put aside from us his great benevolence? Where are the atrocious crimes that we have committed? Where are the uprisings and the acts of violence, the plots and the treason? Which of us has failed to honour the true God or fallen into perverse idolatry? We are the children of Christian fathers and of pure mothers free from the stain of heresy.

Such protests against the stereotypes through which they were perceived speak eloquently of the difficulties faced by the new *mestizos*. Born from paradox, from desire, outside the law and often in defiance of it, they disturbed the quest for fixity in the Spanish colonial order, and yet they could not be ignored any more than they could be integrated. It would take revolutionary transformation in the twentieth century in many Latin American countries before the *mestizos* at last became fully reclassified as legal and moral persons.

120   Sexuality and legitimacy

NOTES

1 Annual report of 1602 from Padre R. de Cabredo to Padre Claudio Acquaviva *Monumenta Peruana* 1970: Vol. VIII: 272–3.
2 Teresa Gisbert, personal communication.
3 Cardaillac shows the extent to which Moriscos were rejected to the edge of society by the punishments inflicted upon them by the Inquisition (Cardaillac 1979: 48–57).
4 Quoted by Cardaillac 1979: 52.
5 Fletamento Alonso de Valdes con el Maestre de Campo Dn Joseph Pastines Justiniano, La Paz, 8 April 1669 quoted by Money 1983: 90.
6 The foreigners included Portuguese, Corsicans, Italians and Flemings (Vazquez de Espinoza 1969[1629] Comp. 605, num. 1706.
7 In what follows I shall mainly be referring to boy children, since it was they who would have been liable for tribute exactions and forced labour in the mines if they were classified as Indians.
8 Letter from Padre L. Lopez to his Jesuit superior Padre Borgia, 1569, *Monumenta Peruana*, Vol. I, (1954).
9 Padre José Acosta, letter to Philip II, 1585, *Monumenta Peruana*, Vol. V, (1964).

REFERENCES

Archivo General de Indias (Seville), EC 868 A.
—— Cont. 1760 A.
Bouysse-Cassagne, T. (1988) *Lluvias y Cenizas: Dos Pachacuti en la Historia*, La Paz: Hisbol.
——(1992) 'Le lac Titicaca; histoire perdue d'une mer intérieure', *Bulletin de L'Institut Français d'Etudes Andines*, 21: 89–159.
Cardaillac, L. (1979) *Moros y Cristianos: Un Enfrentamiento Polémico (1492–1640)*, Buenos Aires: Fondo de Cultura Economica.
Cieza de León, P. de (1979[1553]) *Descubrimiento y conquista del Perú*, F. Cantú (ed.), Roma: Instituto Storico Italiano.
Fernandez de Oviedo, G. (1851[1549]) *Historia General y Natural de Las Indias, Islas y Tierra Firme del Mar Océano*, Madrid: Academia Real de Historia.
Garciliaso de la Vega, I. (1960[1609]) *Comentarios Reales de Los Incas*, Madrid: Biblioteca de Autores Españoles Vols. 133–5.
Huaman Poma de Ayala, F. (1980[1615]) *El primer nueva corónica y buen gobierno*, J.V. Murra and R. Adorno (eds), Mexico: Siglo XXI.
Konetzke, R. (1945) 'La emigración de mujeres españolas en America durante la época colonial', *Revista Internacional de Sociologia*, 3: 123–50.
Lopez Martinez, H. (1964) 'Un motin de mestizos en el Perú', *Revista de Indias*, XXIV.
Money, M. (1983) *Los Obrajes, el Traje y el Comercio en la Audiencia de Charcas*, La Paz: Instituto de Estudios Bolivianos.
Monumenta Peruana (1954–1970) Roma: Institutum Historicum Soc. Iesu.

Ragon, P. (1992) *Les Indiens de la Découverte, Evangélisation, Mariage et Sexualité*, Paris: L'Harmattan.

Salomon, F. (1988) 'Indian women of early colonial Quito as seen through their testaments', *The Americas*, XLIV: 325–41.

Solorzano Pereira, J. de (1648) *Política indiana sacada en lengua castellana de los dos tomos del derecho i govierno municipal de las Indias*, Madrid.

Vazquez de Espinosa, A. (1969[1629]) *Compendio y Descripción de Las Indias Occidentales*, Madrid: BAE Vol. 231.

Zárate, A. de (1947[1555]) *Historia del Descubrimiento y Conquista de la provincia del Perú*, Madrid: BAE, Vol. 26.

Part III

The complicity of religion and state

Chapter 7

Living their lives in courts
The counter-hegemonic force of the Tswana *kgotla* in a colonial context

Ørnulf Gulbrandsen

Recent studies of the colonial encounter emphasize the penetration of Western law. Among many others, Channock has forcefully argued that '[l]aw was the cutting edge of colonialism, an instrument of the power of an alien state and part of the process of coercion' (Channock 1985: 4, cf. Snyder 1981; Roberts and Mann 1991: 9ff.). However appropriate this notion is to depict certain important aspects of colonial encounters, it needs to be taken into consideration that in many non-European societies formal bodies for administration of justice and legislation existed prior to colonialism. It is true, of course, that such bodies were often marginalized, transformed or even destroyed by the colonizing power. In the case of India, for example, Cohn explains that what some idealist colonial officers 'had started . . . as a search for the "Ancient Indian Constitution" ended up with what they had so much wanted to avoid – with English law as the law of India' (Cohn 1989: 151). But the colonial powers did not erode indigenous politico-jural bodies everywhere. In particular, where the colonizers had a strong interest in taking advantage of the option of 'indirect rule' and where indigenous politico-judicial institutions were available, the situation was much more ambiguous.

The Northern Tswana of the then Bechuanaland Protectorate, upon which the present chapter focuses, is a case in point. I shall argue that in this particular colonial context, legislative and judicial bodies, well established at the time the British formed the Bechuanaland Protectorate, were, in important respects, strengthened. In particular, rules applied in litigation, based upon a genuinely Tswana normative repertoire, known as *mekgwa le melao ya Setswana* ('Tswana custom and law', see Schapera 1984: 35ff.), were recurrently modified and amended by the indigenous political bodies, as active and creative responses to new kinds of conflicts and problems arising within Tswana societies at the different stages of colonialism. These changes involved qualifications only of an extensive enduring body of customary rules, rather than facilitating Tswana adaptation to market forces and other external impacts (Roberts 1990). In other words, this was not a case that readily sustains Channock's bold claim that 'customary law far from being a survival, was being created by these changes and conflicts' (Channock 1985: 2, cf. Merry 1992: 365; also cf. Sahlins 1993 and Thomas 1993).

This chapter argues that the colonial encounter involved processes which promoted, to some extent, the Northern Tswanas' consciousness of their distinct mode of jurisprudence and legislation, and thereby strengthened their own cultural integrity. Similarly, in the case of the Southern Tswana (of the present Republic of South Africa) and their encounter with the evangelizing missionaries, the Comaroffs suggest that '*mekgwa le melao*... was now rising to consciousness, in increasingly reified form, under the impact of colonizing culture' (Comaroff and Comaroff 1991: 212–13). They indicate, moreover, that 'much of the Tswana response... was an effort to fashion an awareness of, and gain conceptual mastery over, a changing world' (1992: 259). This notion remains, however, rather undeveloped in their works. Instead their chief concern is with the missionaries' alleged 'colonization of consciousness', involving 'the inculcation of the hegemonic forms, the taken-for-granted signs and practices, of the colonizing culture' (1992: 9). They assert that this endeavour 'had enormous impact' upon the Southern Tswana (1992: 258, cf. 1991: 251).

Such processes of 'inculcations' were certainly at work more or less everywhere along the colonial frontier. Yet, the analysis of this aspect of the intercourse between the colonizer and the colonized should be complemented with the examination of discourses conducted among the colonized themselves. In the case of the Northern Tswana, it seems particularly efficacious to focus upon the politico-jural field, the well-established hierarchy of courts (*lekgotla*, sing. *kgotla*). These fora constituted, throughout the colonial era, a much more important context for everyday social, political and ritual discourse amongst the Northern Tswana than that staged by missionaries.[1]

Tswana courts in particular, located in the midst of people's life world, not only served to settle disputes and deal with criminal cases; they also held a competence to replace custom (*mokgwa*) by law (*malao*). Here is Professor Schapera's judgement of the content of these transformations, based on a comprehensive review of legislation in Northern Tswana *merafe* between 1795 and 1940:

> [I]n their capacity as law-givers, [*dikgosi*] have seldom borrowed important elements from Western civilization.... [C]onfronted with the impact of Western civilization, [they] have tried in the main to adjust tribal life to the new forces bearing upon it; they have aimed at what we may term 'adaptation' rather than at wholesale 'assimilation'.
>
> (Schapera 1970: 57)

I take this to indicate that the legislative activity of the *dikgosi* represented a major factor counteracting the penetration of 'hegemonic forms' of the colonizing culture. This chapter aims to identify factors which worked to such an effect, an effect which Roberts (1985) recognizes in suggesting that Tswana custom and law 'have provided a barrier with which the Tswana ... have kept the world at bay, rather than a device employed by those outside in controlling Tswana society' (1985: 85).

I shall certainly not argue that the Tswana have remained entirely unaffected by the colonizing culture; towards the end of the chapter I indicate how a minor category of people were taken by the spirit of economic enterprises and constituted the core of a movement of economic and political modernization which took the lead from the final stage of the colonial era and gained political control over the national state of Botswana. However, the concern in this chapter is the fact that such peoples as the Northern Tswana were, during the colonial era, by no means passive victims of European dominance, but remained in command of a socio-political order with considerable potentials to counteract the penetration of European categories and valuations. In order to come to terms with processes underpinning the persistence of Tswana categories and symbolism – in particular the normative repertoire of *mekgwa le melao* – it is crucial to recognize the centrality of the *kgotla* in the lives of the Tswana. Its centrality was, of course, conditioned by the fact that it was generally accepted by the British as instrumental to the indirect rule policy. Yet, although it was never in question to replace the politico-jural bodies of the Tswana polities, these bodies did not remain entirely unchallenged. As we shall see, sincere efforts were made to introduce Western principles of administration of justice which were fundamentally in disagreement with Tswana practices of legislation and litigation. This chapter identifies processes which countervailed such initiatives and effectively ensured the autonomy of Tswana jurisprudence, leaving the people largely beyond the reaches of the British magistrates and legislators.

I shall be especially concerned with the cultural meanings and socio-political implications of the fact that practically every adult man recurrently participated in judicial activities by virtue of his membership in the *kgotla* of his descent group and often participated in *kgotla* proceedings at higher levels. Thus, while scholars have predominantly analysed *kgotla* activities as a matter of negotiations and dispute settlement (e.g. Comaroff and Roberts 1981), I make the case for a more comprehensive approach to the study of the Tswana court which enables me to bring into the analysis the fact that these fora represented an all-embracing field of discourse which not only involved the practice of Tswana judicial forms. They also activated pervasive categories and signs by which essential male identity relations were constructed and embedded in an hierarchical socio-political order. The identification of these inherent aspects of the *kgotla* is important in order to explain the Tswana's enthusiastic participation in the administration of justice. I argue that such a strong attachment to the *kgotla* has been essential for the *kgotla* as counter-hegemonic force.

When I speak of the counter-hegemonic force of the *kgotla*, I consider the discourses of the *kgotla* both as a matter of cultural insulation and transformation. It was a matter of insulation in the sense of restraining the naturalization of European categories in Tswana contexts. In this respect, I shall address the distinctively Tswana aspirations, concerns and valuations which limit the relevance of European categories. On the other hand, I aim to identify processes which involved the transformations of European forms in ways that gave them meaning in terms of Tswana categories.

The fact that these processes were often tacit is important because the British rarely acted as agents of the colonizing culture in ways which involved severe political confrontations with the Tswana. The counter-hegemonic force of the *kgotla* basically depended upon its attractiveness as a field of discourse where values and notions prevailed other than those 'inculcated' by the missionaries, exercised by the colonial administration or brought with market forces. As we shall see, the most conscious and explicit efforts to counteract what were conceived as adverse impacts of the larger world were exercised through legislation.

And yet, however significant these countervailing forces were, the latter part of this chapter indicates their limitations. Many of those who were strong adherents to this order were, paradoxically, also those who through their entrepreneurial practices paved the way for socio-economic modernization.

THE CULTURAL CONSTRUCTION OF POLITICO-JURIDICAL DISCOURSE

The Tswana *kgotla* has customarily incorporated the population at large in ongoing discourses on moral and normative issues springing from their recurrent conflicts and disputes. Significantly, in contrast to the discontinuity between everyday life and legal institutions in Western societies (Conley and O'Barr 1990: 169; cf. Fuller 1994: 11), virtually all adult male Tswana used to participate in the resolution of each other's conflicts and disputes, primarily by virtue of their membership in a descent group court. The frequency of this pattern has declined only recently, in the wake of the substantial economic and political changes after the establishment of the national state of Botswana. Yet the *kgotla* still works essentially according to customary practices. Thus, even though this chapter mainly addresses the question of how the *kgotla* constituted a counter-hegemonic force during the colonial era, I can draw upon my observations during fieldwork conducted after Botswana's independence.[2]

Conflicts and disputes are not dealt with by the deployment of rules in the Western 'legal' sense, but through a much more inclusive mode of litigation (cf. Comaroff and Roberts 1981). The already mentioned corpus of normative rules (*mekgwa le melao ya Setswana*) constitutes a repertoire of norms which regulates every aspect of interpersonal relationships. Although knowledge about this vast body of norms varies considerably, it is a normative repertoire with which all adult Tswana used to be familiar through everyday experience and, in particular, through participation in litigation.

These are typically initiated in the immediate local context, often within the domestic yard (*segotlo*). If unresolved at this level, the case is brought into 'the open', i.e. the public domain of the descent group court, from where it may be appealed through several court stages, ultimately reaching the royal court (*kgotla kgosing*) over which the *kgosi* or one of his deputies presides (cf. Schapera 1984: 98ff.). In this way everybody is closely attached to courts which are both situated in the midst of family compounds, and linked up closely with the formal, politico-jural hierarchy.

The pre-colonial villages were, as they in fact still are, divided into administrative wards.[3] Each of the wards was under the administration of a headman who was ideally the senior male member of what is recognized as the most senior patrilineal descent group. The headmen exercise their authority within limits defined by the *kgosi*. In some cases there is an intermediary level between that of the *kgosi* and the ward headman, occupied by a *kgosi*'s representative. The wards were, and still are to a great extent, composed of descent groups, recruited on the basis of strictly enforced principles of patri-virilocal residence,[4] and organized according to principles of agnatic rank. The senior man in this group constitutes the link between the ward headman and the descent group, presiding over its *kgotla*.

The *kgotla* has thus always been essentially an agnatic field and a public domain where common affairs are recurrently discussed. In particular, the *kgotla* functions as a court in which internal conflicts and disputes, typically between agnatic kin, are tried. When I refer to the Tswana as 'living their lives in court' it is not only in the sense that it constitutes a forum in which men used to participate almost daily, exercising their most essential identity relations (see below), but also because the *kgotla* is located in the midst of the homesteads of the descent group. In fact, the entire complex, comprising the homesteads as well as the court, is also called *kgotla*.

The fact that the *kgotla* is encompassed by everyday family and community life gives it a flavour of informality. Often the interaction in the *kgotla* is relaxed and informal, especially in the evening when it used to take the form of 'the men's house' where the men of the *kgotla* enjoyed each other's company, drinking traditional beer (*bojalwa*) and occasionally eating meat, after slaughtering a beast appropriated as a fine. But once an issue is presented, the interaction shifts to a highly formal pattern. During court proceedings every male adult is, in principle, entitled to speak, to participate in cross-examinations and to counsel the head of the court before he makes his judgement. Increasingly women have been allowed to present their own cases and, today, older women often participate in cross-examinations.

While the *kgotla* is popular in the sense of being the principal arena for all adult males, it is also intrinsically hierarchical. It is chaired by the genealogically most senior man surrounded by a group of elders who serve as his councillors called *bagakolodi* ('remembrancers', signifying their experience and their capacity as conveyers of customs). Hierarchy is symbolized in various ways, most conspicuously in the spatial organization of the *kgotla*, with the elder next in rank to the headman located at his right hand, and the others in successive order according to their seniority. Furthermore, before the headman makes his decision after the *kgotla* has debated an issue or examined a case, each of the elders expresses his view on the matter in an inverse ranked order, with the most senior elder speaking last, before the head of the *kgotla* pronounces the concluding decision.

When I asked about the rationale behind this order, many Tswana simply said that 'this is the Tswana way' or 'we found it like this'. This is an order which is passed on without questioning. Others referred to the proverb 'there can only be one bull in the kraal', signalling their appreciation of unambiguous decision-making as the chief means of ensuring social stability. They also value the experience and wisdom vested in the elders, especially the most senior one, the *kgosi* – also denoted *motswadintle*, the one from whom good things come. Adherence to this order is, thus, motivated by the appreciation of seniorhood as a source of welfare and protection.

This notion is further anchored in Tswana cosmology: the senior elders are believed to be the ones who have the capacity to communicate with the principal source of experience, wisdom and morality: the ancestors (*badimo*). Among the dead, too, agnatic descent lines are hierarchized, so that the *kgosi* constitutes the exclusive mediating link between the people and the ultimate source of morality and guidance, the royal ancestors. It is in the idiom of this scheme that the heads of the respective levels of the politico-jural hierarchy are tacitly justified as essential to welfare, protection and social harmony.

The strong association of the *kgotla* with social harmony (*kagiso*), and thus prosperity, is particularly relevant in the present context. Thre is much more to the value of *kagiso* than an appreciation of the recurrent punctuation of tensions and resolution of conflicts. In Tswana thought tension and conflicts are inherently associated with a state of 'heat' which, if allowed to prevail, carries the potential for destruction far beyond the particular antagonistic parties. The notion of 'heat' connotes illness, infertility, stock death and other serious disasters.

Since the elders and, by extension, the ancestors are appreciated as the principal agents of conflict resolution, they are valued as the source of cooling. Thus, the notion of *go fodisa* connotes both to cure and to cool down tensions and conflicts. This notion is firmly inscribed in Tswana space: the ancestors, buried in the cattle kraal, are counterpoised with the bodily epitome of 'heat', menstruating women, representing a destructive force which is associated with the backyard of the *lolwapa*, the *segotlo* (Comaroff 1985: 67–8). Significantly, the head of the *kgotla*, surrounded by the elders, is situated along the wall of pools adjacent to the kraal, and thus closely associated with the principal source of cooling – the ancestors. The centrality of the *kgotla* in the lives of the Tswana follows from this: as an agency of reconciliation and thus *kagiso* it represents a fountain of 'coolness', countervailing the destructive heat of, in Tswana conception, the ever-present threat of tensions and conflicts.

This conception of the *kgotla* in a structuralist paradigm of binary oppositions reveals some basic features of Southern Bantu modes of culturally constructing notions of gender, hierarchy and space (see Kuper 1982). An analysis along these lines in the case of the Tswana is helpful to explain the cognitive structures underpinning the valuation of hierarchical order as the major source of health, welfare and prosperity, and how this order is reified in terms of the organization of space in which the *kgotla* is located prominently at the centre at any level of the polity. Yet, it fails to account for the fact that the people who engage in this order are paradoxically motivated by ambitions which may be in contradiction to its ideals. In fact, my observations of court proceedings, and the discussions and gossips surrounding them, made it apparent to me that the essentially agnatic field of the *kgotla* itself represents an important source of controversy, springing from rivalry over positions within this hierarchically constituted forum. To be sure, the Tswana sincerely idealize the value of *kagiso*, especially in the context of the *kgotla*; they appreciate a person who has a good character (*maitseo ntle*), a person who obeys the orders of his seniors, who is easy to discipline, and who does not behave in a challenging way. The domestic sphere constitutes the primary context for the inscription of such dispositions in 'the body schema and the schemes of thought' (Bourdieu 1977: 15) which are required to cope with all the intricacies of Tswana etiquette in hierarchical social relations. The *kgotla* represents the major field of discourse where patriarchal ideals of discipline are explicated and connected to social harmony and ancestral morality.

Nevertheless, in terms of self-identity, these are at the same time valuations and dispositions which may encourage a person to act in ways which cause tension and conflict. The motivating force is vested in the esteem of seniority and most conspicuously expressed in the idiom of agnatic rank. The pattern of interaction within the *kgotla* epitomizes the fact that virtually all the relationships of a Tswana community express the value of seniority and their notion of *tshisimogo* – social respect – which includes elements of reverence and even fear. While these are notions of seniority which pervade Tswana social relations in general, the *kgotla* is the principal forum in which these values are exercised. Above all, the *kgotla* is essential to Tswana male self-identity because this is where seniority is established, where negligence towards seniors is punished, and where disputes over rank are settled. In this sense, the discourses of the *kgotla* are, in important respects, matters of control and competition for the symbolic capital vested in the hierarchical order. By extension, the discourses of the *kgotla*, especially those of the royal *kgotla*, are dominant in the Tswana context: this is where the etiquette governing senior–junior relations is at its most elaborate, where a person's performance is most carefully watched, commented upon and sanctioned, and where a person's social identity is established and acknowledged; important for his standing in all other contexts.

It is true that senior–junior relations are prescribed to a considerable extent in terms of genealogical seniority. One may well speculate that this cultural practice serves as a measure to limit the prevailing potentials for rivalry. Yet there is considerable scope for elevating one's position through various achievements. This is, of course, most evidently illuminated in succession disputes (at all levels of authority) which were particularly common in pre-Christian times when polygyny prevailed. Here I shall place emphasis upon the more subtle ways in which a person might advance his standing in the *kgotla* (and thus in the wider societal context). For example, there are culturally recognized options for the achievement of a higher position in the *kgotla* by demonstrating efficiency in cross-examination, wisdom in judgement, and knowledge of Tswana custom and law. Above all, the Tswana sincerely admire the ability to express such capabilities through oratorical poise. The aesthetics of a speech as well as the lucidity of the argument are carefully observed, assessed and commented upon. The performer's reputation may be boosted by the head of the *kgotla*, attaching him to the inner circle of confidential advisors and – not infrequently – getting him to act as his mouthpiece during *kgotla* proceedings.

Such advancements might, however, provoke bad feelings and cause antagonism and even severe tensions and conflicts which are typically manifested in sorcery (*boloi*) accusations. This is even more likely when pursued in culturally disapproved ways; for example, if a man challenges the authority of his older brother, or if he dominates a junior brother beyond accepted limits. Cattle, the predominant form of wealth among the Northern Tswana, are a marker of social esteem. They have always been very unequally distributed, yet in ways which do not always correspond to the recognized hierarchy of descent groups and ranked seniority within them. A wealthy man (*mohumi*, pl. *bahumi*) can act more independently in the *kgotla* than his rank would indicate, readily causing jealousy among his closest agnates. Indeed, jealousy (*lehuha*) is a prevailing theme amongst the Tswana and it typically finds expression in suspicion about the exercise of black magic (*boloi*).

Precisely due to the feeling of a pervasive threat of antagonism amongst members of the *kgotla*, and thus the danger of destroying the fertilizing force of *kagiso*, behaviour in the *kgotla* is carefully watched. This manifests in a conspicuous condemnation of emotional, especially aggressive, language in addressing the *kgotla*. Typically senior members of the court put such a person down by stating: 'do you want to make "sorcery" (*boloi*) for us?'

In short, the politico-jural universe of the *kgotla* is founded upon ideals of social harmony and of a social order based upon agnatic seniority which is cross-cut by rivalry over positions, recognition and property. Indeed, the inherent discourses of the *kgotla* itself, fuelled by a stream of court cases, thus contribute to some extent to the form of its reproduction. Moreover, the fact that people are often eager to lodge an appeal in their conflicts and disputes with what they conceive as the ultimate source of justice, the supreme court of the *kgosi*, contributes to the integration of the hierarchy of *kgotlas*. Above all, as people take their cases up through the various court levels, not only do they gain knowledge of more elevated modes of reasoning and judgement, but they are also exposed to the symbolism of hierarchical relations as ever more elaborate and potent, yet essentially replicating the familiar lived-in socio-cultural microcosm of their own *kgotla*, involving strong emotions towards the participation in this order.

Hence conflicts and disputes, even those deriving from antagonism generated in the *kgotla* itself, do not generally involve a centrifugal force, motivating people to stay away from the *kgotla*.[5] On the contrary, such conflicts contribute rather to a centripetal force vested in the attraction of the symbolic capital of the hierarchical order and the *kgotla* discourses (cf. Gulbrandsen 1993b: 571–2).

To be sure, the discourses of the *kgotla* involved the patriarchal exercise of discipline and control at all *kgotla* levels. In this sense it can be seen as hegemonic within a restricted Tswana context, especially in relation to those who were excluded from the *kgotla* but made subject of its discourses: women, children and servants. However, in the context of the colonizing culture, the centrality and autonomy of *kgotla* discourses were challenged. None the less, this challenge was to a significant extent warded off and that the Tswana retained their strong adherence to the *kgotla*; perhaps even more intensively than before they were 'living their lives in courts'. On the basis of the preceding account of the categories, identities and values vested in the discursive field of the *kgotla*, the following sections aim to explain how it retained its integrity and often tacitly transformed European forms into Tswana categories and signs.

AMBIGUITIES OF THE COLONIAL ENCOUNTER

The interface between agents of the colonizing culture and the Tswana was characterized by direct confrontation only to a limited extent. Rather, as we shall see, it was a matter of ambiguity. The Tswana polities with their hierarchy of *kgotlas* were well established at the time the first evangelizing missionaries settled amongst them. They were impressed by the civic government they encountered in these societies (Burchell 1924: 499, 533ff.; Mackenzie 1871: 317ff.; Moffat 1842: 248f.), and they were quick to realize the strength of these institutions:

> I have briefly glanced at the national council as the stronghold or shield of the native customs, in which speakers have, in a masterly style, inveighed against any aggression on their ancient ceremonies, threatening confiscation and death to those who would arraign the wisdom of their forefathers.
>
> (Moffat 1842: 250)

The case of the Northern Tswana is peculiar in the sense that several rulers were baptized at a very early stage, and before most of their people. Being committed to Christianity they had transformed or abandoned several national ritual practices. But the hierarchy of courts remained a Tswana stronghold, a fact which the missionaires were very worried about:

> On the whole, the feudal power of the native chiefs is opposed to Christianity; and the people who are living under English law are in a far more advantageous position as to the reception of the Gospel than when they were living in their own heathen towns surrounded by all its thralls and sanctions.[6]

This statement reflects the fact that even though several of the *dikgosi* let themselves be baptized at an early stage and many followed them as – nominally – Christians, participation in church life was low key, and was to a great extent restricted to women. When the missionaries wanted to do away with the entire socio-political set-up, it was certainly reflecting their sense of men's spiritual satisfaction gained from their extensive participation in the court proceedings. And this was for good reasons: for, as we have seen, the *kgotla* was morally constituted as a politico-religious field. The fact that the Tswana had few rituals which can be labelled 'religious' prior to Christianity and relatively easily gave up or transformed several of those they had when required to by the missionaries, is comprehensible if court proceedings and the debates on moral issues are seen as celebrations of ancestral morality. It has been because of this inherent character of ancestral agency in what appeared to the missionaries as a secular politico-jural domain, that the *kgotla* constituted a significant force by which the Tswana have attempted to incorporate Christianity into their own cultural system (Gulbrandsen 1993a: 69).

The discourse of the *kgotla* was so dominant that, when the *morafe* was dealing with legislative issues, missionaries often participated, acknowledging *de facto* the congruence of Christian and Tswana morality (Gulbrandsen 1993a: 70). Indeed, with limited popular participation in the Christian congregation, the royal *kgotla* was a major forum in which the male establishment in particular could be reached.

The ambiguities of the colonial encounter were apparent also in the Tswana's ability to take advantage of the polyvalency of the items introduced by the missionaries in their broader 'civilizing' efforts. It is true that such European practices as, for men, wearing a suit, significantly distinguished the 'saved' from 'heathens', connoting enlightenment, being civilized. But once the *dikgosi* started to wear a suit in the *kgotla*, whether Christian or not, it soon became a sign of eminence in that particular discursive context, subsequently imitated down the ladder. In due course, every family head, even in the most humble local *kgotla*, was habitually wearing a dress jacket as a marker of seniority. The 'tswana-ization' of Western forms is further illuminated by the practice adopted by *dikgosi* of constructing elaborate Victorian-style, rectangular houses in the royal court. This practice was similarly copied by headmen and others who could afford it in their respective *kgotlas*, though with smaller and more modest constructions, as a sign of prominence in the indigenous hierarchy. In other words, Western forms were fused with Tswana categories.

Not only Western forms, but even Western 'rational' knowledge, to which the Tswana were exposed in missionary schools, was not replacing that of the Tswana tradition. To be sure, in their various modernizing efforts as well as their administration of justice and legislative activity, the *dikgosi* depended on these sources of knowledge.[7] But this knowledge was readily subordinated to the discourses of the *kgotla*. Command over 'Western' knowledge added to the repertoire of distinctions symbolizing seniority in the context of the *kgotla*. Yet this was so only if such a capacity was combined with eminent control over the body of knowledge known as Tswana custom and law and, above all, the demonstration – through oratory skills – of the ability to bring these sources convincingly together. The extent to which the Tswana endeavoured to subordinate Western knowledge to the dominant discourse of the *kgotla* is perfectly illuminated by their notion of *rutegile* – being a learned person. This is an intrinsically Tswana notion which, in the face of missionaries, colonial administrators and other agents of the hegemonic culture, was explicated and reinforced, serving to esteem what they identified as their own heritage of a politico-jural culture.

After decades of evangelizing work, the persistent dominance of the discourses of the *kgotla*, and limited attendance of men at the church services, made missionaries rather disillusioned, as expressed in a complaint by one of them towards the end of the nineteenth century:

> The character of the people discourages... [especially] their un-rivalled niggardliness.... We live in a heathen atmosphere, which is often unspeakably depressing. Around us, a living immovable mass of active heathenism, & one feels that this mass, however silent & invisible it may be, is always, night & day, year in & year out, in daily & implacable opposition to our work for the Lord Jesus Christ.[8]

Yet, however much the missionaries attributed this state of affairs to people's strong attachment to the *kgotla*, they had no powers to undermine it. In fact, as time went by, they became increasingly dependent upon the *dikgosi*, whose control over their people was exercised by virtue of people's strong attachment to the *kgotla*. This dependency increased as a competing 'independent' Christian congregation, evolving in the industrial and mining centres of South Africa under African leadership, entered the local scene.

Moreover, with the establishment of the Bechuanaland Protectorate in 1887, the Northern Tswana polities were boosted. The Protectorate was established on the request of the *dikgosi* who increasingly felt threatened by the expanding frontier of Boers in the Transvaal. Significantly, the British accepted the request largely because these Tswana polities appeared favourable for the establishment of their supremacy at the lowest possible cost, i.e. by governing through indirect rule. In contrast to the missionaries, the British had thus considerable interest in retaining the hierarchy of *kgotlas*. The *dikgosi* should continue to rule their people much as they had, within some broad limitations. Of particular relevance to the present context, it was established that the High Commissioner should 'respect any native laws and customs' regulating 'civil relations', 'leaving the Native Chiefs and those living under their authority almost entirely alone'.[9] The British restricted the judicial authority of *dikgosi* only in severe criminal cases and in cases where Europeans were involved; they were also denied the right to pass capital sentences.

Such limitations have sometimes been taken as signs of a wholesale diminishing of the powers of *dikgosi* during the colonial era, ignoring all the new sources of power which the colonial era brought (Gulbrandsen 1994: ch.4). This trend reflects what I have already indicated in the case of the missionaries: an increasing dependence upon the executive powers of the *dikgosi* and their control over the *merafe*. This dependence is especially clear in their administration of justice. With the progressive integration in the larger world through labour migration and the penetration of the market economy, a wide array of new kinds of disputes and conflicts arose on family and community levels. Acknowledging the fact that these conflicts were genuinely Tswana in nature, the British found themselves heavily dependent upon the *dikgosi*'s judicial, as well as legislative, authority. But the increasing powers of the *dikgosi* were subsequently manifested in ways which did not always please the Administration.[10] A concern also emerged over what was conceived as the autocratic role of the *dikgosi* and the uncertainty about how well grounded their decisions were in popular consultations, as expressed by one energetic Resident Commissioner, who confided to his diary (in 1929): '[The *dikgosi*] practically do as they like – punish, fine, tax and generally play hell. Of course their subjects hate them but daren't complain to us; if they did their lives would be made impossible' (Rey 1988: 4).

Such images of Tswana rulers were motivated by a general reconsideration of the principle of indirect rule, reflecting the British desire to adopt more active policies which required a firmer control over indigenous rulers and their institutions in many parts of the colonial empire. In the present case, the Colonial Administration found itself increasingly uneasy with one particular aspect of the customary set-up of the Tswana polities, which involved the notion that the council of the *kgosi* is the entire nation. An extensive initiative was made to reform the 'tribal administrations', including the requirement that the councils of *dikgosi* should be composed of selected named individuals, patently in agreement with Western legal principles of individual accountability.[11]

The requirement for bureaucratic codification of positions and accountability within indigenous institutions, as well as between the Administration and the *kgosi*, was profoundly expressed in the field of the administration of justice. The High Commissioner issued a particular 'Natives Tribunal Proclamation' in 1934 (no. 75), which framed the Tswana courts into two classes of Tribunals, designated as Senior Tribal Tribunals and Junior Native Tribunals. According to this system, ward and descent group courts were no longer recognized. The Tribunals were to be composed of identifiable members, who should be paid a fixed salary. They should keep written records of their proceedings, available in the case of appeal to the British magistrate courts and for inspection by the local magistrate.

During the preliminary discussions preceding this Proclamation, the issues involved were subject to heated debates in the *merafe* and the Native Advisory Council.[12] At certain points the Tswana were not in full agreement with themselves. Most importantly, several senior tribal representatives to the Native Advisory Council expressed their attraction to the idea of being paid a fixed salary. It was argued, for instance, that such a system would prevent nepotism among unwealthy people who held a high position in the *kgotla* by virtue of high rank. It was even stated that 'these are European modern times and we see that everybody who has something to do is paid'. The *dikgosi* strongly condemned such notions, establishing that 'native ways of doing things are not the same as European ways'. In rejecting the whole idea of identifying the members of the Tribunals as well, they rhetorically asked: 'If anybody is to be paid are we going to pay all the Chief's Councillors, which implies the whole tribe?'[13]

Despite the fact that this became the 'official' view of the Tswana, the High Commissioner enforced the mentioned Proclamation. In a British assessment (in 1953), it was admitted, however, that

> [i]n insisting on the establishment of a formally constituted Tribal Council and of Tribunals of a fixed composition to take the place of traditional trial by Kgotla, the law made a radical change in some of the most characteristic institutions of the Bechuana people... the people saw a menace to a system of trial to which they were as deeply attached as is a Briton to the procedure of trial by a jury.
>
> (Hailey 1953: 222)

In fact, the Administration itself had, when revising the Proclamation in 1943, recognized and accepted the fact that it was unfeasible to give effect to these particular provisions (Hailey 1953: 222).

These ambiguities illuminate British dependency upon the indigenous polity. The fact that it proved very difficult to impose certain Western principles indicates that these polities retained considerable strength. More fundamentally, it reflects the distinctive character of the socio-cultural construction of the Tswana polities and its incompatibility with European modes of government, based upon (Weberian) principles of bureaucratic rationality. The British had, to a significant extent, the choice between accepting or replacing the whole of it. The latter alternative was out of the question, and the ambiguities characterizing the relationship prevailed throughout the colonial era, occasionally involving considerable turbulence, but, on the whole, leaving the *dikgosi* and their polities with considerable autonomy.

TSWANA CONSCIOUSNESS ABOUT THE VALUE OF THE *KGOTLA*

In view of the high degree of popular involvement, the persistence of the distinctive character of the Tswana polities is certainly attributable to the tremendous value which they placed upon participation in court proceedings which, in principle, included 'the whole tribe'. The strong adherence to this mode of litigation found one of its most apparent expressions in their avoidance of the magistrate courts. These courts were established by the British in all capital villages in order to provide the Tswana with a judicial alternative and a court of appeal from where a case could be appealed further to the High Court. The fact that this pattern is not attributable to the repressive power of *dikgosi* is testified by the fact that still, almost thirty years after the curtailment of much of the powers of *dikgosi* by the establishment of the national state of Botswana (1966), the vast majority of cases are still brought to these traditional courts. Moreover, numerous courts have been formed in urban neighbourhoods and the government has instituted a national 'Customary Court of Appeal'.

This is not simply a matter of habitual practice but of conscious preference. One obviously felt problem is the magistrates' lack of competence in Tswana custom and law, according to which the vast majority prefer their cases to be tried. For example, I often heard the Tswana complain that 'in the magistrate courts, people are encouraged to fight'. The high value which they place upon their own mode of litigation as a way of 'cooling' matters rather than intensifying the destructive 'heat' associated with social conflicts, may be traced when contrasted with salient features of the Western system, as summarized by Roberts. In a Western court room

[o]nce the issue is before the judge he is expected to decide the matter, rather than act as a mediator between the two disputants.... Inherent in this method of adjudication is [often] the result that one party wins and the other loses...; it is not an objective of the system that both parties should go away feeling that they have won, or even honours have been shared.

(S. Roberts 1979a: 20–1)

This feature conflicts radically with the Tswana ideal of reconciliation and social harmony (*kagiso*), which depends on the principle that everybody is allowed to express their views. This is particularly important in family disputes where a much broader network of social relationships is involved than would be recognized by a Western legal code. Thus, as the Tswana say, 'people become desperate in the magistrate courts, because they are not allowed to talk as they are used to'. An important consequence of the method of dealing with disputes in these courts is

that once the matter is in the hands of the legal specialists, the lawyers and the judge, they impose their own construction upon it in such a way that both the form and the course which the dispute takes are largely beyond the disputants' control. What is in dispute and how it is to be dealt with are determined by the reach of *legal rules*.

(S. Roberts 1979a: 21, emphasis added)

Conversely, issues for which no legal rules apply are not within the jurisdiction of the magistrate court, irrespective of any sense of grievance a disputant may feel. This is contrary to the Tswana mode of litigation which draws upon the broad, undifferentiated body of norms, the *mekgwa le melao*, and is also typified by the way that the outcome of cases

> can never be decided by the application of single rule or set of rules; it is beyond their intrinsic nature to do so.... [T]he successful contrivance of a relationship depends on the construal of as much of its history and contemporary character as possible in relation to the widest available set of normative referents.... [V]eracity subsists... in the extent to which events and interactions are persuasively construed and coherently interpreted.
>
> (Comaroff and Roberts 1981: 237–8)

This context-bound mode of invoking the normative repertoire places high value on oratorical skills and makes the outcome of cases often unpredictable. Both factors contribute to the perceived dramaturgical value of court proceedings, a value which, I have already explained, is essential for the construction of male self-identity in the context of the *kgotla*.

Of course, adherence to the Tswana court system did not make people immune to British laws; in fact it was established that particular Tswana customs and laws should be cancelled when incompatible with laws framed by the High Commissioner. But such incompatibilities were rare, and when they existed Tswana *dikgosi* occasionally found ways to give preference to *mekgwa le melao* (e.g. S. Roberts 1979b: 48). To the extent that British laws were invoked in Tswana courts, they were applied in the context of the proceedings peculiar to the *kgotla* and not that of the magistrate court. Accordingly, although the Tswana were faced with new kinds of conflicts and problems, they were to a significant extent able to deal with their cases in accordance with their own cultural categories and valuations.

The unsuccessful attempt by the British to reform the Tswana administration of justice was an exceptional occurrence. If this endeavour had any impact at all, it was mainly to raise Tswana consciousness of the merits of their own cultural tradition, particularly in the face of the mode of jurisprudence practised by the magistrate courts.

The requirement to keep written court records was observed, and Tswana *mekgwa le melao* was, on the basis of a joint request by the

Administration and the *dikgosi*, rendered in written form. The Tswana had no objection to this, in fact many of them strongly appreciated Professor Schapera's work, as published in his celebrated *Handbook of Tswana Law and Custom* (1938). In their view, it represented, in the face of the British, a solid manifestation of the comprehensive and coherent 'legal' base for the administration of justice in Tswana courts. Yet this endeavour involved, of course, a kind of reification of *mekgwa le melao* which, if used like a Western law book, would have been incompatible with Tswana litigation practices. The point is that nobody found themselves required to use it in such a way. I have never heard anybody refer to it during court proceedings, nor is there any account of such a practice in scholarly studies of Tswana law. On the contrary, discussing the impact of the *Handbook*, Roberts assures us that '[w]hen we hear Tswana talking about their norms . . . , what we hear is still unmistakably forms of a part of an oral culture . . . rich in proverb and metaphor. This remains the language of *mekgwa le melao* today' (S. Roberts 1985: 84).

I conclude from all this that the discourse of the *kgotla* prevailed throughout the colonial era, meaning that the categories and values essential to the construction of Tswana selfhood were forcefully reproduced. The extent to which they were brought in touch with British law, consciousness arose of the value of their own mode of litigation as particularly conducive to their ideal of reconciliation and 'cooling' matters. Moreover, the ambiguity of the colonial encounter is emphasized by the tacit ways in which European people (missionaries), material items, and knowledge gained significance in terms of Tswana categories and values in the discursive context of the *kgotla*.

REPLACING CUSTOM BY LAW – A CASE OF WESTERNIZATION?

The intensification of judicial activities during the colonial era facilitated their peculiar form of defending and elevating social identities in terms of Tswana categories and values. This intensification of *kgotla* discourses was driven by the increasing number of court cases and legislative issues which, to a great extent, was significantly affected by such external forces as labour migration and trading. In view of the prevalence of these forces, one might well ask if they had any impact upon the *content* of the discourses of the *kgotla* and, by extension, Tswana categories and values.

It should be noted that the Administration gave the *dikgosi* considerable autonomy in the field of legislation, only denying them the right to establish laws incompatible with those proclaimed by the High Commissioner. In fact, the Administration's dependency upon the Tswana rulers' administration of justice found one of its expressions in the Administration's encouragement of the Tswana's rulers to frame particular laws.

Tswana legislation represents an important manifestation of responses to new kinds of conflicts and problems. This is a significant field, because it is not readily given that *kgosi* legislation was entirely a matter of preserving the *status quo*. In their policy-making capacity many of the *dikgosi* took the initiative in modernizing ventures, especially in respect of public services and infrastructure (e.g. Schapera 1970: 96ff.). More relevant to the present context, the *digkosi* held the authority to replace custom by law. As the Tswana say: '*gae lome ka le bolela laengwe*' ('one bee does not use another's sting', i.e. a *kgosi* should rule according to his own ideas, and not those of his predecessors' (Schapera 1970: 19)). This did not mean that the *kgosi* could legislate as he liked. Legislation was always based upon extensive consultations with councillors and headmen, and the *kgosi* proclaimed a new law only after public debate in the royal *kgotla*.[14] Moreover, '[t]he tribe believes that the "chief's law" is an application of ancestral law to a new condition, just as our legislators believe that their statutes are in accord with Common Law' (Willoughby 1923: 99). The Tswana expect that the *kgosi* communicates with the ancestors on this kind of issue, i.e. receiving instructions through dreams.[15] Yet they do not hesitate to criticize what they conceive as insensible legislation, implying that there has been poor communication with the ancestors.

Yet this notion does not readily involve a force in favour of the *status quo*, since the *dikgosi* are, as indicated, expected to legislate pragmatically with reference to the changing historical context. There is thus no need to phrase the new laws in ways which involve a practice of 'inventing customs'. Rather it is a matter of an explicit replacement of customary practice (*megkwa*) with law (*melao*), justified as conducive to social harmony (*kagiso*).

In the historical context of colonialism, the question is therefore whether the recurrent replacement of custom by law involved the penetration of the hegemonic culture. This question is pertinent because several laws concerned property, inheritance and marriage in ways which may readily be seen as encouraging individuation of the social field. This kind of change is often, in anthropological discourse, conceived squarely as a movement from traditionalism to modernity, from collectivism to individualism. One might expect that these new laws would erode core Tswana cultural notions, those which construct hierarchical identity relations.

The commodization of the Tswana economy has certainly involved a partial emancipation from the iron hand of the hierarchical order. But since this order prevailed during the entire colonial era, and has survived significantly since the establishment of the 'liberal democratic' state of Botswana, I shall, within the limits of this chapter, concentrate on how a variety of legislation was conceived by the Tswana as measures to maintain social harmony and, thus, safely situated on ancestral grounds.

Changes pertaining to family property relations are a case in point.[16] For example, *kgosi* Seepapitso III of the Bangwaketse (1910–16) legislated that the earnings of migrant labouring sons were no longer the property of their fathers, as custom dictated, but available to the sons for the purchase of their own livestock. To Western eyes this might seem to be the epitome of the individuation of property relations, undermining patriarchal authority materially as well as symbolically. The substantial changes of rules to inheritance in favour of women and junior men invite a similar interpretation. For instance, it was customary practice that at a man's death, his property was kept under the custodianship of his oldest living brother until his sons had reached an age at which they were able to take care of their inheritance. The widow and her children were thus made dependent upon this man.

Kgosi legislation replaced these customs by new laws in several respects. While the inheritance was customarily divided unequally amongst the sons in favour of the eldest one – who was responsible for looking after his mother, unmarried sisters and junior brothers – the new laws specified that not only the wife, but also unmarried daughters were entitled to inherit from the deceased man. Laws were also passed against polygynous marriage and, concomitantly, against the practices of levirate and sororate (see Schapera 1970: 134ff.).

Changes of this kind have been celebrated by such different agents of Western morality as early missionaries and spokespersons for women's emancipation, although these groups clearly embraced radically different versions of Western morality. It is therefore not surprising that the Tswana are able to construe these new laws in terms of their own moral categories and valuations. This point came home to me after a conversation with one of the most prominent Tswana rulers during the colonial era, the now late *kgosi* Bathoen II who ruled one of the major Tswana kingdoms (Ngwaketse) for more than forty years. He explained:

> Yes, these inheritance laws had something to do with the fact that we were entering a money economy. But they were not made in order to promote that development. On the contrary, the point of the laws was to limit the destructive effects of the new situation. The thing was that as new economic opportunities came to us, there were more and more men who, rather than looking after the widow and children of their late brother, used the wealth he had left them for their own purpose. When we began to see such irresponsible behaviour, which was totally at odds with our communal way of life, it was my father's [Seepapitso III] and my responsibility to stop it by law. In order to ensure order and harmony in our society, it was our duty to look after the weak and vulnerable, not the rich and the greedy.
>
> The reason why we insisted that migrant workers should be entitled to the cattle they had bought with their wages, rather than their being included in the fathers' herd, was that the fathers used to take the money brought home by their sons, so the young men started to spend their earnings on girls and other useless things before they went home. This was a very destructive situation which had to be corrected by law.
>
> As for the legislation against polygyny, this was carried through under the influence of the missionaries, though as leaders of the people, we were not their puppets. For instance, I insisted on the retaining bridewealth (*bogadi*) as the basis for legitimating marriage, against their protests. This was necessary in order to stop the growing disorder in matrimonial matters. An increasing number of illegitimate children were being born who had to grow up without a proper father. In fact, in some cases they did not even know who their father was.[17]

In other words, the old *kgosi* construed these new laws as a matter of patriarchal morality, rather than simple submission to Western ideals of family and division of property. Such patriarchal responsibility is an important corollary of Tswana hierarchical values. Ideally, seniority is not only a matter of privilege, but also a responsibility. If you suffer mistreatment from your senior, there is always somebody else he is a junior and who has the responsibility to protect you.

There are many other examples of this kind of legal initiative to limit the destructive impact of external changes on Tswana life. Another important, and often controversial, field was that of restricting the production, sale and consumption of alcoholic drinks. This was enforced on the same patriarchal pretext of sustaining social peace and order, and, in particular, preventing a selfish father from ruining his children's home. Furthermore, while the Northern Tswana rulers did not legislate significantly to regulate exchange *amongst* their own people, they framed, in a highly patriarchal fashion, a number of laws and regulations in order to limit their sale of crops and livestock to European traders. For example:

> At first people tended to sell crops recklessly after a good harvest. The result was that if a bad season followed, as it often did, they usually had to buy back supplies, for food or seed, at prices sometimes three to five times as much as they had been given. Because of this [a number of *dikgosi*] ... adopted the practice ... of periodically forbidding the sale of sorghum and other crops (to traders, but not to fellow tribesmen) without special permission. ... The legislation ... was meant to prevent people from being improvident with their basic food supplies. It was for somewhat similar reasons that ... chiefs also forbade the sale to traders of heifers and young cows.
>
> (Schapera 1970: 111–12)

Similarly, the *dikgosi* regulated labour migration to the South African mining and industrial centres; young men had to request permission to leave from the tribal authorities. This was denied 'if it was thought that [the applicant] was trying to evade his tribal responsibilities or that his absence would be *detrimental to the welfare of his family*' (Schapera 1970: 116, emphasis added).

In conclusion, the legislative examples reviewed here illuminate that however 'Western' in origin were the forces which gave rise to new kinds of conflicts and problems, these were always manifested in distinctively Tswana contexts. They were culturally conceived as such, and they were, with very few exceptions, dealt with by Tswana legislators in courts and legislative assemblies in the *kgotla*, in accordance with the categories and values residing there. Most apparently, legislation is typically justified by reference to the supreme goal of sustaining social order, in which values of caretaking, commensality and submittance to seniority are held in high regard. These valuations are rarely expressed by contrasting Tswana ways with those of the Europeans, who constituted after all a small category of people whose life was only to a limited extent transparent to most of the Tswana during the colonial era. Rather they are thematized with reference to the pervasive tendencies of individual endeavours amongst themselves. That is, tendencies which are, as we have seen, epitomized by rivalry for position, property and prestige.

THE LIMITS OF THE *KGOTLA* AND THE AMBIGUITY OF MODERNITY

In the context of the *kgotla* individuating tendencies often cause resentment and jealousy. Such effects are, however, not inevitable, and jealousy is equally disregarded as is increasing wealth by exploiting, for example, a younger brother and his family. On the other hand, there exist honourable ways of accumulating property through hard labour, and some people have given more weight to the attraction of wealth than the danger of causing jealousy, i.e. sorcery (*boloi*). The attraction of wealth, which in this context means cattle, involves more than material security. Cattle have always been a highly significant political asset, as the Tswana say: 'A man who has got cattle, that is a *mohumi* is a man who can speak', meaning that a man with wealth (*mohumi*) is politically independent in the sense that he can often express his view more freely in the *kgotla* than what follows from his genealogically determined rank, while controlling the political behaviour of other people depending upon him through cattle clientship (*mahisa*). Cattle wealth thus features prominently in the symbolism of the hierarchical order; the discursive practice of the *kgotla* in important respects not only justifies highly unequal distribution of cattle wealth, but also the individual accumulation of this kind of property.

It is in the light of this inherent incitement for individuation, combined with the growing opportunities for commercial agro-pastoral production, that one should understand the emergence of a particular category of entrepreneurs during the colonial era. These were often exceptionally industrious individuals, occasionally re-cruited from families of quite modest rank. They increasingly manifested as a network of people who devoted much more time to their economic activities and to discussing their commercial pursuits than participating in the discourses of the *kgotla*. Eventually they formed the core of what became the state-bearing political party of the Independent Botswana, which forcefully advocated the ideology of economic liberalism and development in an utterly Western sense.

While there had practically been no urban centres in the entire Protectorate – people were to a great extent concentrated in exceptionally large villages of tens of thousands of people – urban areas emerged and national capital (Gaborone) was established with a rapidly expanding state bureaucracy, university and commercial activities. This development involved the formation of new arenas in which Western categories of bureaucracy and market relations prevailed, gradually reducing the centrality of the discourses of the *kgotla* in the lives of the Tswana.

And yet, although Western modernity has taken a firm hold in post-colonial Tswana society, the issues addressed in this chapter emphasize the extent to which the Tswana nevertheless retain their attachment to the *kgotla*. This is, to a great extent, attributable to the fact that they still strongly adhere to the Tswana court. Yet there is more to it than that: to most people the practising of the patri-virilocal mode of residence and attachment to their ancestral *kgotla* is still essential for establishing self-identity. This is true even for many of those who pioneered modern elite careers in the urban centres. Conversely, traditional elite persons have followed suit and many of them have used their considerable herds in pursuit of commercial pastoralism.

These apparently ambiguous features reflect the fact that the notions of 'traditional' and 'modern' elite blur the tacit, but structurally significant, coalescence of interests, as epitomized by the supreme value of cattle – at once symbolic in the context of the *kgotla* and material in the context of the *realpolitik* of the nation-state institutions. One may even argue (Gulbrandsen 1994) that they have jointly taken advantage of the control over these institutions, with a privileged access to the wealth accumulating in the state treasury. This is a kind of tacit control ensured, in part, through the prevailing adherence of most rural people to the *kgotla*. Only recently does the political significance of these intrinsic controls show signs of erosion, as a consequence of mass migration and class formation in the urban centres of Botswana since the 1980s.

CONCLUSION

This chapter has been concerned with the reproduction of Tswana judicial and legislative fora in the face of colonialism. I have focused on the inherent dynamics of the *kgotla*, in order to identify processes counteracting the impact of the colonizing culture. These processes were of different orders. Most obviously the Tswana resisted several attempts to westernize the constitution of their politico-jural bodies. It is true that such practices as keeping court records and reducing Tswana custom and law to writing satisfied the British, but they had little impact upon Tswana jurisprudence. Moreover, the establishment of magistrate courts was of very limited significance, because the Tswana retained a strong preference for their own mode of litigation. What was more threatening to the Tswana – the British plans for reforming the constitution of the Tswana court system in ways which significantly reduced its popular element – was successfully resisted. Through these encounters and challenges the Tswana became increasingly conscious of the value of their own mode of litigation.

I have related their strong appreciation of particular procedural practices of the Tswana court to the high value placed upon performance in the *kgotla*, the centrality of the *kgotla* in establishing and negotiating male self-identity at all court levels, and the appreciation of the ideal of reconciliation in court proceedings – the use of the *kgotla* as a cooling source. This ideal, I argue, is closely connected to the notion of *kagiso* (social harmony), essential for fertility, health and material prosperity and highly vulnerable to the 'heat' caused by aggression, conflict and tension. Even though *kgotla* discourse connotes rivalry, discipline and punishment, the symbolic wealth thus vested in it explains why the Tswana avoid, in their view, the conflict-generating proceedings of the Western court, and have, until recently, participated intensely in the *kgotla* proceedings.

Now, even though the Northern Tswana expressly and consciously repudiated British forms such as that of the magistrate court, it does not necessarily follow that they isolated themselves from the colonizing culture. As the Comaroffs argue with particular reference to the missionary endeavour, the Southern Tswana 'frequently rejected the messages of the colonizers, and yet are powerfully and profoundly affected by its media' (Comaroff and Comaroff 1991: 311). Moreover, in their attempt to reform the indigenous practices of architecture, clothing and cultivation, the missionaries were 'ever more successful in their implanting the cultural forms of bourgeois Europe on African soil' (1991: 311). In particular, once the plough was adopted, a radical transformation of property relations and division of labour was set in motion, contributing significantly to individuating the social and the political field and thus eroding the 'tribal' structures.

Evangelizing missionaries, working among the Northern Tswana, were governed by a similar objective of fundamental reform but, as we have seen, they failed. In spite of the fact that Tswana communities showed, in many respects, an increasing receptivity to certain apparently European forms (clothing, furniture and house construction) as well as the content of European culture (knowledge obtained through education), the *kgotla* – the epitome of the Tswana polity – remained the dominant discursive field which, in part, reduced the relevance of European forms and, thus, involved a degree of cultural insulation. In part the *kgotla* worked to fuse such European forms as clothing and house constructions with Tswana categories – even command over European 'rational' knowledge became an asset in the discourses of the *kgotla*. Above all, the tendencies of individuation amongst the Tswana themselves, fuelled by the commodization of the economy, triggered legislative responses in the *kgotla* by which *dikgosi* effectively enforced the Tswana scheme of patriarchy; the taken-for-granted notions of protection and commensality upon which authority relations at all levels were justified. It is in this sense that I refer to the counter-hegemonic force of the *kgotla*. This force was reproduced by virtue of the exercise of Tswana custom and law in the hierarchy of *kgotlas*, ensuring the maintenance of a high degree of cultural uniformity in spite of the increasingly diverse ways in which various categories of the people were interacting with agents of the colonial administration, labour migration, commercial trading, Western education, membership in missionary congregations and so on.

This kind of tacit, inherent counter-hegemonic force is particularly important in the present context because there were few instances of conscious and explicit rejections of Western forms, such as that of the magistrate court and of bureaucratic constitution of courts and councils. It is true, of course, that the colonial era had a great impact upon aspects such as marriage and family economic adaptation which gave rise to a number of new kinds of conflicts. Yet *kgotla* discourses on judicial and legislative matters meant, to a significant extent, that the Tswana were dealing with the effects of colonialism, in the form of its repercussions, *amongst themselves*. For example, in terms of increasing marriage instability, pre-marital pregnancy, and senior men exploiting or ignoring their juniors. And the Tswana were doing so within the context of the *kgotla*, where they were left with a high degree of freedom to base decisions on their own normative rules, the *mekgwa le melao ya Setswana*.

The preceding section acknowledged the fact that elite men, in particular, were increasingly brought into discursive domains where Western categories and values featured with greater prominence. But it was not until the establishment of the independent Republic of Botswana that they, by virtue of their considerable entrepreneurial ambitions, manifested themselves as forceful agents of Western modernity. In particular, they spearheaded the establishment of the modern politico-administrative institutions of the national state and the expansion of the market economy, promoting a development which gradually engaged people in arenas where the rules and resources of the *kgotla* did not feature. Still the *kgotla* is central in the lives of many Tswana, because it remains crucial to them as an arena for the establishment of self-identity. Above all, its everyday reproduction is attributable to the people's strong adherence to the customary court, epitomized by the fact that *kgotlas* are being established all over the urban centres of Botswana.

Due to the intensification of disputes and legislative issues during the colonial era, family heads were increasingly involved in discursive practices which exposed them to these counter-hegemonic processes, since they were all incorporated in the hierarchy of courts. This was not a matter of compulsory incorporation, although the discourses involved an element of disciplinary inculcation of obedience and submission within the context of strictly enforced senior–junior relations. The force and efficiency of the system was ensured by the strong attraction of the cultural wealth vested in those relations which were most profoundly manifested in the discourses of the *kgotla*: participation in these discourses was a matter of asserting the most essential aspects of one's selfhood.

In a restricted Tswana context, the discourses of the *kgotla* can themselves be seen as hegemonic, as a set of categories and signs underpinning the largely taken-for-granted authority relations and, thus, the exercise of dominance by senior men *vis-à-vis* their juniors and, above all, men *vis-à-vis* women, who were only marginally associated with the *kgotla*. In the larger context of colonialism, however, they were all advantaged by the fact that the strength of the *kgotla*, and thus that of the Northern Tswana polities, kept the British willing to retain the Protectorate in the face of the continuous pressure for annexation to the apartheid regime of South Africa.

ACKNOWLEDGEMENTS

This is a revised version of a paper read at the workshop *Inside and Outside the Law*, EASA 3rd Biennial Conference, Oslo, 24–27 June 1994. I am grateful for the useful comments received from the participants at the workshop: Jan-Petter Blom, Georg Henriksen, Edvard Hviding, Olaf Smedal and, in particular, Olivia Harris, whose comments on content as well as form have helped me very much to improve the chapter. I am sending this chapter to press just as Professor Isaac Schapera, the doyen of Tswana studies, is reaching his 90th birthday. On this occasion and in gratitude for many stimulating conversations on the Tswana over the last decade, I dedicate this chapter to him

NOTES

1   Although several Northern Tswana rulers accepted Christianity at an exceptionally early stage and many became nominally members of the missionary church, the actual participation in the activities of the missionaries remained very limited, especially for adult males (cf. Schapera 1958).

2   A number of field studies, mainly among the Ngwaketse who are a major Northern Tswana group located in present south-eastern Botswana, were conducted between 1975 and 1992.

3   See Burchell (1924: 512); Livingstone (1857: 13); Okihiro (1976: 11ff.); Schapera (1935, 1984: 91ff.); Schapera and Roberts (1975); Gulbrandsen (1993b).

4   The enforcement of this principle was relaxed by Botswana's independence and the curtailment of the power of *dikgosi*, yet it has been practised to a significant extent also since then.

5   The antagonism between certain members of a descent group or ward *kgotla* has on some rare occasions been so severe and persistent that one party has been removed to another *kgotla*.

6   Mackenzie to Mullens, 'On the way to Kuruman from Shoshong', August 1876, London Missionary Society Archives, South Africa 38/3/C.

7   In the Ngwaketse, for instance, *kgosi* Bathoen II (1928–69) chose most of his closest confidential advisors and councillors mostly amongst people who had, like him, been educated at missionary schools.

8   Lloyd to Thompson, London Missionary Society Archives, Africa South, 14 February 1894.

9   Orders in Council established by the High Commissioner, as quoted after Schapera 1970: 51–2.

10   A case in point is *kgosi* Sechele II of the Bakwena whom the British dispossessed and exiled (see Ramsay 1987).

11   Opening Address by the Resident Commissioner at the Fifteenth Session of the Bechuanaland Protectorate Native Advisory Council, *Minutes*, Mafeking, 10 July 1933: esp. pp. 12–13.

12   This Council was established in 1920, composed of the *dikgosi*, some of their senior advisors and representatives of the Administration, for

mutual consultations on major issues concerning the Protectorate. The Council was chaired by the Resident Commissioner.

13 See Minutes of the Fifteenth Session of the Bechuanaland Protectorate Native Advisory Council, Mafeking, 10 July 1933.

14 The *melao* were written down and filed; they have been carefully compiled and examined by Schapera (1943, 1947, 1970, 1984).

15 It should be noted here that the *dikgosi* legislated independently of each other, meaning that the *mekgwa le melao* was revised differently in the various Northern Tswana kingdoms (cf. Schapera 1943, 1970).

16 For the Northern Tswana there is a unique, comprehensive corpus of records of legislation which have been carefully compiled by Professor Schapera (1943, 1947, 1970, cf. 1984) and which are the source for the following analysis.

17 Edited from a conversation with Bathoen Gaseitsiwe (the former *kgosi* Bathoen II who abdicated in 1969), December 1985.

REFERENCES

Bourdieu, P. (1977) *Outline of a Theory of Practice*, Cambridge: Cambridge University Press.

Burchell, W.J. (1924) *Travels in the Interior of Southern Africa, Vol. II*, London: Longman.

Channock, M. (1985) *Law, Custom and Social Order: The Colonial Experience in Malawi and Zambia*, Cambridge: Cambridge University Press.

Cohn, B.S. (1989) 'Law and the colonial state in India', in J. Starr and J. Collier (eds) *History and Power in the Study of Law, New Directions in the Anthropology of Law*, Ithaca, NY: Cornell University Press.

Comaroff, J. (1985) *Body of Power – Spirit of Resistance: The Culture and History of a South African People*, Chicago: The University of Chicago Press.

Comaroff, J. and Comaroff, J.L. (1991) *Of Revelation and Revolution: Christianity, Colonialism, and Consciousness in South Africa*, Chicago: The University of Chicago Press.

Comaroff, J.L. and Comaroff, J. (1992) *Ethnography and the Historical Imagination*, Boulder: Westview Press.

Comaroff, J.L. and Roberts, S. (1981) *Rules and Processes. The Cultural Logic of Dispute in an African Context*, Chicago: The University of Chicago Press.

Conley, J.M. and O'Barr, W.M. (1990) *Rules versus Relationships. The Ethnography of Legal Discourse*, Chicago: The University of Chicago Press.

Fuller, C. (1994) 'Legal anthropology, legal pluralism and legal thought', *Anthropology Today* 10: 9–12.

Gulbrandsen, Ø. (1993a) 'Missionaries and the Northern Tswana rulers: who used whom?', *Journal of Religion in Africa* 13: 42–83.

—— (1993b) 'The rise of the North-Western Tswana kingdoms: the dynamics of interaction between internal relations and external forces', *Africa* 63: 550–82.

—— (1994) *Poverty in the Midst of Plenty: Inequality of Rank, Power and*

Wealth in a Tswana Society. Bergen Studies in Social Anthropology, No. 45, Bergen: Norse Pub.

—— (1995) 'The king is king by the grace of the people: the exercise and control of power in ruler–subject relations', *Comparative Studies in Society and History* 37(3): 415–44.

Kuper, A. (1982) *Wives for Cattle*, London: Routledge & Kegan Paul.

Livingstone, D. (1857) *Missionary Travels and Researches in South Africa*, London: Ward, Lock & Co.

Mackenzie, J. (1871) *Ten Years North of the Orange River: A Story of Everyday Life and Work among South African Tribes*, Edinburgh: Edmonston & Douglas.

Mann, K. and Roberts, R. (eds) (1991) *Law in Colonial Africa*, London: James Curry.

Merry, S.A. (1992) 'Anthropology, law and the transnational process', *Annual Review in Anthropology* 21: 357–79.

Moffat, R. (1842) *Missionary Labours and Scenes in Southern Africa*, London: Snow.

Okihiro, G. (1976) 'Hunters, herders, cultivators and traders: Interaction and change in the Kgalagadi nineteenth century', unpublished Ph.D. thesis, University of California.

Ramsay, J. (1987) 'The neo-traditionalist: Sebele II of the Bakwena', in F. Morton and J. Ramsay (eds) *The Birth of Botswana. A History of the Bechuanaland Protectorate from 1910 to 1966*, Gaborone: Longman Botswana.

Roberts, R. and Mann, K. (1991) 'Introduction', in K. Mann and R. Roberts (eds) *Law in Colonial Africa*, London: James Curry.

Roberts, S. (1979a) *Order and Dispute: an Introduction to Legal Anthropology*, Harmondsworth: Penguin.

—— (1979b) 'Tradition and change in Mochudi', *African Law Studies* 17: 37–51.

—— (1985) 'The Tswana polity and *Tswana Law and Custom* reconsidered', *Journal of Southern African Studies* 12: 75–87.

—— (1990) 'Tswana government and law in the time of Seepapitso, 1910–1916', in K. Mann and R. Roberts (eds) *Law in Colonial Africa*, London: James Curry.

Sahlins, M. (1993) 'Cery cery fuckabede', *American Ethnologist* 20: 848–7.

Schapera, I. (1935) 'The social structure of the Tswana ward', *Bantu Studies* 9: 203–24.

—— (1943) *Tribal Legislation among the Tswana of Bechuanaland Protectorate: a Study in the Mechanism of Social Change*, London: Percy Lund, Humphries & Co.

—— (1947) *Political Annals of a Tswana Tribe*, Communications, n.s., no. 18, Cape Town: School of African Studies, University of Cape Town.

——(1958) 'Christianity and the Tswana', *Journal of the Anthropology Institute* 88: 1–9.

—— (1970) *Tribal Innovators: Tswana Chiefs and Social Change 1795–1940*, London: Athlone Press.

—— (1984[1938]) *A Handbook of Tswana Law and Custom*, London: Oxford University Press.

Schapera, I. and Roberts, S. (1975) 'Rampedi revisited: another look at a Kgatle ward', *Africa* 46: 258–79.

Snyder, F.G. (1981) 'Colonialism and legal form: the creation of "customary law" in Senegal', *Journal of Legal Pluralism* 19: 49–81.

Thomas, N. (1993) 'Beggars can be choosers', *American Ethnologist* 20: 868–76.

Willoughby, W.C. (1923) *Race Problems in the New Africa*, Oxford: Oxford University Press.

Chapter 8

A public flogging in south-western Iran
Juridical rule, abolition of legality and local resistance[1]

Manuchehr Sanadjian

One morning in late August 1981, a crowd of several hundred people gathered to watch the public flogging of four Luri men in the centre of the small town of Deh-dasht, a sub-provincial capital in the south-western province of Kuhgiluyeh, Iran.[2] The men were guilty of gambling in a private house in the town. They had been discovered playing cards for money by the Islamic Revolutionary Guards (*pasdaran*), and convicted by the ruler of the Islamic jurisdiction (*hakim-e shar'*), a ruthless non-native shaikh, who operated mainly from Yasuj, the provincial capital.[3]

Earlier in the morning the Islamic Guards had announced the public punishment over a loud-speaker, driving through the town's main streets. From early morning women carrying their children or holding them by the hand could be seen moving towards the place of the flogging, referred to as a *shalaq-zadan* and declared to be the rule (*hukm*) of the Islamic Revolutionary Court. No mention was made of the word *marasim* (rituals), a term often used in the official organiza-tion of other events, such as mourning and marches (*azadari va rahpaymai*),[4] for which the attendance of all Muslim sisters and brothers was obligatory. In this case there was no direct requirement that the spectators attend the flogging. Nevertheless, the very public announcement, and the spatial and temporal centrality of its enact-ment, indicated that a large audience was expected to assemble to confirm the gamblers' violation of the 'collective sentiments' of the Muslim community (*ummat*),[5] of which the Lurs were supposedly a part. Such acts of witnessing involved a restrained, distanced participation but still a necessary one.[6]

The site chosen for the flogging was adjacent to a public park on the main east–west thoroughfare. It was highly focused, the largest open space in the centre of town, where the local assumed a national character and events were made meaningful by reference to official history. As a public domain, where the state made its presence palpable in everyday local life, it was the arena in which 'well-honed messages' (Handelman 1990: 9) were circulated, articulating the local with the national.

The main entrance to Deh-dasht was from the east, where the road connected it to the town of Dugunbadan some ninety kilometres away. The awkward, blocking presence of the park at its centre had denied the town the typical space in which official national events were organized. Unlike many other Iranian towns and cities, modern Deh-dasht, which developed in the late 1960s, had never had at its entrance a large square dominated by a menacing statue of the Shah or his father, Reza Shah.[7] As one approaches from the east one passes the main clinic and the countryside police (gendarmerie) head-quarters before reaching the large rectangular park with eucalyptus, oleander and willow trees, surrounded by government offices, the school, shops and private houses. The informal environment of the park, contrasting with the surrounding official formality, is a distinctive feature of Deh-dasht. It denies officialdom an important space to define the experience of the visitor at the entrance to the town,[8] and offers Luri visitors to the town a refuge from the scorching heat, where they can eat and rest before returning to their villages. It is a space of respite in an increasingly alienating and tense environment. As a result the Lurs in the park at the time of the flogging were drawn to join the assembled crowd.

Apart from its location, the timing of the flogging also ensured it would be the focus of attention. Life in the town is dominated by official rhythms, and work in government offices sets the pace for relationships with the surrounding villages. The town is a privileged locale with reference to which the villagers measure time. Late morning was the peak time for visitors from the villages to attend clinics, the agricultural bank, and other government agencies. Government employees were more likely to be available early in the day, and Luri clients had a better chance of finding them in a reasonable mood. The non-Luri civil servants usually considered Luri clients recalcitrant and their requests unreasonable and incomprehensible, and their tolerance declined as the working day progressed in scorching heat. In their timing of the punishment, therefore, the Islamic authorities clearly aimed to communicate their message beyond the town's boundaries.

CIVIL SOCIETY AND LOCAL/NATIONAL ARTICULATION

The Lurs are part of the category known as the *ilat/'ashayir*, normally translated in anthropological discourse as pastoral nomadic 'tribes'. The main distinguishing features of the *'ashayir* – tent-dwelling and pastoral nomadism – have been invoked to fix their shifting relationship with non-*'ashayiri* Iranians. The Lurs' 'remoteness', their rugged mountainous habitat, and their allegedly nomadic way of life[9] have made their status as Iranian citizens ambiguous, placing them potentially outside the law, insofar as the historically constructed realm of law asserts not so much the liberty of the individual as the sovereignty of the state. The *'ashayir* were thought typically to live along Iran's borders, where they were alternately celebrated as national guardians and feared as potential traitors, especially at times of crisis such as the Revolution and the Iraq–Iran war. However, their potential for insubordination was perceived not so much in political, legal terms but as a force of nature opposed to urban culture. It was this potential for insubordination that had secured first a governorship and later provincial status for their homeland in the 1960s and 1970s, out of proportion to their population and land.

After the Revolution, encompassing notions of culture and society in the construction of the nation gave way to an urban-based conception of the Muslim community (*ummat*). This was not merely the creation of the *ulema* (the Islamic clerics) but of an all-out confrontation between Iranian civil society and the state from which the *ummat* emerged victorious, speaking for the people/nation (*mardum/milat*) as the latter asserted itself in the streets of the cities. This unity was predicated on the suppression of multiple sources of social conflict based on race, class and gender. In the period of mass mobilization, participants had resolved their differences with reference to a transcendent unity and shared project of salvation. Paradoxically, after the Revolution the separation between social and political sources of power was intensified as the Islamic state used its popular base to prevent people from mobilizing in the newly-liberated political space. The social and cultural forces which underlay the revolt of civil society against the Pahlavi state brought it also into acute conflict with the Islamic state. That the Muslim community provided little room for the assertion of local communities could be seen from the growing number of regional protests that the Islamic state had to face – in Kurdistan, Turkaman-Sahra, Khuzistan,

Baluchistan, Azarbayejan. Furthermore, the official refusal of discourses of culture and social difference could no longer account for the differences between Lurs and non-Lurs, which had previously been defined in cultural terms. This was particularly clear in the case of the supposed heresy and paganism of the Lurs' religious beliefs. The territorial basis of the *ummat* exposed even further the incompatibilities of the Lurs within the Iranian nation-state.

The creation of the Muslim community required the operation of Islamic norms which sought to turn individuals into subjects, members of the community, and the creation of the Islamic state involved the comprehensive incorporation of these norms into a juridical model which defined them in terms of 'that which is permitted and forbidden' (cf. Macherey 1992: 176). Diverse practices were classified into the opposed Islamic categories of the permitted (*halal*) and the prohibited (*haram*). Islamic norms had been an integral part of Iranian civil society before the Revolution, especially in rites of passage. At that time, however, the lack of a tight juridical framework allowed a flexible, even if inconsistent, practice of these norms in the rapidly-developing capitalist economy and society. Their codification in Islamic jurisprudence (*fiqh*) after the Revolution transformed their role in the construction of the civil society, and they became the means of including some and excluding others from the *ummat* by subjecting secular domains to their rule. The subsumption of Islamic norms into a tight juridical model meant that the heterodox social relationships within which they had hitherto been practised were progressively denied.

For example, the body was previously the subject of Islamic acts of purification – in eating, washing and clothing – but at the same time it was the object of desire and pleasure in an expanding market economy. As the defining role of Islamic norms became more decisive they also became less participatory/inclusive and more juridical/negative, denying the social and cultural contexts within which they were embedded. This was particularly significant given that Islamic norms have characteristically permeated social life to a degree unparalleled in Judaism and Christianity (Guilaume 1956). This denial involved the displacement of local customs by Islamic rules. The abolition of local customs, however, did not mean that marginal local groups such as the Lurs were incorporated 'inside the law' of the nation-state. On the contrary, it was accompanied by a drastic reduction in the relative autonomy of legal practice. For example, the existence of brothels in large Iranian cities before the Revolution was a tacit recognition of a distinct social domain where sexual relations were organized outside the sphere of morality itself hardly separable from Islamic norms (see Hirst 1989). Their abolition after the Revolution was not so much an attempt by religion to regain control over lost domains as to assert ascendancy over new ones, such as sexuality, leisure, ideology, food and the body. If previous recognition of sexuality as a social practice granted it a degree of autonomy, its post-revolutionary subsumption within Islamic norms removed it from its social context – e.g. family, youth.

One important outcome of the abolition of a distinct social domain by Islamic jurisprudence was the denial of relative autonomy to legal discourse. The independence of legal discourse derives from the recognition that society is differentiated and that legal institutions are part of this differentiation. From this perspective, the legality of Islamic jurisprudence was undermined in that it failed to recognize the existence of the social domain and tried to replace it with the *ummat*. Despite its heavy reliance on the Islamic courts, the unitary Muslim community (*ummat*) is not a legal creation in a modern sense of the word but only a juridical one.[10] In fact, the courts' rulings have consistently worked towards abolishing the distinction between the illegal, the immoral and the sinful. Since Islamic jurisprudence treated crime, vice and sin as synonymous, the notions of society and culture, within which specific social relations functioned independently, became redundant. In the public announcement of the floggings no reference was made to gambling as a legal object, a *jurm*. It was the authorities' normal practice to emphasize Islamic rules rather than the secular, legal definition of an offence, without which the distinction between sin and crime disappeared.

In this case the state's use of the body as its immediate object of power is complemented by grounding it as a Muslim subject, a member of the *ummat* (cf. Foucault 1982: 781). The state embarked simultaneously upon the use of force which stripped the body of its social and cultural bearings and reinserted it into an officially organized cultural setting. The complementary exercise of power through discourse derives from the state's continuous efforts to negotiate the consent of its subjects.[11] Despite its noted anomaly for refusing to recognize the social and cultural nature of relationships of power the Islamic state, even in this early stage, could not afford to rely entirely on a juridical mode of power.

The state's juridical mode of power had already exposed the lack of shared cultural basis for power exercise among the Lurs. It also revealed the attempt by the state to construct such a basis. The shaikh's resort to a cowboy image was an attempt by him to sustain his construction of the Islamic jurisdiction using the 'civilization'/ 'savagery' contrast. The Luri visitor's plea to the ruler to stop the dangerous imitation did not only derive from the fact that swinging a loaded pistol around his finger was an odd way of handling a gun to a Lur. It also reflected a mismatch between the shaikh's assumed role of a mischievous western cowboy and the Lurs' image of an elderly religious man whose authority was traditionally based on impartiality and mediation in their conflicts. The Lur's humorous reference to the incident revealed the paucity of a shared cultural repertoire inside the Islamic court to which they could resort (cf. Rosen 1989). Outside the court a similar paucity was disclosed through the official ritualistic construction of the community. The scope for resistance by the Lurs to political domination by the state was geared to the latter's attempt to sustain its juridical power by grounding it in social relations.

THE SPECTACLE OF FLOGGING

The uniformed Islamic Revolutionary Guards kept the Luri visitors lined up at some distance on the pavements, although many towns-people had secured a good view by climbing over the roofs and walls of the surrounding shops and houses. The confident demonstration of gaze by the crowd was matched by the Islamic officials' efforts to keep it at a distance from the site of the punishment, so that there would be a clear space for the condemned bodies to perform.

The spectators' attempt to get a good view of the flogging, i.e. to turn it into the object of their gaze, indicated the absence of clear rules for behaviour on such occasions. They pushed forward, undermining the authorities' attempts to create a climate of solemnity around the punishment of those who had violated Islamic rules.[12] The convicts' presence was evidently designed to create fear, representing the state as a force both for subjugation and for reintegrating them into the Muslim community. The convicts' identity as individual sinners had to be superseded in a redemptive act in which the crowd would participate as witnesses, not merely as spectators.

The ritual was designed to construct a liminal space within which to enact the sacredness of the Muslim community. The 'script' for the performance, a 'negative rite', evoked the sacred/profane opposition which is central to Islamic collective representations (Lacroix 1979; Durkheim 1965) acted out through spatial positions (Parkin 1992).

With a very restricted opportunity for convicts and crowd alike to invoke a narrative and employ a temporal device in constructing community, space was the main organizing principle, not only in creating the collectivity against which the convicts' 'criminal' acts were gauged, but also in transforming the actors through redemption – the essential feature of the *ummat* (Ayoub 1978). The redemptive act of punishment required that the participants act out the roles assigned to them as sinners and as witnesses, but the assumption of these roles was continually undermined by the crowd's eagerness to get closer and turn the condemned bodies into objects of fun and curiosity.[13]

The spectacular punishment represented a further attempt by the Islamic government to introduce the Lurs into the 'circle of power' in which they were supplied with the categories of 'proper' and 'right' in the double sense of the word (Lacroix 1979), and the profanity of daily experience was 'refracted' through the collective ideas of the Muslim community, and the constructions of the rights of rulers and the wrongs of the ruled. The Lurs' enthusiasm undermined this attempt, through their refusal to bear witness to the sin of gambling in exchange for being represented as the redeemed.

To my chagrin, I found the crowd in a relaxed and even festive mood. This seemed surprising at a time when the Islamic regime's other forms of bodily punishment were characterized by horrific blood-letting executions. The Lurs were fully aware that the exercise of power on bodies in the public flogging was likely to be followed, as in reality it happened, by the state disposing of them in executions. To me the convicts were the victims of repression, whose rights, both as citizens and as human beings, had been violated by the state's brutal domination of their bodies.[14] Their position as legal subjects, in my view, had been reduced to their status as subjects of the state.[15] A critique of the state's repression inevitably involved me in discourses of citizenship and natural human rights (Hunt 1992). Whatever reservations I might have had about the adequacy of these universalist notions did not affect my perception of the violence perpetrated by the state. Had it not been for my anthropological interest I would have left the scene, for I desired to be neither spectator nor witness. Like the Lurs I was not prepared to cast myself in the role of audience of an officially organized ritual. But unlike them I saw myself as witness of the violation of the convicts' rights. The Lurs' response was on a different level. They seemed not to share with the Islamic authorities a sense of gambling as a criminal offence, but neither did they share my interpretation of the flogging as a violation of human rights.

Paradoxically, the legal frame of reference in my interpretation of rights and their violation brought me close to the Islamic officials' way of defining the offence and its punishment. The officials had defined juridically an offence committed by a number of Lurs; I defined in legal terms the offence of the government. The Lurs by contrast showed equal disregard for both the official notion of Islamic jurisprudence and my universal notion. In this instance I had no means of enforcing my notion of legality, while the Islamic authorities were able forcefully and brutally to replace ambiguous local practices by clearly defined Islamic laws. Significantly, the Lurs' reaction implicitly recognized the two externally defined sets of rules, one juridical and the other legal.

A NOVEL MEDIATION

An unmarked van brought the convicts to the scene, accompanied by a number of uniformed Islamic Guards. The convicts were mostly in their twenties. A few days later a group of Lurs in the town referred to them in a brief, detached way as coming from particular villages and *dastehs* (territorially-based groups), i.e. they were from the country-side.[16] A well-respected local turbaned old Sayyed officiated at the event.[17] He sat cross-legged on the roof of the van holding a loudspeaker, and made an informal speech, remarkable for its conciliatory tone. He cited no other Quranic verse than the most common one 'In the name of Allah, the Beneficent and Merciful'; nor did he refer to prophetic and *imami* traditions (*hadith*) characteristic of sermons by Muslim preachers. He made scarcely any attempt to enter into sacred time; he left almost unused the Quranic language which, however unintelligible to most of the audience, was regarded as potent and was the source of his own authority, and he deliberately played down the semantics of the flogging in order to highlight its 'pragmatic meanings' (Tambiah 1979: 166). His language was geared to appeasing his local audience. He began by almost seeking to excuse the government which, because of its Islamic character, had no choice but to take punitive action against gamblers. The punishment had to be carried out in order to observe Islamic rule (*hukm*) which prohibited gambling. It was not intended to harm the personal reputation and social standing of the convicts; they and their relatives should not in any way feel degraded by it. It was simply a religious duty the government was carrying out, and should be seen as such.

However, the old Sayyed devoted most of his speech to explaining how gambling was a violation not of Islamic rule but of local sensibility towards what was proper and right. He explained gently how damaging it was, squandering resources which should be spent on wives and children and preventing men from meeting their contractual obligations and promoting business.

After the Sayyed's reassuring speech, the convicts were taken in turn out of the van and made to lie face down on a bench. A long leather thong served as the whip (possibly a man's belt). The flogging did not seem to cause much physical pain and the Guard in charge did not show a great deal of enthusiasm. As a result, the Guard standing on the roof of the van supervising the operation, apparently unhappy with the inadequate severity of punishment, asked his fellow Pasdar to flog the first convict again. When the crowd heard this, those close by – particularly those standing near or sitting on the roofs and walls – started clapping in jubilation. Their reaction infuriated the Guard on the van and he jumped down frowning and shouting, 'Who was that clapping?' and marched up and down the crowd scrutinizing them. The crowd stayed silent, and having failed to find a culprit he returned to his supervision duty. The convicts remained quiet throughout, showing no sign of unrest or resistance.

The themes of the Sayyed's speech reflected the changing ethos in Deh-dasht as it expanded. The town was one of several places in the province where the Lurs' relation to pasture, land, herds and labour was changing, with an increasing emphasis on individual ownership. There was a rapidly-developing market for unskilled labour which contributed less and less to the reproduction of a social position, but instead was being exchanged for money. This change potentially threatened the dominant position of men since female labour could also be exchanged outside the domestic sphere. Economic viability was a struggle in the new situation. The sale of land or herds, wage-labour and borrowing were common strategies for forming capital to set up a small enterprise in town, such as a shop. The theme of loss from gambling in the Sayyed's speech testified to the new individualist and accumulating attitudes of Luri townspeople. In traditional Luri life, possession had been associated with redistribution in the form of feasts and meeting needs. Now it was subject to calculation and risk avoidance.[18] Traditional Luri possession of livestock, pasture and land was characteristically risky, but the risk was compensated by the autonomy and power of their unsettled life (Sanadjian 1987). It was an indication of changed circumstances that the traditionally high value that Lurs attributed to pillage (*gharat*) – risky but if successful bringing with it both economic and political gain – had given way to a more measured conception of loss in the risk-taking of gambling. Raiding was traditionally the occasion for the Lurs to test and display their bravery. Gambling was discouraged by the local mullah because of the risk of economic loss. Paradoxically, it was a similar reorientation to economic gain that drove the Lurs to the risks of gambling.

LOCAL SENSIBILITY

The Sayyed addressed his audience not primarily as Muslims and subjects of the Islamic state, but as Luri men, heads of local households (*khanivar*) and families (*khanevadeh*). The terms indicated an emerging structure of domesticity among the Lurs in Deh-dasht, an increasingly privatized space set apart from male-dominated public space, in sharp contrast to the traditional Luri patrilineal descent group, *tash* (fire). The Lurs' recent migration to the town has usually involved selling their herds, letting their agricultural land, and engaging in intensive wage-labour. The money raised is used to purchase land and materials for a house in town, a shop, a pick-up, or for their sons' formal education. Survival of Luri domestic units in the new climate has become more precarious as the Lurs can no longer take for granted the support and security of the village community.

In Deh-dasht, Luri households are linked through monetary transactions, which create autonomy as well as vulnerability. An increasing private appropriation of resources for consumption has led to greater distance between households and tension within kin groups, weakening traditional forms of support, and increasing their insecurity. The strain of demonstrating publicly the viability of the new households is borne by men. The Sayyed's speech addressed the rejuvenated patriarchy of the new situation. The household's unstable boundary with the wider economic and political structures gave men a prominent position not only to control its resources but also to represent it. The changed intersection between the domestic unit and the wider context had brought about the enhancement, the 're-enchantment' of the role of Luri men as the protectors of their household (Sanadjian 1994a) although it did not necessarily imply a central role for them in the economic organization of the domestic unit. But it did mean that male domination was not confined to public domains.

The Lurs are conscious of their increasingly moral and economic independence from the kin group. By identifying gambling as the factor which undermined the viability of Luri households, the Sayyed was pointing to the instability of their family relationships. His emphasis on the family was not on its integrative role within the society but its vulnerability as an autonomous unit. In his speech women were represented as dependent on the male household head and exposed to seduction by outsiders. The expanding public spaces in Deh-dasht and elsewhere were sites of female vulnerability, where the moral viability of the families' household must be maintained. The development of public space in this region has often been sponsored by the state in attempts to promote the sense of the nation. It has led to the development of new eating habits and the seeking of friendship with influential outsiders, giving Luri patriarchy a new visibility and vulnerability which was what the Sayyed addressed in order to mobilize the local audience.

The mullah's implicit recognition of the shifting boundary between Luri households did not draw *primarily* on their economic performance, but their ideological-moral viability, which depended on their continuous recognition by outsiders. The interdependence of domestic units in terms of honour and shame gave gambling a different meaning here from the way in which it was defined nationally in religious and juridical terms. Instead of describing the gamblers' deeds in terms of abstract notions of sin and vice to an imagined Muslim audience, the local preacher addressed his local constituency, who defined the problems of gambling primarily in terms of its effects on families. By so doing he was subverting the national religious-political significance of gambling. The local dignitary who had been asked to help the Islamic state redefine a locally ambiguous practice – gambling – as a criminal offence defined it rather as unreasonable, irresponsible and unjust. He actually ended up subverting the universal status of Islamic law and neutralizing the central authorities' initiatives. The local mullah implicitly disarticulated the 'invented' national practice from the local situation.

In the past, gambling was mostly the prerogative of Luri chiefs. The risks involved affected not so much their financial as their social standing. To rob another chief, even in this non-Luri manner, was part of the continuous plotting in which all Luri chiefs were involved in order to maintain their power base among their followers. Gambling constituted the boundary of the Luri community unless an external threat forced a greater degree of unity. Luri commoners were discouraged from speculating on each other's possessions by close kinship ties. The chiefs' more extensive contacts with the outside world had also increased their openness to the notion of private property and, consequently, their inclination to treat each other's possessions as 'things' divested of their social meanings (Kiernan 1976); and they were sufficiently distant from each other in kin terms to contemplate taking away each other's possessions under the agreed rules of gambling. It was only when the role of community in defining Luri material possessions was weakened due to the growing impact of the market, that Luri commoners came to define their relation with material possessions in terms of ownership, i.e. *external* to each other, and that the seizure of someone's property, hitherto part and parcel of inter-communal conflicts, was transmuted into the individualized, speculative act of gambling.

Thus, the speech reflected a shift away from the official definition of Lurs as members of the Muslim community, through performative acts of flogging, to their reinstatement as members of Iranian civil society. It invoked the central value of the family-household instead of that of the *ummat*. The Sayyed directly addressed all Luri household heads, bracketing the Islamic notion of jurisprudence on the basis of which the punishment had been defined, and addressing the sensibilities of his local audience by situating the offence within local customary practices.

A NEW ECONOMY OF POWER AND THE BODY

Public floggings were one of many innovative techniques on the part of the Islamic regime to constitute the Muslim subject, complementing the network of other institutions such as courts, prisons, schools, and mosques. The creation of these spectacles was designed to short-circuit the process of turning the individual into the object of power, by erasing the institutional relationships which had previously mediated between ruler and the ruled. Massive rural–urban migration, large-scale proletarianization, the state's economic role, and the expansion of market relations had split the old forms of social agency into new ones based on money and profit: investors, producers, consumers, proprietors, the unemployed and waged workers. It was recognized that these changes had brought with them social ills such as delinquency, sexual seduction, greed and cheating. The novelty of the Islamic state was to withdraw such recognition, turn these social ills into the object of outright condemnation,[19] and reduce the object of its power to a thing – a body stripped of its social bearings (Foucault 1982). It did away with the notion of social process where the offence is committed (instead of considering it as a set of social relations to act on), and targeted the offender as the immediate object of power.

The reappearance in post-Revolutionary Iran of the body as the major target of the penal system had much to do with the ground lost by the state during the revolutionary upheaval. In pre-Revolutionary times, the state was the enemy of the people; after the Revolution individuals became the immediate enemy of the state. Through an unprecedented assertion of collective will Iranians had destroyed the earlier state as a juridical/political entity, and the Lurs had played a part in this, even if a peculiar one (Sanadjian 1987). The new Islamic state had to reclaim these liberated individuals, to subjugate them and turn them into subjects – self-acknowledged Muslims. But the Islamic state's restoration of control over its subjects did not take place in the juridical/political realm of the liberation, where discourses of freedom, independence and republicanism predominated, but through denying the idea of society.[20] In requiring Iranians to witness the formation of the *ummat* it gave little recognition to social distinctions and individuation. The new technique, a 'pastoral', salvation-oriented power, was directed at an abstract Muslim subject, divorced from his or her social context.[21] This pastoral power derived its strength from the rejection of social forces which the state defined as corrupt and criminal.

The state's negation of social networks gave it power over things rather than relationships (Foucault 1982: 786). Instead of using power through relationships, the state targeted the body, in order 'to close the door on all possibilities' for its subjects (Foucault 1982: 786). In this way it denied human actions, which as products of interactions could not be the immediate object of its power. To exert diffuse power in relationships between individuals and groups had practically been ruled out by the Islamic state as 'non-economical' (Foucault 1980).[22]

Having denied the social basis of its exercise of power, the state needed to find a totalizing context in which to mobilize its subjects by drawing on the body's symbolic significance. The new 'economy of power' adopted by the state was based on criminalization. By defining an increasing number of offences in criminal terms, it progressively reduced the autonomy of the civil, and punished those who transgressed Allah's inalienable 'bounds' (*hudud*)[23] through the restoration of theatrical elements. The result was a further shift from tort to crime in Islamic jurisprudence (Maydani 1955). The public visibility of crime through punishment-as-spectacle reduced the space for tolerance, which sustained the notion of right as a legal rather than moral category. Instead, it promoted a notion of justice which oscillated between an immediate need for retaliation and a theological quest for retribution. It undermined the dispersal of blame characteristic of a modern conception of justice which derives from a social definition of crime. In this conception, a notion of society was essential to the tolerance shown to criminals.[24]

In post-Revolutionary Iran, punishment-as-spectacle operated on the body as the immediate object of the exercise of power (Foucault 1975: 10–11). This control over the body, evidenced in the punishment of the gamblers, denied the liberty of the condemned because the institutions of civil society within which it would have been inscribed were not recognized by the state. It was the erasure of civil society that was celebrated by the state's spectacular control over the bodies of convicts. Paradoxically, the dissociation of Muslim subjects from their social relationships required not only the presence of 'criminals' but also the testimony of witnesses. This presence was all the more necessary as the state's control over the bodies of its subjects was far from complete, given the increasing commodification of labour-power. Every day a growing number of Luri wage-labourers gathered early in the place of the public floggings to sell their labour, and the Islamic state watched closely to prevent any political interference with this economic autonomy.

The principle which had traditionally guided punishment among the Lurs was retaliation and flight. Those guilty of adultery, homicide or serious injury usually took refuge in a safe, distant place. The threat and fear of retaliation related the offender to the offended in a reciprocal exchange, which became even more egalitarian when the Lurs acquired rifles, especially the long-range Bruno.[25] The homo-genizing impact of rifles on Luri power structure forced 'crime' out of the community, which became increasingly the place where men were safe from their rivals. The local base was the tower, fort and castle, whose construction was recounted as a major event in the history of each community. The Lurs' punishment for the violation of shared values was not concentrated on the offender's body, since it stayed out of reach of the offended community.

Incarceration and beating often reflected asymmetrical power relations. Pillage was a form of retaliation against enemy outsiders. Within the community punishment was less visible. Indeed, there was very limited public space in the community for the assertion of political power (Clastres 1977). Disobedient Lurs were imprisoned in their chiefs' castles or camps. Beating (*kutak*), especially when it took place in public as in bastinado,[26] reflected attempts by the chiefs to consolidate their position in relation to the outside world. The beating was intended to provide the chiefs with a power base in order to act on behalf of outsiders. It was designed to make visible an offence beyond the boundary of community, in the wider sphere within which the chiefs negotiated for power. This conferred on the position of Luri chiefs an oppressive, exploitative character (see Taheri 1978 for a vivid Luri semi-fictional account). However, in so far as a chief's externally endorsed position had to be made internally viable (bearing in mind that nomadism made it much easier for the Lurs to escape an oppressive rule), communal sentiments had to be maintained. Thus, acting as external agents the oppressive chiefs could hardly do away with a local base to be negotiated from among the Lurs. There is a significant difference between the Luri chiefs' use of beating, and the public flogging organized by the Islamic state or the less spectacular but no less humiliating and coercive beating by the Shah's security men searching for the Lurs' hidden rifles.[27] While both the Pahlavi and Islamic states have used the body as object of power in order to integrate the local community within the state, Luri beatings served an autonomous assertion of power by the local community.[28] Even bastinado was used by chiefs in the past primarily to *extend* their local power base. The public flogging, on the other hand, represented the assertion of the predominantly national power in a local context. Even the Luri agents instrumental in this assertion could not fail to express their reservation about this external dimension, as noted above, in the hesitation of the guard in charge of flogging and the interpretation of the preaching mullah.

SILENT SUBVERSION

The convicts' persistent silence bestowed a 'connective character' on an otherwise condemning act of punishment (Foucault 1975), signalling a refusal to reproduce themselves as the object of the crowd's gaze and the official ritual of redemption. Although known to many spectators, the convicts refused to acknowledge them.[29] Their lack of response and interaction with the crowd allowed them to maintain a certain anonymity. The convicts also undermined the national, Islamic sense of redemption and showed little sense of shame or guilt, which obstructed their passage to the anti-structural space of the *ummat*, where they would become the object of juridical,

moral and political exercise. Their reluctance to take part in the rite
was matched by the crowd's refusal to act as witness, all the more
significant given the strategic importance of repentance (*tubeh*) in
Islamic law (Schacht 1964). The convicts' silence and passivity
subverted the visibility bestowed on their 'crime' through the
spectacular punishment. The crowd's cheerful response was the
subversion of the state's total reconstruction of the sacred, the
redeemed. The convicts' subversion consisted in disrupting the state's
construction of the profane, the sinful.

The clapping by the crowd and the pleasure it generated subverted
the Muslim community, as the angry Guard testified. The *ummat* was
to be enacted in the public spectacle of flogging, which could only be
realized if a distance was maintained between the spectators and the
object of punishment. The convicts' persistent silence, the Sayyed's
speech, the crowd's jubilation, even the informal layout of the park
itself revealed a disjuncture between the local and the national, and
reflected the problematic nature of extension of rule through the
introduction of clearly defined juridical categories. As the different
reactions demonstrated, the creation of local sensibility to law had to
be negotiated by other means than simply introducing a juridical
mode of power. The sphere of the 'legal' was not the same as the
domain of law (Geertz 1983; Rosen 1989).

A contrast with the commemoration of national martyrs is
instructive. The celebration of martyrdom places the dead beyond
the reach of the contaminated world. For example, the martyr's body
does not need to be washed before burial – a practice strictly observed
by Muslims. Although introduced to the Lurs from outside, the
official notion of martyrdom allowed them to connect local practice
to a wider frame of meaning. I used to hear the Lurs praising their
kinsmen killed on the Iran–Iraq battlefields using traditional epics for
the brave. Although the Luri version of the brave (*shuja'*) was not the
same as the official Islamic notion of martyr (*shahid*), the celebration
of martyrdom was a political space in which local practice could also
be articulated. But in the case of these floggings, the Lurs were denied
the opportunity of articulating local understandings of gambling to
national juridical rule despite the local mullah's mediation. His
conciliatory speech sought to delineate a local ground for defining
the offence in non-Islamic utilitarian terms, but he could not overrule
the demand by the Islamic officials that the Lurs – both as convicts
and their audience – be witness to the creation of an Islamic anti-
temporal space in which local differences were erased.

RESTITUTORY vs. REPRESSIVE LAW

The Islamic Revolutionary court's verdict was not a sentence passed on gambling as a legal object. This would have required a discourse on legality that, even if inspired by religion, was autonomous enough to withstand the contingency of power exercise. The crowd was not called upon *to give* their evidence against the condemned but *to receive* the verdict of the Islamic authorities who were punishing those who had violated Allah's inalienable rights. The testimony the crowd was called upon to give was not primarily *against* the convicts, but *for* their own membership of the Muslim community. The Islamic court's rule (*hukm*) was far from a legal exercise designed to produce the criminal object (*jurm*).

Before the Revolution it was illegal to make a living from gambling, but private acts of gambling were not as such criminal offences. Gambling only became an issue when it was publicly visible, and sanctions against it only applied when civil pressure failed to keep it invisible. Before the criminal threshold was reached, the community had discretionary power to deal with it. The *Qur'an*'s reference to gambling is arrow-shuffling (*maysir*), a local game for which at the time of the Prophet the stake was a number of slaughtered beasts, mainly camels.[30] The growing number of animals slaughtered in each game led to its prohibition, but no penalty is fixed for the game in the *Qur'an* despite its grouping with other sinful acts (*Encyclopaedia of Islam* 1991; Schacht 1964: 13). Prohibition was later justified by Islamic jurists with reference to its risk-taking (*gharar*), speculative nature (Rayner 1991: 289; Rodinson 1974: 16). It was defined in terms of losses and gains within individual transactions, and gave a secondary role to the *ummat* to apply repressive sanction. The virtual absence of reference to gambling in discussions of Islamic penal law reflects its ambiguous position as a tort or a crime (Doi 1984; Maydani 1955). The little evidence of punishments against gamblers in the past suggests that courts played a less important role than social pressure. The Prophet is said to have ordered believers not to acknowledge gamblers (Rayner 1991: 295–6). The introduction of Iranian civil code in 1936 legally formulated a long ambiguity in Islamic jurisprudence between tort and crime in relation to gambling. Gambling was recognized as a crime by the state *if* it was recognized as tort by the society.

ERASURE/INTEGRATION AND CUSTOM/LAW

The Islamic state now prohibits gambling not primarily for its risk-taking (*gharar*) character, but as a betrayal of the Muslim community. The shift of focus from the individual's loss towards the destruction of the *ummat* undermined the civil protection gambling had hitherto enjoyed. The Muslim community within which gambling was defined as crime was the product of a double process, the erasure by the state of local variations and their integration into a transcendental order. While the erasure took place on an ideological level, the prime site of the imagined Muslim community, the state's rule required a more pragmatic response, i.e. non-interference with the sale of the body in the form of commodified labour. It was also in response to a marked local/non-local difference that the Islamic state relied on the mediation of the Sayyed in the local construction of the *ummat*. Paradoxically, the more the state was forced to take local differences into account in practice, the more it sought to erase them in ideology. Islamic law is built on the ruins of local customs, where its imposition has been historically resisted (Anderson 1976). The Iranian state's growing translation of the ambiguous language of custom into pointed and clearly formulated laws increased this resistance. One feature that distinguished the Islamic state from the Pahlavi one was that the latter, unable to resolve the tension of imposing national law on a local setting, often incorporated customs into a vague Iranian nationhood in order to avoid exacerbating the local/national incompatibilities.

The Islamic state, by contrast, used the popular mandate it had been granted in the revolutionary upheavals to abolish the dichotomy between custom and law. It did not abandon the public/private distinction that continued to be the basis of the separation between civil and criminal offences. This in theory left certain areas free from state intervention. The concession was designed to defuse widespread anxieties. However, as an integral part of the strategy of constructing the Muslim community, the Islamicization of the legal system inevitably redrew the distinction. The latter marked less the restrictions on the power of the state than the threat of its intrusion. The customary ushered in the domination of the state's law over the body of individuals – a tangible object of its power – as the basis of the Muslim community.

In contrast to the ambiguity of the notion of *haqq* (right) among the Lurs, in which the legal and the moral are inextricably linked, the

Islamic state took upon itself to define *haqq* within the limits appropriate to its own rules, or *hukms*. The potential discrepancy between the two – *haqq* and *hukm* – was to be overcome within the ritual practice of the *ummat*, so that *haqq* would correspond to the requirements of state rule (*hukm*). Local spectators were called upon not to watch the flogging but to be the witness of an a-temporal Islamic order which united duty (defined primarily in terms of rule) and right, reflecting the members' demands of the Muslim community. For rulers and ruled alike, the 'identity between the right and the real' was far from clear (Geertz 1983: 189). The appeal to God, the prime and ultimate source of identity between right and real, who speaks through the *Qur'an* and the words and deeds of his Prophet, only indicates the constant need for mobilization to bridge the gap between them. The opposed forces of Paradise and Hell are occasionally mobilized by the contesting parties, but the direction they take is determined within a locality. Such mobilization cannot be effected by an a-historical conception of Islamic law (Arjomand 1989) nor deduced from an equally a-historical notion of Muslim sensibility to legality (Geertz 1983). In both these cases the notion of legality tends to homogenize time and space, eclipsing the significance of the incompatibility between the right and the real in a particular locality. Moreover, the equation of juridical and legal power negates the historical process by which the rule's hegemonic position is secured outside the distinct domain of legality from within which the ruler is authorized to articulate right (*haqq*), drawing on the term's ambiguous moral meaning. It is the tension arising from the uneven formation of the right and the real in the context of the nation-state that informs 'the Islamic legal sensibility' (Geertz 1983). As I have argued above, even a mullah whose position was geared to the permanent validity of Islamic law could not afford to ignore the distinction between norms and facts. The significance placed on witness in the ritual celebration of the Muslim community derives precisely from the need to bridge the gap between the right and the real in a local context. It is this continuous call for witness to testify to the universal validity of the Islamic law that subjects the latter to local customary practices. Paradoxically, the more the law extends, the more vital do local customs become for the law's claim to supremacy. The wider the sphere of law, the more problematic prove to be the connections between *there* – both in metaphorical and literal sense – and *here*.

CONCLUSION

Law has been present in anthropological discourse by proxy. Anthro-pological versions of the 'Hobbesian problem' or the 'problem of order' (Mennell 1980; Giddens 1990) were not legal discourses on sovereignty. Maine's influence on Evans-Pritchard and Dumont is seen through these anthropologists' search for equivalent institutions to law in primitive societies (Appadurai 1992). Unlike political philosophers whose main concern was the state, anthropologists were preoccupied with social integration. Malinowski (1926) saw little difference in obligations created by custom and the 'legal fetters' between individuals and society. Anthropological concern with dispute (e.g. Roberts 1979) left intact the Hobbesian problem as the custom/law dichotomy did not challenge the functionalist premise. The cohesion of social totality was maintained either through the ascendancy of predictable customs or through the uncertainty of the rule of law in human relations (Leach 1977).

The functionalist approach made it impossible to examine the law as a means of domination (Lukes and Scull 1983). The recent shift towards symbolic representation of interests has highlighted the question of domination (Starr and Collier 1989). A characteristic feature of law has been its refusal to acknowledge its own historical/ spatial contingency, which has made it a means for the state to homogenize and dominate the political space as a domain of universals (Hegel 1952; Marx 1963). The state has progressively incorporated local customs by re-defining them and transforming them into laws, thus dissolving the specificity of the local into the generality of the national. Hence the widespread attribution of law as the 'emissary' of the state (Baxi 1990). It has to be recognized that the articulation of specific customs through the generality of law entails more than a juridical mode of power. The symbolic terrain in which legal power is asserted requires a close look into the negotiation for power in the course of which domination is transformed into hegemony, a rule based on consent (Gramsci 1971). Foucault's remarks concerning juridical and social modes of power can be employed to examine the mobilization of meaning at the local level required for a hegemonic construction of legality (Foucault 1982; Macherey 1992). It is through this construction that resistance by the ruled to domination through law can be shown to involve little, if any, recourse to the discourse of law. As a major source of tension in community–state relationships the efficacy of law is not determined

through its articulate use in court, but checked against the recalcitrant, even if non-articulate, reaction of the community. Although
local people can exert little control over the ways in which law
individualizes them as legal subjects, they can more effectively subvert
the process in which they are totalized as members of the community/
society over which the state presides.

NOTES

1   I would like to thank Olivia Harris and Marilyn Strathern for their
    comments. I still remain frustrated by my inability to specify the friend-
    ship and trust I enjoyed among the Lurs during this critical time.
2   Fieldwork was carried out in the province of Kuhgiluyeh and Boir-
    Ahmad between 1979 and 1982 (Sanadjian 1990). The province was
    divided into three sub-provinces of which Kuhgiluyeh with Deh-dasht as
    its capital was the largest.
3   Luri visitors to his office regularly found him sitting behind his desk
    ostentatiously handling an uncovered and apparently loaded pistol
    which he swung around his finger from time to time conjuring up the
    familiar image of a western cowboy among his visitors. Among the harsh
    judgments issued by the old shaikh were several death sentences,
    including a high school boy's, but not before showering abuse on his
    pleading mother.
4   The organization of marches to mourn, say, the death of those killed in
    the battlefields of the Iraq–Iran war, was a post-revolutionary re-
    enactment of the revolutionary dramas of 1977–1979, where the funeral
    processions for those killed during the anti-Shah protests had been
    transformed into mobilization against the state. In the post-Revolu-
    tionary period, the official appropriation of the death of individuals
    became a daily routine for the negotiation of legitimacy by the state.
5   This is a Persian version of Arabic *umma*.
6   The situation described here happened only two and a half years after the
    February 1979 revolution that toppled the Pahlavi regime. The Islamic
    state formed in the aftermath of revolutionary change went through
    stages of increasing repression, each characterized by an attempt to
    resolve social conflict, and each representing a further abdication from
    the political field of the social classes and strata that had constituted the
    backbone of the Revolution. The context described here belongs to a
    period when the Islamic regime, having ousted the first president of the
    Islamic Republic in June 1980, and put opposition groups in their
    thousands in front of firing squads, was consolidating its position in a
    war-torn country and using terror to deal with everyday forms of
    resistance . Although I have not visited the place nor been able to write
    to local friends since I left Iran in the summer of 1982, I understand that
    the situation of the Lurs has remained unstable. The firm grip of the
    regime has not been loosened but its moral authority has been dented by
    corruption scandals, local and national, in an ever deepening economic

crisis characterized by soaring inflation and chronic shortages of basic necessities. Today abuse of power seems to have been displaced by a more quantifiable abuse of economic resources. The use of repressive methods, although it has by no means disappeared, seems to have been exhausted, a fact reflected in the current efforts by the former prominent agents of the regime to make conciliatory gestures towards local people. I have tried to remain attentive to the need to historicize this unstable context by avoiding historical extrapolation. Hence the apparent inconsistency in the use of present and past tense in my ethnographic account.

7   These statues typically represented less a sign of stability (Handelman 1990: 4) than the instant monitoring of the public sphere of which it was a monumental expression. In the eyes of the Shahs, everything public necessarily assumed the threatening character of the political (cf. Heller 1991: 342).

8   The planner of Deh-dasht, a young non-Luri political dissident, had told a Luri friend in confidence at the time that he had deliberately provided no space for the silencing statues and the associated ceremonies of the Shah's officials.

9   According to the national census of November 1976, there were only 794 *'ashayir* households in the province, i.e. 1.9 per cent of its population (*Farahang-i* n.d.: 3). The *'ashayiri* (tribal) household is defined in the census as one 'dependent on tribe or sect' and 'not living in a permanent residence at the time of enumeration'. The discrepancy between the recorded reality of nomadism and its popular conception raises an issue beyond that of numerical accuracy. As a signifier *'ashayir* – 'nomads' – does not need to match its signified. This is important in the light of the anthropological obsession with pastoral nomadism in Iran and elsewhere in the Middle East. One cannot adequately understand what the *'ashayir* signifies unless one sees the 'nomad' as a 'handyman' (*bricoleur*), which allows them to take a creative part in the encompassing system while remaining outside of it. The bricolage of nomadism places the *'ashayir* simultaneously inside and outside the law.

10   The distinction made here between the juridical and the legal is not designed to highlight the pre-modern character of the Islamic regime. Drawing on Foucault, I define the juridical mode as a negative form of power exercise, primarily concerned with what is permitted and forbidden. The object is made accessible in this mode of power as a 'thing' divorced from social relationships in which the body is embedded, the site of production of the subject. The legal, on the other hand, is distinguished as an action upon a set of relations and geared to the production of the subject. Although Foucault has examined the emergence of the legal as the product of modern social and economic change (Foucault 1975) it is not equated here with modernity. The juridical/legal distinction is used as an analytical tool to examine various forms of power in a rapidly changing situation. I have used them to investigate how the Islamic regime attempts to reorganize civil society by denying it the relative privilege it had previously been granted to exercise power on its members. This enables the state to turn the latter into its immediate object of the exercise of power. The Islamic state's abolition of dis-

ciplinary procedures in which the members were produced as subjects, including legal ones, was, however, far from even. For example, there was little interference with disciplinary processes, in which labour was turned into commodity.

11   Foucault's approach to power has the merit of going beyond the use of force and looking for power relations in all aspects of human life. His interest, however, in the anatomy of the 'microphysics of power' has been at the expense of due consideration for what Stuart Hall has called the 'macrohydraulics of power' (Hall 1988: 70). Although attentive to non-discursive forces which bear on discourses (Dirks et al. 1994), Foucault refuses to recognize the determining effect of organization of these forces not only by the state but also civil society. My aim here, on the other hand, is to look at the interchange between the concentrated area of power which Foucault largely fails to consider, and dispersed forms of power of which he is a brilliant investigator. I have tried to demonstrate the organizing impact of the post-revolutionary state on power relations inscribed within the society in Iran. Such a focus on the agency of the state and civil society makes it possible to examine a new 'economy of power' used by the Islamic state to overrule the social and the legal as distinct, relatively autonomous domains of action. The revitalization of this juridical mode of power by the state militates against the Foucaul-dian notion of discipline based on the society's organization of surveil-lance expressed in legal terms (Foucault 1975).

12   The status of gambling in Islamic rules is in fact quite ambiguous, as I shall discuss below.

13   The Islamic state's concern to construct a homogeneous national semantic space in this remote locality militated against a more flexible, local-based interaction between spectators and convicts. This was in contrast to a predominantly local response to spectacular punishments of regicide (Foucault 1975; Rejali 1994), or local robbers reported from previous centuries (Blok 1989).

14   My distress at taking part in this depressing event was quickly somatized in a severe, persistent neck pain.

15   It has to be noted that the scarcity of different forms of property, landed or otherwise, among the Lurs had historically endowed them with a meagre source of rights compared with the ones available to many other Iranians.

16   This is not a 'bloodless' ethnographic account. The relative absence of the 'voice' of those who took part in these dramatic events in this account is not a positivistic device to enhance scientific objectivity. Indeed, for me to remain silent was an essential part of participating in the Lurs' social and political life under the circumstances. Away from the scene of the public flogging I did not find the Lurs' reaction anything but muted. Even in much more tragic situations when I found a Luri friend grieving for a son or brother executed by the regime's firing squads the restraint shown was remarkable, despite their detailed accounts of painful efforts to recover the dead bodies of their kin. The silence was not the result of a discrepancy between my curiosity and Lurs' lack of response, as I often felt compelled to remain silent, but reflected the lack of space in which

they could express the new grief. Their response to death, particularly the death of young relatives, is typically expressive of the tragic occasion. For example, on one occasion a young Luri friend was sitting next to me in a car and describing the unexpected execution of his high school student brother. I would not have realized that he was crying if he had not moved to get a handkerchief out of his pocket and the driver had not passed to him quietly a pack of cigarettes. Paradoxically, participation in such tormenting experiences forced me to share with the Lurs this lack of space which had made them 'voiceless'.

17   He was locally respected because he chose to make a living from his own work, including working the land, despite his entitlement to donations as a descendant of the Prophet and as a learned person.

18   One Luri man who had recently become *haji* revealed the growing tension between accumulation and redistribution. Explaining to me why he had made the pilgrimage to Mecca, he complained that once people see your (economic) situation is improved they start to remind you that it is now incumbent on you to become *haji*. Pilgrimage diverted a man's accumulated resources towards negotiating a social position.

19   That this was a new economy of power rather than autarchy is detectable in the growing call in the West for retaliatory, quick response to crimes.

20   The negation of the notion of society in the construction of the Muslim community is more explicit in literary Islamic sources (Sanadjian 1994b).

21   Foucault attributes the strength of individualizing forces in modern western states to the pastoral power of Christianity since the eighteenth century (Foucault 1982: 783). Thus, by refusing to recognize the 'macro-hydraulics of power' of civil society (see note 11 above) whose colossal force Europe began to feel in this period, Foucault is able to mystify the process of individualization. In post-revolutionary Iran the Islamic state resorted to pastoral power in order to short-circuit access to its subjects. The source of this pastoral power cannot be dug out of Shi'ism but lies in the attempt by the Islamic state to neutralize the individualizing forces of an unevenly developed civil society that the state sought to transcend.

22   A significant difference between the Pahlavi and Islamic penal system was that the latter regarded imprisonment not as a punishment but as a 'coercive measure which aims at repentance' (Schacht 1964: 176). The Islamic regime's use of the prison demonstrated vividly this 'economy of power'. Political prisoners were frequently reminded by Islamic officials in prison assemblies of the dire consequences of failing to show repentance. It was not the regime's concern to feed them. This attitude towards prison made it far more dangerous for political prisoners. By contrast, prison offered the Shah's political prisoners some of protection against the harassment and intimidation they were subjected to outside jail.

23   'In Islamic jurisprudence, the word *huddud* is limited to punishment for crimes mentioned by the Holy Qur'an or the Sunnah [traditions] of the Prophet while other punishments are left to the discretion of the Qadi [judge] or the ruler which are called Ta'azir' (Doi 1984: 221).

24   A differentiated, complex notion of society and the concomitant recognition of social processes were particularly lacking in the treatment of political offenders by the Shah's regime. The torture systematically used

against its opponents was not only physical, but involved stripping the offenders of their social agency by dubbing them as incestuous, anti-God, 'communist'. A Muslim political activist was reported to have called upon God loudly to help him withstand the pain while being beaten by a SAVAK agent. The call made the agent stop torturing the prisoner immediately and seek God's mercy! By evoking God the political prisoner placed himself on the same terrain on which his Muslim torturer operated, from which the agent had excluded him in order to use his body to obtain information.

25 Many Luri couplets are about rifles, particularly the Bruno (Ghafari 1983).

26 The official punishment in nineteenth-century Iran. The convict was beaten with a stick on the soles of the feet.

27 Beating is used fairly widely by Luri men against women in the domestic sphere. Such use of physical force has been geared to a clearly demarcated private domestic domain which is a recent phenomenon. It was harder for Luri men to use force against women in the past without visibly offending the wider kin group.

28 There seems to be little gain in using the notion of right to compare these different contexts of beating. The concept of human right cannot be meaningfully raised outside a 'horizontal comradeship' and homogeneous time within which individuality, the basis of a notion of right, can be sustained. However important a means of comparison, right is not the sole or even the most effective means of a cross-cultural comparison of violence. As I have described here, my notions of rights actually obstructed my appreciation both of the Lurs' noisy subversion and their silent resentment. Power and the interest at stake provide a more tangible framework for understanding violent acts.

29 It was the likely presence of many relatives of the convicts that had motivated the Islamic officials to seek the arbitration of the respected Sayyid.

30 'O you who believe! intoxicants [wine drinking] and games of chance [arrow-shuffling] and (sacrificing) to stones [idols] set up and (divining by) arrows are only an uncleanness, the Satan's work; shun it therefore that you may be successful' (*Holy Qur'an* 1985: 109 [Chapter V, 90]). The only other reference to arrow-shuffling (*maysir*) in the *Qur'an* is in Chapter II, 219, where it is prohibited along with wine drinking (*khumr*) (*Holy Qur'an* 1985: 30). The Qur'anic prohibition later lost its local reference in the hands of Islamic jurists who translated it into a generic term of gambling (*qimar*) (see also Rayner 1991: 292).

REFERENCES

Anderson, N. (1976) *Law Reform in the Muslim World*, London: University of London/The Athlone Press.

Appadurai, A. (1992) 'Putting hierarchy in its place', in G. E. Marcus (ed.) *Reading Cultural Anthropology*, Durham: Duke University Press.

Arjomand, S. A. (1989) 'Constitution-making in Islamic Iran: the impact of theocracy on the legal order of a nation-state', in J. Starr and J. F. Collier (eds) *History and Power in the Study of Law: New Directions in Legal Anthropology*, Ithaca: Cornell University Press.

Ayoub, M. (1978) *Redemptive Suffering in Islam: A Study of the Devotional Aspects of 'Ashura in Twelver Shi'ism*, The Hague: Mouton Publishers.

Baxi, U. (1990) ' "The state's emissary": the place of law in subaltern studies', *Subaltern Studies* vii: 247–69.

Blok, A. (1989) 'Symbolic vocabulary of public executions', in J. Starr and J. F. Collier (eds) *History and Power in the Study of Law: New Directions in Legal Anthropology*, Ithaca: Cornell University Press.

Clastres, P. (1977) *Society Against the State*, Oxford: Basil Blackwell.

Dirks, N. B., Eley, G. and Ortner, S. B. (1994) 'Introduction', in N. B. Dirks *et al.* (eds) *Culture/Power/History: A Reader in Contemporary Social Theory*, New Jersey: Princeton University Press.

Doi, 'Abdur Rahman I (1984) *Shari'ah: the Islamic Law*, London: Taha Publishers.

Durkheim, E. (1965) *Elementary Forms of the Religious Life*, trans. J.W. Seain, New York: Free Press.

—— (1983) 'From repressive to restitutory law', in S. Lukes and A. Scull (eds) *Durkheim and the Law*, Oxford: Martin Robertson.

Encyclopaedia of Islam (1991), new edition, vol. 6.

Farhang-i-abadiha-yi kishvar, ostan-i-Kuhgiluyeh va Boir Ahmad, n.d. vol. 17, Statistical Centre of Iran.

Foucault, M. (1975) *Discipline and Punish: The Birth of Prison*, trans. A. Sheridan, London: Penguin Books.

—— (1980) 'Lecture Two: 14 January 1976', in C. Gordon (ed.) Foucault, *Power/Knowledge*, Brighton: Harvester.

—— (1982) 'The subject and power', *Critical Inquiry* 8(4): 777–95.

Geertz, C. (1983) 'Local knowledge: fact and law in comparative perspective', in C. Geertz *Local Knowledge: Further Essays in Interpretive Anthropology*, New York: Basic Books.

Ghafari, Y. (1983) *Nimuneh-'i az ash'ar-i mahali-yi mardum-i Kuhgilueh va Boir Ahmad va sharh-i kutahi az zindigi-yi 'Kiy Luhras'*, Yasuj, 1362/1983.

Giddens, A. (1990) *The Consequences of Modernity*, Cambridge: Polity Press.

Gramsci, A. (1971) *Selection from the Prison Notebooks*, London: Lawrence & Wishart.

Guilaume, A. (1956) *Islam*, Harmondsworth: Penguin Books.

Hall, S. (1988) 'The road to the garden: Thatcherism among the theorists', in G. Nelson and L. Grossberg (eds) *Marxism and Interpretation of Culture*, Urbana: University of Illinois Press.

Handelman, D. (1990) *Models and Mirrors: Towards an Anthropology of Public Events*, Cambridge: Cambridge University Press.

Hegel, G. W. (1942) *Philosophy of Right*, Oxford: Oxford University Press.

Heller, A. (1991) 'The concept of the political revisited', in D. Held (ed.) *Political Theory Today*, Cambridge: Polity Press.

Hirst, P. (1981) 'The genesis of the social', *Politics & Power* 3: 67–82.

Holy Qur'an (1985), trans. M.H. Shakir, London: Muhammadi Trust.

Hunt, A. (1992) 'A socialist interest in law', *New Left Review* 192: 105–19.

Kiernan, V.G. (1976) 'Private property in history', in J. Goody, J. Thirsk and

E.P. Thompson (eds) *Family and Inheritance: Rural Society in Western Europe, 1200–1800*, Cambridge: Cambridge University Press.

Lacroix, B. (1979) 'The elementary forms of religious life as a reflection of power', *Critique of Anthropology* 4(13/14): 87–103.

Leach, E. (1977) *Custom, Law, and Terrorist Violence*, Edinburgh: Edinburgh University Press.

Lukes, S. and Scull, A. (1983) 'Introduction', in S. Lukes and A. Scull (eds) *Durkheim and the Law*, Oxford: Martin Robertson.

Macherey, P. (1992) 'Towards a natural history of norms', in T.J. Armstrong (ed.) *Michel Foucault: Philosopher*, Hemel Hempstead: Harvester Wheatsheaf.

Malinowski, B. (1926) *Crime and Custom in Savage Society*, London: Routledge & Kegan Paul.

Marx, K. (1963[1843]) 'On the Jewish question', in T. Bottomore (ed.) *K. Marx: Early Writings*, London: C. A. Watts.

Maydani, R. (1955) 'Uqubat': Penal Law', in M. Khadduri and H. J. Liebrsny (eds) *Law in the Middle East*, vol. 1, Washington DC: The Middle East Institute.

Mennell, S. (1980) *Sociological Theory: Uses and Unities*, 2nd edition, Walton-on Thames, Surrey: Nelson.

Parkin, D. (1992) 'Rituals as spatial direction and bodily division', in D. de Coppet (ed.) *Understanding Rituals*, London: Routledge.

Rayner, S.E. (1991) *The Theory of Contracts in Islamic Law*, London: Graham & Trothman.

Rejali, D. M. (1994) *Torture and Modernity: Self, Society, and State in Modern Iran*, Boulder: Westview Press.

Roberts, S. (1979) *Order and Dispute: An Introduction to Legal Anthropology*, Harmondsworth: Penguin Books.

Rodinson, M. (1974) *Islam and Capitalism*, Harmondsworth: Penguin Books.

Rosen, L. (1989) 'Islamic "case law" and the logic of consequence', in J. Starr and J. F. Collier (eds) *History and Power in the Study of Law: New Directions in Legal Anthropology*, Ithaca: Cornell University Press.

Sanadjian, M. (1987) *The Articulation of Luri Society and Economy with the Outside World: A Growing Paradox in a South-Western Province of Iran*, Unpublished D.Phil. thesis, University of Oxford.

—— (1990) 'From participant to partisan observation: an open end', *Critique of Anthropology* 10(4): 113–34.

—— (1994a) 'State and civil society', London: Goldsmiths' College.

—— (1994b) 'Witnessing, an Islamic rite of passage and a local/non-local articulation', unpublished paper.

Schacht, J. (1964) *An Introduction to Islamic Law*, Oxford: Clarendon Press.

Starr, J. and Collier, J. F. (1989) 'Introduction: dialogues in legal anthropology', in J. Starr and J. F. Collier (eds) *History and Power in the Study of Law: New Directions in Legal Anthropology*, Ithaca: Cornell University Press.

Taheri, A. (1978) *Mamiru*, Yasuj.

Tambiah, S. J. (1979) 'A performative approach to ritual', *Proceedings of the British Academy* LXV: 113–69.

Chapter 9

Which centre, whose margin?
Notes towards an archaeology of US Supreme Court Case 91–948, 1993 (*Church of the Lukumí vs. City of Hialeah, South Florida*)

Stephan Palmié

On 11 June 1993, the US Supreme Court unanimously overruled a set of ordinances passed some six years earlier by the City of Hialeah, a Cuban-dominated, largely blue-collar incorporated city within the Greater Miami metropolitan area. Though two lower courts had previously upheld these ordinances, the Supreme Court found that they unlawfully suppressed practices protected under the US Con-stitution's First Amendment's guarantee of Freedom of Religious Exercise. The practices in question were what adherents of the Afro-Cuban religion *regla ocha* or Santería call *dar de comer al oricha* ('to feed the god[s]'), and consider indispensable to the maintenance of human–divine relations. As Chief Justice Kennedy correctly stated, though powerful, the deities of *regla ocha* are not immortal: 'They depend for survival on the sacrifice [of animals]'. Moreover, '[g]iven the historical association between animal sacrifice and religious worship', the court's opinion continues, the 'petitioners' assertion that animal sacrifice is an integral part of their religion cannot be deemed bizarre or incredible' (Justice Kennedy, quoted in *New York Times*, National Edition, 12 June 1993). If so, the City of Hialeah had overstepped the bounds of its legitimate authority. By prohibiting 'to unnecessarily kill, torment, torture, or mutilate an animal in a private or public ceremony not for the primary purpose of food consumption' (Ordinance 87–52, City of Hialeah), it had tampered with behaviours which the nation's founding document explicitly locates beyond the reach of its power to prosecute. By placing the Santeros' catering to their deities' appetites under constitutional protection, the Supreme Court turned Hialeah's law-makers into law-breakers.

Here, it would seem, we have a prime case of centripetal movement, driven by the power of the American legal system to discursively constitute its own object. The artefact that emerged from the process,

US Supreme Court case number 91–948, *Church of the Lukumí Babalu Ayé vs. City of Hialeah*, unmistakably located the margin in the centre. 'Although the practice of animal sacrifice may seem abhorrent to some', reads Justice Kennedy's opinion, 'religious beliefs need not be acceptable, logical or comprehensible to others in order to merit First Amendment protection' (quoted in *New York Times*, 12 June 1993). The logic of its own forensic discourse compelled the secular state to safeguard the dietary habits of the divine. Though perhaps only by legal proxy, the *oricha* are now residents of the United States. If it accomplished anything, the case inscribed their presence into the law of the land.

The decision's more mundane consequences seemed immediately obvious. As Herman Cohen, chief law enforcement officer of the ASPCA, put it in an interview with the *New York Times* on the day of the verdict, '[u]ntil today, taking an animal into a living room, cutting its throat, and saying a prayer was prohibited ... I don't know if that's true anymore'. 'Changó has blessed us at last' the same article reported as the reaction of Ernesto Pichardo, the man who had originally sued the City of Hialeah; 'the future is to institutionalize the Santería religion. We will do it as soon as we can.' Enoelia Martinez, owner of Hialeah's Botanica La Luz, a store selling Afro-Cuban ritual paraphernalia, commented: '[t]his is very good for me', anticipating, presumably, not only a brisk pickup in business, but the potential for future exemption from city retail licensing fees (*New York Times*, National Edition, 13 June 1993).

By projecting the semantic reach of its legal apparatus into an unsettled area of discourse, the American state had created a frontier on which several interested parties were already busily relocating their projects. It is too early to gauge the results of these activities. At face value, it would seem that Pichardo is right in predicting that the thrust of movement will be directed inward, leading to further acts of appropriation across increasingly porous borders between centre and margin. On the other hand, spatializing the history of *Church of the Lukumí Babalu Ayé vs. City of Hialeah* as a movement from the margin of a landscape of power and legitimacy to its centre is in itself a problematic manoeuvre. Most obvious is the danger of confusing legal discourse with its referent by collapsing a multifaceted processual turbulence into a singular, and seemingly transparent, event marked 'outcome'. More importantly, such a view fails to address the fact that *in relation to process* topical notions such as centre and margin presuppose narrative. Their relationship cannot be known, or at least remains arbitrary, unless it is told. This raises the possibility of multiple centres and margins constituted within a variety of stories arising out of a heterogeneous universe of discourse, and informed by various positioned subjectivities. Legal discourse frames one such narrative, and, as I will try to show, case 91–948 is but a thinly spread icing on a thickly layered cake of stories. Cutting into this hetero-glossic cake is a modest archaeological task. To this end I switch to narrative myself.

KNOW THINE ENEMY

Though constantly brewing somewhere, trouble always starts at a fixed point. There is no narrative without a point after which nothing will ever be the same. Empirically, there is always a profusion of such points or thresholds hidden in the plot of events, waiting to be overridden in retrospective – or sometimes prospective – construc-tions. Wielding some narrative authority myself, I shall pick one such point and say that trouble started in mid-May 1987, when a sign reading 'Iglesia Lukumí Babalu-Ayé' appeared in front of a small brick building on a former used car dealer's lot in a moderately depressed area of Hialeah. Its unpretentious appearance suggested another addition to Hialeah's growing number of Hispanic storefront congregations, but the Church of the Lukumí Babalu Ayé represented something unique. It was the first legally accredited institution of worship serving a group of practitioners of *regla ocha*, an Afro-Cuban religion popularly known as Santería. In the fall of the preceding year, these Santeros had managed to gain official recognition as a church organization from the State of Florida and, having consulted their gods for guidance in selecting a propitious location, had set up shop at the corner of West Fifth Avenue and Okeechobee Road in Hialeah. Within days they were facing fierce opposition.

The most obvious problem was that Santería worship entails animal sacrifice – a fact that had enraged Dade County residents ever since the first reports of such practices appeared in the press in the early 1970s. By then, the ongoing exodus from revolutionary Cuba had strengthened the ranks of a reconsolidating Afro-Cuban reli-gious community in exile[1] to a degree where its ritual activities were bound to attract the attention and disapproval of the general public. Fuelled by the local media – quick to exploit the sensationalist potential of Santería in headlines like 'drums beating and animals shrieking frighten South-West Dade residents' (*Miami Herald*, 25

November 1979) or 'ritual sacrifices turn Miami River red' (*Miami Herald*, 30 May 1981) – the controversy over what many of Dade County's 'Anglo' residents perceived as a morally subversive foreign cult infiltrating their community surfaced again and again throughout the 1970s and early 1980s. Yet despite a rising tide of repression, the growth of Santería continued. Today maybe 10 per cent of Greater Miami's more than 600,000 Cuban-American citizens practise *regla ocha* and/or other Afro-Cuban religions, and there are strong indications that these religions are branching out into other ethnic sectors as well.[2]

There were other problems, too. Whether or not the gods had planned this in sanctioning the choice of Hialeah as a location for the church, the members of the Church of the Lukumí Babalu Ayé must have known that they were courting confrontation. Santería had not descended upon South Florida out of the blue and for many of Dade County's Anglo residents, its spread merely represented a symptom of a more pervasive malaise: the perceived loss of control over the economy, social life and culture of their environment, brought about by post-1959 Cuban immigration. Especially in Hialeah, 'Hispanization' had been rapid and thorough, leaving the town squarely in the hands of a Cuban majority by the end of the 1970s. In that sense, Hialeah had been heading towards an inter-ethnic confrontation for quite a while, and for many of its disgruntled Anglo residents a Santería church opening in their hometown represented not only the ultimate affront, but also a welcome opportunity for the externalization and focusing of diffuse anti-Hispanic feelings.

Tension quickly spilled over into the public arena. In a city council meeting on 9 June 1987, Hialeah saw the first of a series of impassioned debates on the legitimacy of what most participants considered an atavistic superstition, 'devil worship', or, worse yet, an outright assault upon American civilization. Though in itself of little consequence, this event is worth attention, for it set the stage for the confused transcultural dialogue that ensued, and established some of its discursive conventions. Most notable was the tendency on the part of Hialeah's concerned citizens to construe themselves into a community under attack, not so much by a group of individuals contending the boundaries of legally permissible behaviour, but by an ill-defined, even mysterious, force threatening to corrupt the moral and physical fibre of Hialeah's social body. By the same token, the obscure nature of the malignant agent did not preclude knowing: Santería was one of the things that are 'always already known', but beg telling. For example Pat Keller of the Allapattah Community Association, who claimed to have lived 'next door to Santería for 7 years', recalled in phantasmagoric detail that her

> nights were filled with horror: drums beating and animals crying. I witnessed the throat-cutting. The animals' life ebbed away. The madman danced around the animals and I saw the stark terror in the creatures' eyes as they died. . . . The heavy involvement in drugs with the people in Santería is well known. It was written up in the *Miami Magazine*. I witnessed the drug scenes involved with Santería. The madmen, the Santeríans ingested the drugs as they proceed with their horror scenes. The little white bags are distributed afterwards and that's the end of the horror scenes as the animal's life ebbs away. Our health is threatened . . . I can't make any definite statements, but I'm going to ask that we ask ourselves some questions. AIDS is transmitted by blood. . . . Santería, as I told you, engages in the drinking and exchanging of blood. [. . .] We do know that AIDS is spread by drug users; Santeríans are heavy users of drugs. Under the influence of the drugs more blood is exchanged; the human and animal blood. The dead creatures, as you know, are thrown into our waterways or streets and our vacant lots. Some have jobs in the restaurant field. There could be blood on their hands. Under their nails. And your gracious waiter may be a Santería practitioner who drank blood the previous evening. I am forced to ask the question, conclude with a question: AIDS has spread like wildfire. Santería has grown like wildfire here in Miami, Hialeah. Are the two related?
>
> (Hialeah City Council, 9 June 1987, tape recording)

Apart from fears of contamination unleashed by the fantastic transgressions attributed to the Santeros, the tape recording of that meeting imparts an equally strong sense of sacred abomination and divine wrath: ' . . . if we allow such a thing, a satanic, satan worshipping church in this city', the Reverend Reynaldo Medina exhorted the council,

> the city that prospers may not be so prosperous anymore! Because the blessing, the prosperous blessing of god over this city could just turn into a dark cloud, because instead of a blessing this will bring a curse upon the city!
>
> (Hialeah City Council, 9 June 1987, tape recording)

Julio de Silva, Chaplain of the Hialeah Police Department, put the matter even more succinctly: 'Nations that are controlled by this system of religion are in darkness, and the Bible says that these things are an abomination to the Lord' (Hialeah City Council, 9 June 1987, tape recording). Clearly, there was a higher mandate the council itself had invoked when asking the Lord's blessings in the meeting's opening prayer. There *did* exist a central authority to which their own discursive practice had made them answerable.

DARK CLOUDS

In a three-hour symbolic purge, the Santeros were accused of every evil thought to be plaguing South Florida: from drug abuse and the corruption of public morale to cannibalism, the poisoning of Hialeah's water supplies, and the spread of AIDS. Yet it was not only the predictable antagonism of nativistic community organizations, animal protection agencies, and fundamentalist Christian groups that the Iglesia Lukumí Babalu-Ayé found itself contending with: what may have come as a surprise to the Santeros was how eagerly a majority of Hialeah's Cuban-Americans joined the crusade against them. 'No hay peor cuña que la del mismo palo', *Miami Herald* reporter Patricia Duarte would later write:

> Didn't it strike you that five out of Hialeah's seven council men are Cubans? That the pastors and ministers who have protested against the Iglesia Lukumí Babalu-Ayé over the radio and in front of the Council are Latins, too? That so far no Hispanic organization has entered the battleground in *public* defence of the Santeros?
> (*El Herald*, 21 June 1987)

By branding the Afro-Cuban religions as deviant and 'un-American', the adversaries of the Church of the Lukumí Babalu Ayé struck a responsive chord. Like Martha Lechuga, a twenty-six-year-old college student who implored Hialeah's councilmen to 'help her keep her pride in being a Cuban-American', many other members of 'the community in exile' sensed the danger of losing control over a version of 'cubanidad' that did *not* employ the symbols of Afro-Cuban religious culture as emblems of contrast against their North American host society. Although Santería had been practised privately even by members of the pre-revolutionary Cuban elite, in public it had always carried the stigma of a former slave religion and had acquired even more pernicious connotations in the United States. Though the issue rarely surfaced in public discourse, a major factor in structuring the reaction of Dade County's Cuban community was their knowledge about, and strategic appropriation of, American constructions of 'race'.

Cuban racism takes different, and in many ways more subtle, forms than the rigid colour line typical of North American society. Yet although most Cubans reject large parts of their host society's racial ideology, they cannot help being impacted by it. Living in a society which collapses their traditionally fluid, or, at least, multi-tiered racial typology into the two categories of 'Hispanic' and 'black', and whose value system attaches extremely negative connotations to the latter, has added a new dimension of racial self-consciousness to their culture. Ever since the large-scale influx of dark-skinned lower-class Cubans during the so-called Mariel Exodus of 1980, and the tremendous social problems that followed tarnished their image as upwardly mobile Caucasian immigrants, South Florida's Cubans react rather sensitively to the issue of race – especially when faced with the possibility of being cast, *pars pro toto*, as a 'coloured' group by indiscriminately racist Southern whites.

The surfacing of an ostensibly African-derived piece of Cuban cultural baggage as a marker for their collective identity evoked deep-seated fears of public degradation; fears that overrode not only whatever attachment they felt towards the Afro-Cuban part of their cultural heritage, but also whatever feelings of ethnic solidarity they entertained towards the Santeros who, after all, were Cubans too. To compound their conceptual and moral problems, what they were confronting was only nominally a 'black religion'. At the time, the Church of the Lukumí Babalu Ayé was almost exclusively composed of persons phenotypically 'white' even by American standards. Though its President, Ernesto Pichardo, claims religious descent from nineteenth-century enslaved Africans hailing from what he calls 'the *ara takuá* nation',[3] he likewise takes pride in being of 'pure' Spanish–French extraction, not much more than four generations removed from Europe. Like many of his fellow Santeros in exile, Pichardo projects the image of a dapper, fluently bilingual Cuban-American businessman – just what South Florida's economic elite looks like today.

Whether conscious of the fact or not, in defending a favourable definition of 'cubanidad' they had developed in relation to their host society, many of Miami's 'good Cubans' wound up in an uneasy coalition with the same nativistic elements of South Florida's Anglo-American society they were fighting on other accounts. A good example of the mounting confusion about where to locate centre and margin in a moral landscape cluttered with colour-coded value markers is an anonymous letter Pichardo received in the summer of 1987, in which 'Concerned Citizen' demanded that Pichardo 'go back where you crawled from some pigsty in Haiti', because 'we find your kind so ugly that I want to throw up if I see your black faces'. Tellingly, the letter concluded 'no future here for you, some Cubans will get rid of [you] some way'.

Still, while publicly marginalizing Santería as a ludicrous black lower-class superstition, many Cubans have highly ambivalent feelings about the possible reality of the powers Santeros wield. For one commentator in a tabloid geared to a Cuban audience, the events of the spring of 1987 fed a nightmare peculiar to a community for whom the state of exile had become a *raison d'être*: reporting the honours Fidel had bestowed upon a Yoruba king visiting Cuba, Pedro Roman speculated that by facilitating a meeting of local *babalaos* (divination specialists) with this representative of the African culture from which Santería had taken its origins, the 'red monster' himself had launched yet another attack – this time supernaturally reinforced – against his exiled opponents. Was not the constant fractioning of political groups in exile, Roman suggested, evidence of the effects of African witch-craft harnessed to Communist goals? (*Teve-Latino* no. 61, 12–18 June 1987).

A POLITICAL CURSE

The situation was aggravated by the unexpected turn things had taken in the June council meeting: while outbursts of fear and aggression from Hialeah's Anglo minority mingled with Cuban-American pledges of allegiance to mainstream values and the apocalyptic rhetoric of fundamentalist ministers, Hialeah's City Council was facing a legal impasse, because Florida's so-called 'kosher law' explicitly allows the slaughter of animals for religious purposes. Although the council passed an emergency ordinance against animal sacrifice to appease the raging audience, even city attorneys openly voiced their doubts about its legality. Pressure built up during the next few months. Council as well as mayoral elections were coming up in the fall, and as Reynaldo Medina, pastor of one of Hialeah's many Cuban-American Protestant congregations, had stated in the June meeting, these elections would tell 'who voted for what or against what!'. However, for Hialeah's political elite the situation was more complex, and it seems likely that some of them had private qualms about taking a decisive stand against the Santería church. Five years earlier, Maurice Ferré, the ex-mayor of Miami and a decidedly more cosmopolitan politician than any of them, had been accused of spending $1,500 of campaign funds for a Santería ceremony staged by a former campaign worker who had allegedly delivered the votes of 2,000 Santeros (*Miami Herald*, 18 July 1982 and 1 July 1984). Puerto Rican Ferré had retorted at the time that criticizing a politician for attending a Santería ritual would be 'like telling a politician in Boston he shouldn't go to St. Anthony's parade or the St. Patrick Day's parade'. Santería was 'a reality in the Cuban world' and 'a reality in Miami politics' (*Miami Herald*, 18 July 1982).

The truth of that statement must have dawned upon Hialeah's notables as the controversy dragged on. One of the ironies of the case was that the property on which the Santeros had planted their church had recently played a significant role in the downfall of one of their colleagues, councilman Sebastian Dorrego, who had offered to sell his vote on a commercial re-zoning for a $15,000 bribe. The bribe never materialized, Dorrego went to jail and the landowner, Julio Navarro, leased out the place to the Santeros instead – not without malicious intent, as some people in Hialeah think. 'A political curse hangs over the home of South Florida's first public Santería church', the *Miami News* reported on 8 June 1987, and Dorrego was not to be its only victim. As became known in 1990, mayor Raul Martinez himself had previously tried to buy the property in question for a 'steep discount' and, after Navarro had declined, had vetoed the zoning change. As far back as 1984, Navarro had informed the FBI about Dorrego's attempt at extortion and had even taped a phone conversation with Dorrego's middleman. Ironically, the 'distribution of culture' worked in Dorrego's and Martinez' favour: it was not until 1986 when a Spanish-speaking prosecutor was put on the case that these tapes were 'rediscovered' as evidence (*Miami Herald*, 4 April 1990).

Rumour had it that offers to negotiate were ventured by individual politicians trying to get the Santeros to move quietly. By the end of the summer local papers supporting particular candidates for the mayoral elections were levelling accusations of complicity with the Santeros against the respective rivals. The mayor, for one, publicly charged that 'the timing of the opening [of the church], which has attracted the attention of the national press, is calculated to embarrass him in the upcoming re-election' (*Florida Today*, 26 July 1987). 'Que se ponga de pie el verdadero señor Babalu Ayé' – 'will the real Mr Babalu

Ayé please stand up?', asked *El Sol de Hialeah* on 22 October, implicating former councilman and current candidate for mayoral elections, Paulino Nuñez. The Santeros gleefully joined in the fray. On 20 August, the president of the Church of the Lukumí Babalu Ayé, Ernesto Pichardo, confirmed to the *Hialeah Home News* that several city officials were privately tapping Afro-Cuban religious resources. Nor had the legal issue been settled. By July the *babalao* Rigoberto Zamora began running legal notices in local newspapers stating the intent of an organization named Afro-Cuban Lucumí Association to open a Temple of Olofí Babalawo in an unspecified Miami shopping mall (*Miami Herald*, 16 July 1987). Although the venture apparently never materialized, it demonstrated how far the foiled 'landmark decision' had left the door open to religious entrepreneurs steering towards legal recognition in the wake of Pichardo's pilot boat.

In August, finally, after prolonged manoeuvring on the part of Hialeah's city fathers, a provisional decision was made to render the Santería church inoperative by outlawing its sacrificial practices on the grounds both of the questionable ordinances, and of pre-existing zoning regulations prohibiting the keeping of animals on its premises. To preclude all eventualities – such as the church surreptitiously transforming itself into a licensed stockyard – the city's language made clear that Hialeah was *not* zoned for commercial slaughter. On 14 September 1987, mayor Martinez approved the final version of a bill outlawing the sacrifice and possession for sacrificial purposes of animals in the city of Hialeah.[4] The 'Good Cubans' finally had their way, or so it seemed. Less than two weeks later, the city was facing a legal charge of violation of First Amendment rights to freedom of religion backed by the American Civil Liberties Union. Far from being intimidated, and well aware of the workings of the American legal system, Ernesto Pichardo and the Church of the Lukumí Babalu Ayé had chosen their weapons.[5] The case eventually went on trial before the South Florida Federal District Court in August 1989 and followed the classic *Sherbert vs. Verner* (1963) line. Although a burden on the plaintiff's free exercise of religion was recognized, Judge Eugene Spelman found that 'compelling state interest' vindicated limitation of First Amendment rights (5 October 1989). The case went for appeal to the 11th Circuit Court at Atlanta, and eventually found its way onto the agenda of the Supreme Court which produced just what Hialeah's councilman Julio Martinez had prophesized back in June 1987: a landmark decision.

The case followed the lines of the highly publicized *Employment*

Division, Department of Human Resources of Oregon vs. Smith decision (1990) which had reversed the 1964 *People vs. Woody* decision legalizing the ceremonial use of peyote by adherents of the Native American Church. *Oregon vs. Smith* had established the principle of 'neutrality' or 'general applicability' as a test for the constitutionality of legislation curtailing the free exercise of religion. Religious practices can be prohibited only if they do not form an exclusive part of the behavioural repertoire of a religious body. The law must incriminate the same type of behaviour on a secular, socially inclusive level. Since Hialeah's city fathers chose to prohibit only the religiously motivated killing of animals (and not, for example, hunting), they ran up against the logic of a precedent that had earlier restricted the legal range of action of another minoritarian religious body.

Hence *Church of the Lukumí vs. Hialeah* is of considerable legal interest, for it may play a future role with respect to issues associated with the debate over 'multiculturalism'. This becomes clear when one considers how precariously close the Supreme Court's decision in *Oregon vs. Smith* came to deliberating issues of *cultural* instead of merely religious practice (see Lawson and Morris 1991), a tendency that relates to the conceptual problems faced by the secular state when forced to construe 'religion' into a positive legal category (cf. Burkholder 1974; Fields 1982; Rowlands and Warnier 1988; Geschiere 1988; Fisiy and Geschiere 1991). Previous US legislative history shows an uneasy vacillation between morality and *mores* in matters of 'free exercise'. In comparison to the so-called 'establishment clause' cases (most of the recent ones centring around the 'creationism' debate), 'free exercise' cases have tended to involve not dogmatically radical segments of majoritarian faiths such as Protestant fundamentalists, but groups whose distance from the mainstream of American denominationalism could not simply be classified as variant, but was produced by clashes of the enactment of their religious precepts with notions of 'public order', i.e. majoritarian *cultural* norms. Well-known cases include *Reynolds vs. US* (1879) centring on Mormon polygyny (which was, of course, lost), and the more recent case of *Wisconsin vs. Yoder* (1972), where, perhaps for the first time, the concern over the preservation of a 'way of life' structured by religious precepts informed a decision to suspend state interest in favour of what was recognized as the right of the Old Order Amish to 'a culture of their own'.[6]

WHEN THE GODS GO TO COURT

So far, I have sketched the cultural contradictions that generated the conflict Justice Spelman would struggle to cast into a !egal mould in a Miami court room in the summer of 1989. I have referred to several alignments of interest and emotion which, at times, united, at other times and levels of social articulation, drove apart the detractors of the Church of the Lukumí Babalu Ayé. Yet there were still other bodies of 'local knowledge' involved; other perspectives; other ways of construing the bare events, the 'plot', into a coherent narrative. One of these – informed by yet another system of signification – was that of *regla ocha*, and its divine law-giver, *ifá*. It took me a long time to discover this 'subterranean' narrative myself – in fact, I am not even sure about my agency as 'discoverer'. I have known Pichardo since 1985 and had heard of the first trial's outcome in the spring of 1990 while on a visiting appointment at the University of Virginia. Having personal as well as academic interest in the case, I flew to Miami. Expecting to find Pichardo in low spirits – he had, after all, just lost a crucial legal battle – I was taken aback as he began to unravel a story of triumphant victory in a spiritual confrontation: 'una guerra avisada por *egún y ocha*' – a war announced by the dead and the gods.

I knew that Pichardo rationalized his efforts to establish Santería as a legitimate religion as a sacred personal mandate announced to him by divination in the course of his initiation into *regla ocha* as a devotee or 'son' of the god *Changó* in the spring of 1971. But I had not expected him to go into a lengthy explanation of how divination had guided his every move, including his deliberate and well-planned confrontation with the American legal system. It was only in listening to *his* version of the story that I began to realize the complexity of the narratives within which he framed his experience.

In what follows I will attempt a reading of this 'subterranean' story-line threading through the 1989 trial and the events that surrounded it. It seems that this counter-narrative first surfaced into public discourse during the 1989 trial, at the end of a cross-examination of Ernesto Pichardo by the defendant's attorney on 8 August. Dissatisfied with the evidence produced in the course of a lengthy and unpleasantly technical inquiry into the mechanics of animal sacrifice, Judge Spelman himself addressed the witness. And as their dialogue proceeded, one catches a glimpse of a competing set of 'laws and orders'; a *lex divina* entering into a curious dialogue with the

American *leges humanae*. Santeros perceive divine order as partly accessible to human understanding through the 256 *odu* or divination verses of the *ifá*-oracle. *Ifá* is not only a technical means of access to divine order and the will of the gods, but also a personified instance of the divine: having been witness to the creation of the world, *ifá* is the only one to know and communicate its true course. *Ifá* knows all there ever was and will be.

A quote from the trial record illustrates the confrontation between the laws of *ifá* and those of an American judge trying to cut through the tangle of political and cultural semantics surrounding this case:

THE COURT [JUDGE SPELMAN]   You have indicated to the court in your testimony that Ifá never intends to violate the law.

THE WITNESS [PICHARDO]   That is correct.

THE COURT   Now, if the City of Hialeah has a constitutional right to say to any religion because of the mandates of the western world, because of the fact that we have grown up in a more civilized society over the years than maybe the tenets or principles of a particular religion have with regard to the manner in which they conduct themselves, that not only are we going to prevent the disposal of carcasses and things of that nature in certain ways, but that we must say to you that it is against the law to in fact sacrifice animals, what would Ifá's reaction to that be if Ifá does not violate the law?

THE WITNESS   The religious principles would then indicate that the religion will cease being a religion because the sacrifice...

Spelman cut Pichardo short at that point, asking whether 'Ifá gives up that easily' – compared, at least, to other gods that Spelman chose not to name. Pichardo did not delve into the theological intricacies of why gods ultimately depend upon their human worshippers, but merely indicated that since sacrifice was indispensable to the initiation of new priests, attrition would gradually lead to the demise of Santería as a religion. Yet *ifá* had not, in fact, given up. Was not the fact that sacrificial practice had survived even severe persecution evidence of *ifá*'s will? And did not the religious community continue to 'stand on the side of their God rather than [that] of man's law'? 'But my question is', Judge Spelman responded,

THE COURT [JUDGE SPELMAN]   If Ifá is in fact the recognizer of laws and there is a law against it, then how can one interpret one's religion to believe that it ought to violate the law?

THE WITNESS   Because which comes first, God's law or man's law
and we have to obey God's law –
THE COURT   But you are telling me God's law is in fact to obey the
law.
THE WITNESS   Yes. And the first one you must obey is his law.

Here they finally arrived at Matthew 22: 21 ('Render unto Cae-
sar...'), and Spelman let the point go in despair of the momentous
problems it created for a legal system that claims to 'know no heresy',
yet holds itself accountable to unspecified 'ultimate moral principles'.[7]

However, in Pichardo's terms, a different sanctioning authority
was already at work, which would make its powers felt regardless of
the outcome of the trial. In the *apertura del año* of 1987 – a major
oracular ceremony charting the course of the new year – *Changó*, his
ruling *oricha*,[8] had spoken through the sign *Obara Eyioko* (6–2)[9] of
preparing for battle in order to establish Santería as a legitimate
religion. In accordance with this mandate Pichardo had 'gone to war'.
In 1988 *Changó* spoke again, this time in *Obara Meji* (6–6), ruling that
'two kings cannot live in the same city' and that 'truth is born from the
lie'. In 1989, the *refrán* or proverbial saying was '*oreja no pasa cabeza*'
(8–8) – respect your elders, do not confuse hierarchies: profane power
is vanquished by sacred authority. Early in 1990, the goddess *Ochun*
announced change and motion, spoke of losses turning into gains.
The sign was *Oche Meji* (5–5). Its meaning to him, Pichardo told me,
was: 'let them play it out as a winner, let them dig their own grave'. He
was right: by September of 1989, the FBI had begun to investigate
mayor Raul Martinez for shady real estate business and graft. Only
weeks after I had returned to the University of Virginia, I received a
call from Pichardo. The profane king had fallen – '*el rey se cayó*' as one
of Martinez' political opponents put it in an interview with *Herald*
reporters (*Miami Herald*, 4 April 1990). Martinez and several
members of the city council had been indicted for racketeering and
organized crime. 'Remember', Pichardo said, 'how I told you years
ago that all I wanted was to have them put in the book that Santería is
a legitimate religion? And didn't the judge say it was? It's there on
record. Now who's the winner?'

This may not have been the final point at which 'plot' and 'story'
converged for Ernesto Pichardo. Whether intended or not, the
statement about the fallen king points towards another level on
which Pichardo and his religious associates might have read the

events. The Afro-Cuban *oricha Babalu Ayé*'s origins can be traced to the chthonic Yoruba smallpox deity *Sopona*, variously referred to by the euphemistic titles *Babalu Ayé* or *Obalu Ayé*, meaning 'father' or 'king of the world'. Afro-Cuban divinatory traditions recount the following 'historia' (explicatory tale accompanying a particular divination outcome). As a mythical personage, *Babalu Ayé* leads a vicious life, becomes afflicted with infectious diseases and is ousted from his native land. On his journey he encounters *Changó*, who directs him to the neighbouring kingdom of the Arará (a Lucumí term for the Fon of Dahomey). There he kills the morally corrupt and tyrannical native ruler and assumes his place. This myth has a parallel in Dahomean history. Herskovits (1938, II: 136ff.) reports that the alien Aladaxonu rulers banned the indigenous cult of the chthonic smallpox deity Sagbatá from the royal city of Abomey, legitimating their action by reference to traditions attesting that *two kings cannot live in the same city*. Sagbatá, however, returned at least three times to afflict or kill the 'profane' king: we know from historical sources that the Dahomean kings Agadja, Kpengla and Ghezo suffered or died from smallpox! (cf. Herskovits 1938, II: 136ff.).

Could any of the actors involved in the Hialeah affair have been aware of this ironic parallel? Prompted to explain the significance of the 1988 *refrán* to *Obara Meji* (6–6), i.e. 'two kings cannot live in the same city', Pichardo, whose sacred name is, indeed, *obá irawó* – 'king of Irawo' or, as he translates it, 'king of the stars' – volunteered the Afro-Cuban myth. Whether or not he knew the relevant ethnographic literature is impossible to say, but that is beside the point. A moral topology had been restored. Martinez had fallen after confronting not only a son of *Changó*, but *Babalu Ayé* himself. Ousted from his native realm, the sacred king returned to punish the profane offender. The god of sickness restored moral health.

SACRED KINGS AND THEIR SUBJECTS

I have not been to Miami since the Supreme Court decision, but I have little doubt that, by now, Pichardo's narrative about divine centres of authority and their secular margins has been spun around the 1993 decision as well. Pichardo is a divination specialist, and Afro-Cuban divination is an ongoing process, geared towards discursive appropriation of moral territory. By now the voices of the *oricha* and the priestly dead will have lent additional confirmation to a text whose meaning was, in essence, 'always already known'.[10] Moreover, I suspect that the story has also extended its reach in social space, diffusing far beyond the sociological confines of the Church of the Lukumí Babalu Ayé. Like the legal pronouncement about a set of faulty ordinances – 'enacted by officials who did not understand, failed to perceive, or chose to ignore the fact that their official actions violated the nation's essential commitment to religious freedom' (Justice Kennedy, quoted in *New York Times*, National Edition, 12 June 1993) – the story about divine vengeance provides a device for invading alien moral terrain. The ostensible mutuality of this process is stunning. The United States of America and the Church of the Lukumí Babalu Ayé are now, in a sense, constitutive of each other. Indeed, it might appear that discursive convergence had been coming all along, and was only temporarily delayed by interference from a morally corrupt, and legally unsanctioned, margin: the City of Hialeah.

The City has now been silenced. Facing a good half million dollars in lawyers' fees, its present mayor still feels that 'the vast majority of Hialeah's residents support the city's position', but declared his intention to refrain from further attempts at regulating Afro-Cuban religious activity (*New York Times*, National Edition, 13 June 1993). Yet there is another set of stories hidden in the legal narrative of *Church of the Lukumí Babalu Ayé vs. City of Hialeah* which revolves around the question of what margin moved to which centre. The evil city may not have been alone in experiencing massive dislocation. For the plot of case 91–948 harbours yet another irony, predicated on the sociology of Afro-Cuban religion in exile.

It consists less of a story than of an egregious absence in the public record: something unaccounted for, a mute – though by no means voiceless – margin which I, too, am reluctant to foreground. Crucial to this silence is the fact that the American legal system literally invited Pichardo and his associates to construe the Church of the Lukumí into a *pars pro toto* of an entity named, and therefore known, as 'Santería'. Yet the fact that Pichardo *is* a Santero does not necessarily mean that he fought the case for what is, in practice, a sociologically diffuse, and legally invisible, aggregate of small groups of practitioners of *regla ocha*. The disturbing fact about the collusion between the United States of America and the Church of the Lukumí Babalu Ayé seems to be that he did not. And indeed, while the case was pending, Pichardo faced a continuous murmur of protest from within the ranks of what Max Weber would call a community less of intent than of political fate.

Though it is possible to generalize about Santería as a body of socially distributed knowledge and practices, it is hard to pin down a formal organizational structure above the level of widely recognized priestly positions aligned into shifting hierarchies of individually negotiated seniority and religious competence.[11] Incumbents of such positions form the points around which what Santeros call 'casas de santo' or *ilé ocha* crystallize: aggregates of priests (*olocha*) of junior status, initiated neophytes (*iyawo*) and uninitiated clients (*aleyo*), who are linked together by bonds of religious kinship,[12] moral obligations to allocate time and resources to collective ritual activity, and personal motivation by clients to avail themselves of divinatory or therapeutic resources, and attend non-esoteric ritual events. Such 'cult groups' tend towards segmentation. Since junior priests can perform initiations, they often build up a group of junior religious kin while still attached to the 'casa' of a senior priest. A large 'casa' can thus contain not only several 'generations' of fully initiated priests, but may, in case of open conflict, break up into a number of smaller independent 'casas', staffed by the 'following' of former 'junior' priests who now occupy apical positions within new cult groups.

Beyond this basic level of integration, 'Santería' is little else but a referent of often fiercely antagonistic discursive projects, few of which have ever congealed into concrete and lasting social realities.[13] There are, thus, no hard and fast criteria for identifying a 'community of believers', let alone for statistically circumscribing the demography and sociology of Afro-Cuban religious practice. While this creates obvious problems for any 'outside' agency trying to conceptualize 'Santería' in the light of standard notions about American denominational corporations, similar problems plague those who would issue authoritative statements on behalf of their own faith. Since institutionalized mechanisms for enforcing consensus on any other than strictly ritual matters do not exist, no one can legitimately speak for a larger constituency than his or her junior religious kinfolk, if one manages to keep them in line. Though gossip tends to act as a negative sanctioning force (which can destroy individual reputations, and break alliances), there is no universally recognized manner in which legitimation and authority can positively and unequivocally be established beyond the level of single, or a few closely related, casas (Palmié 1987).

A MAN FOR ALL SEASONS

Hence the problem of 'leadership', or, perhaps more adequately, 'spokesmanship'. Although a long tradition of persecution in Cuba has left Miami's Santeros with a repertoire of practices geared towards strategic concealment, to many of them the Hialeah confrontation must have driven home the fact that they cannot avoid the issue of public self-representation. Yet whom to authorize with such a task, and on what grounds? Religious seniority and priestly competence are equivocal criteria, and the few senior priests whose standing is widely recognized are loath to expose themselves to public controversy. The ability to project an image conforming to American standards of 'respectability', bilingual fluency, and rhetorical abilities are the hallmark of a younger generation of priests, many of whom have grown up in the United States. But encouraging their ambitions goes against the grain of deference due to senior authority.

Yet although most Santeros are quick to voice their regrets about this state of affairs, spokesmen[14] abound. Since the early 1970s, diverse outside agencies – among them the Catholic Church, the University of Miami School of Medicine, the Dade County Medical Examiner's Office, the Metropolitan Miami Police Department, the local Schoolboard, newspaper reporters, TV stations, and a few anthropologists – have actively sought information on Santería. In doing so, they inadvertently contributed to the emergence of a new role configuration among Miami's Santeros: the self-styled mediator or spokesman-priest, at the interface between 'internal' and 'external' discourses *about* Santería. By now, one can trace a fairly uniform career pattern salient to the majority of previous aspirants to this role. Beginning with an initial press exposure (often in the context of a public controversy), a single priest turns into the media's informant of choice; in the next few years, his voice increasingly dominates 'external' discourse about Santería, while his position comes under increasing 'internal' attack, mainly through gossip. Finally he disappears from the public stage, often with a severely damaged reputation on both levels.[15]

Though conforming to this new social type, Pichardo is not the first practitioner of *regla ocha* to speak out publicly on behalf of an objectified linguistic construct variously termed 'Santería' or 'la religión', but merely the most successful to date. Part of this relates to his versatility in manipulating culturally heterogeneous discourses in order to effect semantic slippage between them. Whether officiating in his role as cowrie-diviner and ritual expert (*italero*), hosting talk shows on American religious diversity for a local Spanish TV station, or fighting a constitutional law suit, he has managed not only to avoid or subvert attacks on his credibility, but to increase his visibility as an icon of what he thinks is the future of Afro-Cuban religion in the USA: the respectable priestly functionary of a legally recognized *American* denomination worshipping African gods. Believing that in the long run only conformity to 'the American Way' will ensure the survival of his religion, Pichardo has – over a span of almost 20 years – patiently pursued the course of engineering a public 'American' identity for his faith. As he put it in an interview in January 1987, his aim was 'to extricate Santería from the backyards of Little Havana and Hialeah' in order to establish it on par with other legitimate denominations (*El Herald*, 2 February 1987). Pichardo's spectacular legal success would seem to prove him right. Dovetailing with his own constructions of events, the legal narrative emerging from the ultimate centre of secular power drowned the voices of his public opponents. Yet South Florida's self-styled guardians of public morality may not be the only ones to deplore this outcome.

WILL THE REAL MR BABALU AYÉ PLEASE STAND UP?

Another dimension to the controversy that began to unfold around Ernesto Pichardo's church in the summer of 1987 was that he and his fellow church members were – albeit for different motives – as fervently striving for conformity to white American middle-class values as their Cuban-American opponents in Hialeah's City Hall. What is perhaps most striking about the Church of the Lukumí Babalu Ayé is how little it resembles the traditional 'marginal' format of an Afro-Cuban cult group. In order to fashion their religion into an entity capable of being processed by the American legal system, and arrogating peculiarly American emblems of respectability, Pichardo and his associates transformed what may once have been a '*casa de santo*' into a public church. They wrote a 'code of ethics and belief' for a religion largely based on oral tradition, and lacking any form of institutionalized orthodoxy. They devised written rules for member-ship and priesthood qualifications, reserving their right to exclude persons of doubtful repute. They set up a public house of worship for ritual practices that traditionally take place in the privacy of individual homes, and announced their intention to hold formal religious instruction classes terminating with a diploma, in order to standardize and 'purify' a body of religious knowledge which had so far been transmitted informally, and in their view incompletely, by unscrupulous or incompetent priests.

Such initiative did not meet with the approval of South Florida's Santeros. Pichardo's move towards 'legitimacy', once ratified by the 'centre', might result in the further de-legitimation of any version of Afro-Cuban religious practice deviating from the modular pattern which the Church of the Lukumí Babalu Ayé was busily inscribing into public discourse. As one of their more aggressive moves against this emerging 'internal margin', in 1992, Pichardo and his associates distributed a booklet in English entitled *Santería ... : What you need to know, but can't get anywhere* (Church of the Lukumí Babalu Ayé 1992). Though ostensibly cautioning outsiders 'enthusias[tic] to learn more about Santería spirituality' to 'beware of the unscrupulous priest', the booklet's text contained a variety of messages: signals to potential 'inside' detractors, acrid rebuttals of professional 'outside' experts (such as anthropologists), and more oblique messages shrewdly playing upon generalized American constructs of honest practice, consumer control, authenticity, and legitimacy. 'Numerous questions concerning the qualifications of some persons representing themselves as teachers have been raised by lay persons seeking a spiritual path through Santería', reads the opening paragraph:

Many sincere priests have asserted that most books on Santería contain many errors of fact. They feel that such distortions, promoted by irresponsible authors and public speakers, have contributed to the problem of inauthentic teachings and question-able qualifications.

The truly honest priests openly criticize those who exploit Santería's spirituality. Indeed, there are reports of priests insisting on charging substantial fees for crisis-intervention rituals or ceremonies to anyone who wants to play 'religion for a day' and can afford the price. . . . Santería, like any other religion, is bound to have its share of unscrupulous priests, and we need to take seriously allegations made against them. However, we must also equally avoid unfair and unsubstantiated charges. The accused must be regarded as innocent until proven guilty.

There is no reason why anyone should entrust his or her vulnerable psyche to the care of so-called spiritual teachers without first checking their backgrounds for the authenticity of their qualifications. *Here are some valuable tips on how to protect yourself, your friends, and your family from the unscrupulous priest.*[16]

(Church of the Lukumí Babalu Ayé 1992, original emphasis)

Pichardo was clearly playing with fire. What particularly stung his opponents was that he consciously set up an artificial value scale for outsiders intent on charting a moral topography of Afro-Cuban religion in South Florida: given a chance, the honest priest would move to the centre and expose himself to public scrutiny. Only the deviant would choose to remain on the margin. In addition, Pichardo's narrative about a move from margin to centre at least subliminally cross-referenced a variety of larger discourses concerning representations of race and class. The problem here was not so much that Pichardo and his associates had carefully crafted a 'white middle-class Cuban-American' media image for the Church of the Lukumí Babalu Ayé to pre-empt discursive linkages between the African origins or their religion and the semantic spectrum the concept of 'blackness' evoked in the American imagination. It was rather that this move was symptomatic of a more pervasive shift in the political economy of the social distribution of Afro-Cuban religious practices in South Florida. Already in 1986, a black Santera who had emigrated during the Mariel Exodus (and experienced a good measure of discrimination from established Cuban-Americans) bitterly complained to me about the rift opening between the growing number of religious practitioners hailing from Miami's Latin business elite, and those priests of Afro-Cuban descent who found themselves on the social and economic margins of Dade County's Hispanic community. Affluent white Santeros, she claimed, were raising the price 'of just about anything in this religion' to a degree where black Cubans could no longer afford to practise it. Not only were Afro-Cubans 'being despoiled of their spiritual heritage', the religion itself was turning into a commodity in a market increasingly segregated along the lines of colour and class.

Whether or not an exclusionary motive can be ascribed to Pichardo, it is clear that his actions stirred up a number of issues which Miami's Santeros were ill-prepared to address. The central problem was that they lacked a vocabulary in which to voice their dissension. *Regla ocha*'s organizational diffuseness notwithstanding, the tendency to objectify what many Santeros tellingly refer to as 'la religión' is not of recent origin. However, what Santeros haggle about when they accuse each other of profaning The Religion or acting '*contra la tradición*' relates to deviations from a (largely inexplicable) standard of theology and ritual practice, or to individual breaches of secrecy. Pichardo's activities went beyond this type of complaint. Though nobody seems to have ever seriously questioned his priestly qualifications, he has repeatedly been accused of profaning the religion – e.g. when he held educational workshops on Afro-Cuban religion at Miami Dade Community College, or in front of police officers and health workers undergoing cross-cultural training programmes. Prior to the 1993 trial he was widely denounced as a publicity seeker, troublemaker, or pretentious upstart trying to establish himself as bogus pope of Miami. Yet though typical of the tendency of Santeros to try to curb aspirations to leadership within their ranks, such reactions were both largely irrelevant to Pichardo's project, and indicative of more fundamental misgivings.

It seems to have struck many practitioners of *regla ocha* that the narrative Pichardo had publicly spun around Santería might have momentous repercussions within their own universe of discourse. Even before his spectacular legal victory, the modular pattern represented by the Church of the Lukumí Babalu Ayé was being replicated by a rival group, the Cabildo Yoruba Omo Orisha, Inc., headed by a priest named Willie Ramos. As the term '*cabildo*' suggests, Ramos' group defined itself, in contradistinction to the *Church* of the Lukumí Babalu Ayé, as the conservative guardian of tradition. Still, its 'public relations policy' closely paralleled that of the Church of the Lukumí Babalu Ayé during an earlier stage of its career. Just as Pichardo had established ties with 'outside patrons' like the University of Miami, the Miami Dade Community College System, the Metro Dade Police Department, *Miami Herald* journalists and local TV stations, the Cabildo appeared to reproduce this process by aligning itself with Florida International University, and aggressively building up a media image. Pichardo, it seems, had merely opened a door. The model itself was now up for grabs.

The controversy about the Church of the Lukumí Babalu Ayé proved that the margin itself was in flux. Not only at the centre, but also in the periphery borderlines dissolved and categories began to blur. Pichardo was a product of this world of shifting allegiances and *ad hoc* decisions. Instead of redrawing the boundaries of discourse, he had developed what many of his traditionally minded opponents saw as a contaminated idiom, in which the distinctions between self and other, centre and margin would become increasingly harder to make. Pichardo's transgressions were only symptomatic. His priestly and secular opponents were facing the same dilemma. They, too, were caught up in conflicting loyalties and aspirations; suspended in discursive linkages between margin and centre that crosscut their political, social and cultural identities – not only as Santeros, but as Cubans of different social and racial origin, as Cuban-Americans manoeuvring within the value space of their host society, and as American citizens competing for political and economic resources within the context of South Florida's 'plural society'. Whether case 91–948, *Church of the Lukumí Babalu Ayé vs. City of Hialeah* has resolved any of these ambiguities remains to be seen.

NOTES

1   While single practitioners of Afro-Cuban religions may have migrated to the United States as early as the 1940s, cult groups ('*casas*') capable of reproduction by initiating new members did not form before the early 1960s in metropolitan New York/New Jersey, and subsequently in Miami. Today Afro-Cuban religious communities exist in several urban centres of the US, Puerto Rico, Venezuela, Mexico, Panama, Spain and, reportedly, Italy and the Netherlands (cf. Palmié 1991: 184–205).

2   Apart from a sizeable contingent of Central and South American adherents, the Afro-Cuban religions are spreading among members of Miami's native African-American community. To a certain extent this is due to a re-convergence with the so-called 'American Yoruba Movement', which initially emerged from a deliberate appropriation of elements of Afro-Cuban religious culture by black American cultural nationalists (cf. Hunt 1979; Palmié 1995).

3   The term would seem to derive from the Yoruba word *ará* (inhabitant) and *tápà* (a designation for the Nupe), cf. Abrahams (1958).

4   It was this set of ordinances, and particularly their definition of 'sacrifice' as 'to unnecessarily kill, torment, torture, or mutilate an animal in a private or public ceremony not for the primary purpose of food consumption', with which the city of Hialeah set itself up for the eventual 'kill', so to speak. How, the Supreme Court Justices would later ask, did Hialeah's city fathers imagine they could define the 'necessity' which their formulation invoked? Would they yank away the gun from a man who took his son on a weekend hunting trip to the Everglades? Would they stop the local Humane Society from putting to death stray cats and dogs? And if not, were the terms 'sacrifice' and 'ceremony' not clear evidence that their ordinances targeted nothing *but* Afro-Cuban religious exercise?

5   They were not the first group of practitioners of an Afro-Caribbean religion to put America's commitment to its constitution to the test. In July 1850, the New Orleans *Daily Delta* reported a court case that had arisen from a police raid on a Voodoo ceremony in which rather similar arguments were raised:

During the trial a free colored priestess named Betsy Toledano claimed the right to hold Voodoo services on the grounds of the constitutional guarantee of freedom of religion.

In outlining Voodoo's origin Betsy pointed out that it was of African origin and that her version of the religion had been passed on to her by her grandmother. She continued to explain certain objects used in a ceremony. Concerning a necklace she wore was said (sic) to be able to cause rain; a bag of flint and sand pebbles were explained as powerful enough to prevent certain diseases or bring about the love of one person for another. Although the priestess's right of religious practice was not denied, her right to permit slaves to attend was a violation of the law and she was fined.

(Sterkx 1972: 265)

Another case tried in 1863 found entry into the 1876 edition of the Pierre Larousse: charged with 'seditious and secessionist' intent (New Orleans was, after all, under Union control at the time), the Voodoo priests claimed constitutional protection, and, since no political motives could be proven, were eventually acquitted (Larousse 1876, xv: 812).

6   Such ties between belief and aspects of organized ways of life divergent from majoritarian orientations are likely to be of future concern to the American legal system. Given the current controversy over the representation of historic (as well as contemporaneous) 'Others' in public education, it is surprising that the criminalization of alien cultural practices – which has a long history in the United States – has not received more attention.

7   The extent and historical origins of this particular contradiction are usefully surveyed by Derr (1981). There are good grounds for arguing that the subject of religious legitimation of behaviour has counted, in US courts, among those 'topics on which legal discourse must be silent, either because its internal contradictions have to be covered up; or because to state its basic assumptions would be to expose them to discussion, critical scrutiny, and the risk of rejection' (Humphreys 1985: 256). This is hardly surprising given the courts' difficulties to live up to Madisonian standards in a society whose members, according to 1987 poll results, internationally rank second only to Malta in rating the importance of God in their lives (Wills 1990: 16). For an account of similarly unspeakable issues in another area of forensic discourse, see Minow (1990) on the philosophy and politics of silence in the American legal system's handling of social constructions of physical 'difference'.

8   Although practitioners of *regla ocha* are simultaneously initiated into the cult of several *oricha*, one of them is specifically designated as the 'owner of the [initiate's] head' (*olorí*). Individual Santeros regularly refer to this particular divinity as 'their *oricha*'.

9   The bracketed numbers refer to the amount of cowries falling '*boca arriba*' (i.e. with an artificial opening produced by filing of the shell's upper part facing the viewer) when thrown in the two successive divinatory operations that determine a single sign or *odu*.

10   It is worth noting that despite its technical similarity to the *modus operandi* of a common law system (such as that of American jurisprudence), Afro-Cuban divination notionally pronounces canonical truths.

11   Defined by, among other things, verifiable status as an initiate, ascertainable 'religious descent', length of time since initiation, and individually negotiable reputation as someone who is in command of varying amounts of esoteric knowledge ('*conocimientos*') and sacred power (*aché*).

12   Such kin-relations are expressed in the idiom of godparenthood. An initiating priest acquires the status of godparent in relation to the initiate, who becomes a godchild. Lateral linkages ('*hermandad en santo*') extend between godchildren initiated by the same godparent. Vertical linkages are (selectively) reckoned along the line ascending towards the godparent's godparent, and often several 'generations' beyond. Since fully initiated priests can begin initiating others after only one year of neophyte status, 'generations' are of varying length. Being able to trace one's religious genealogy to a famous priest or a prestigious old '*casa*' in Cuba (and getting others to confirm it) is a strategic asset in negotiating religious hierarchies among priests.

13   There is evidence for repeated unsuccessful attempts to forge corporate linkages above the level of single local 'casas' which, in Cuba, appear to date back to the 1930s and 1940s.

14   I am deliberately using a gendered term. Although women are barred from specialized priestly roles (namely those of *babalao* and *italero*), there are no restrictions on their attaining positions of seniority within the ranks of the general priesthood. Several of the most prestigious '*casas*' in pre-revolutionary Cuba were headed by women. Yet so far, no priestess has emerged as a 'public figure'. While the female voice plays a considerable role within the internal discourse of *regla ocha*, in public, it is silenced by a semantic selection process foregrounding male authority. The same holds true for the relatively large group of homosexual male priests.

15   A characteristic example is that of C., a priest who rose to media fame in the late 1970s. At the height of his career, he travelled to Nigeria, where he claimed to have been initiated as a *babalao*, edited an esoteric journal, and published a book on 'The Religion of the Yoruba in Cuba'. By about 1980, C. disappeared from the public stage. When I did fieldwork in Miami, I learned that he had been 'silenced' from 'within': after his return from Nigeria, rumours were launched about his homosexual past, an allegation that (whether true or false) effectively destroyed the legitimacy of his claim to be a *babalao*.

16   In a later section entitled 'Select Your Teacher Well!!', the booklet gives a checklist of twelve questions designed to guide consumers about their 'prospective teacher's qualifications and experience'.

REFERENCES

Abrahams, R. C. (1958) *Dictionary of Modern Yoruba*, London: University of London Press.

Burkholder, J. R. (1974) ' "The law knows no heresy": marginal religious movements and the courts', in I. Zaretsky and M. P. Leone (eds) *Religious Movements in Contemporary America*, Princeton: Princeton University Press.

Church of the Lukumí Babalu Ayé (1992) *Santería . . . : What you need to know, but can't get anywhere*, Miami: no publisher.

Derr, T. S. (1981) 'The First Amendment as a guide to church–state relations: theological illusions, cultural fantasies, and legal practicalities', in J. B. Hensel (ed.) *Church, State, and Politics*, Washington: Roscoe Pound American Trial Lawyers' Foundation.

Fields, K. E. (1982) 'Political contingencies of witchcraft in colonial central Africa: culture and the state in Marxist theory', *Canadian Journal of African Studies* 16: 567–93.

Fisiy, C. F. and Geschiere, P. (1991) 'Judges and witches, or how is the state to deal with witchcraft?', *Cahiers d'Études Africaines* 30: 135–56.

Geschiere, P. (1988) 'Sorcery and the state: popular movements of action among the Maka of southeastern Cameroon', *Critique of Anthropology* 8: 35–63.

Herskovits, M. J. (1938) *Dahomey*, New York: J.J. Augustin.

Humphreys, S. (1985) 'Law as discourse', *History and Anthropology* 1: 241–64.

Hunt, C. (1979) *Oyotunji Village*, Washington, DC: University Press of America.

Larousse, P. (1876) *Grand dictionnaire universel du XIXe siècle*, Paris: Administration du Grand Dictionnaire Universel.

Lawson, P. E. and Morris, C. P. (1991) 'The Native American church and the new court: the *Smith* case and Indian religious freedoms', *American Indian Culture and Research Journal* 15: 79–91.

Minow, M. (1990) *Making All the Difference*, Ithaca: Cornell University Press.

Palmié, S. (1987) ' "La religión del chisme": Klatsch, Informationskontrolle und soziale Organisation in den afrokubanischen Religionen Miamis', *Lateinamerika Studien* 23: 197–207.

—— (1991) *Das Exil der Götter*, Frankfurt: Peter Lang.

—— (1995.) 'Against syncretism: Africanizing and Cubanizing discourses in North American òrìsà-worship', in R. Fardon (ed.) *Counterworks*, London: Routledge.

Rowlands, M. and Warnier, J.-P. (1988) 'Sorcery, power and the modern state in Cameroon', *Man* 23: 118–32.

Sterkx, H. E. (1972) *The Free Negro in Ante-Bellum Louisiana* Rutherford.

Wills, G. (1990) *Under God*, New York: Simon & Schuster.

Index